TO PROVE I'M
NOT FORGOT

TO PROVE I'M NOT FORGOT

Living and Dying in a Victorian City

SYLVIA M. BARNARD

For David

First published by Manchester University Press in 1990
This revised edition published in 2009
Reprinted 2019

The History Press
97 St George's Place,
Cheltenham, GL50 3QB
www.thehistorypress.co.uk

British Library Cataloguing in Publication Data.
A catalogue record for this book is available from the British Library.

ISBN 978 0 7509 5060 2

Typesetting and origination by The History Press
Printed in Great Britain by TJ International Ltd, Padstow, Cornwall

Contents

List of Illustrations

Preface

How difficult we find it to face up to death, to talk about it even. The mere physical proximity of the dying and the dead discomforts us acutely. Perhaps that is why the very old are nowadays shunted off into terminal wards to die and, once dead, their remains are, at a growing rate, cremated, leaving nothing behind but roses and ashen memories.

Things were far otherwise with the Victorians. Exactly like countless generations of Christians before them, they lived in a world in which existence was a struggle, disease was rife, and death struck without warning or mercy. Unable to hide themselves from death, they felt no need, no compulsion, to hide the dead. Far from it. From the domestic deathbed drama to the stately funeral, decked out with all the pomp and circumstance of mourning, our forebears celebrated death as the great climax of the mortal lifespan of each Christian soul; every exit became a solemn, ritual re-enactment of those grand truths of the Christian Gospel: the impermanency of the flesh and the triumphal progress of the immortal soul into life eternal. Indeed, the rites of passage for the departed were highly public events, and (we might sceptically observe) more attention, more expense, often seems to have been lavished on subjects once deceased than when they toiled as factory workers, exhausted themselves out as wives and mothers, or sacrificed their lives under foreign suns for their queen. The theatre of death finally accorded them a more glorious role than when they played their parts on life's stage.

And of no site is this truer than of the tomb. Aghast at life's brief transience, our forebears wanted the grave at least to be permanent, solid, a rock of ages fortified against the sieges of time. The grave needs must be a worthy memorial of the dead, a warning to the living ('As I, so you'), and a finger-post to all, pointing to what was higher and nobler.

Precisely because the grave ought properly to be an emblem of eternity, earnest and improving Victorians were appalled at the treatment they saw all too commonly meted out to the corpses of their recently deceased nearest and dearest: their coffins stacked in overcrowded crypts and vaults, or packed promiscuously into fetid parish churchyards. In what was perhaps their first and boldest act of slum clearance, Victorian burial reformers developed the cemetery, snugly sequestered in suburbia, the first of the garden cities, a sylvan, planned and peaceful final resting-place for those whose lot in life, all too often, had been smoke, stench and struggle.

Amongst the earliest, and the grandest, of the corporation cemeteries the Victorians built was that in Leeds. In her meticulous and moving rec-reation of the founding and fortunes of what the locals came to know as 'Beckett Street' or 'Burmantofts', Sylvia Barnard superbly restores to life this Victorian celebration of death, now almost completely disappeared: the stately funeral cortège, the plumed horses, the streets lined with silent mourners, the Dead March from *Saul*, the gravestone chiselled with urns and angels, all eloquent with pious inscriptions and hopes for futurity. Over the last ten or fifteen years, inspired by the pioneering researches of such French scholars as Michel Vovelle and Philippe Ariès, British historians have belatedly taken up the study of the iconography of rites for the dead. In her sensitive *Death, Dissection and the Destitute: a Political History of the Human Corpse* (London: Routledge & Kegan Paul, 1987), Ruth Richardson in par-ticular has emphasised the overwhelming sense of the sanctity of the corpse, felt by the ordinary men and women of nineteenth-century England. Such penetrating insights into the Victorian way of death are fleshed out and fur-ther developed by Sylvia Barnard's close-up study of daily life in one single dormitory for the departed.

Death was, as every Christian learnt, the great leveller. All manner of men, all walks of life, from brewers to bargees, concert violinists to vagabonds, were interred in Leeds' municipal cemetery. Some died rich in days; others entered the grave before ever reaching the cradle. No small number were struck down in their prime by sudden and shocking providences: drown-ings, traffic accidents, fires, poisonings; one tombstone commemorates the pathetic end of Mary Jane Duckworth, aged eight, run down and killed by an empty hearse, returning from Beckett Street itself. Fittingly, many of those most closely involved with the building and administration of Burmantofts chose to be buried alongside its spreading beeches and sycamores.

But if death levelled in a common mortality, the rules, rituals and respectabilities of Victorian burial reinforced all those hierarchies of class and confessional boundaries which the Victorians upheld so stoutly to maintain divisions amongst the living. The scale and situation of the turfy plot (predictably, first-class graves were on the highest ground), the quality of the stone, the height of the obelisk, the lavishness of the mason's design and inscription – all eloquently bespoke the ranks and divisions of the city itself. For the labouring poor, special cut-price 'guinea graves' were devised, so tightly crammed together that they became for all the world like a mocking reproduction of the back-to-backs in which their tenants once had dwelt. More shameful still was that enduring object of terror, the pauper grave – a mass pit which, even in the present century, was sometimes used to house higgledy-piggledy some two dozen bodies.

In thus recognising that the culture of death replays life itself, in seeing the cemetery as a kind of Pompeii, or as a frozen glacier slice of time, lies the special insight of this poignant book. For Sylvia Barnard's inventory of the dead, grave by grave, acre by acre, above all opens windows upon the living. Every corpse was once a householder, and many of them have been resurrected by the author's dedicated investigations in local archives, directories and newspapers, to afford us a Lowry-like panorama of the teeming life of the living in Leeds before the Grim Reaper gathered in his harvest.

Tall tombstones have their stories to tell; above all, their lapidary inscriptions perpetuate positive and tangible identities, established through civic chauvinism, fierce family and district loyalties, and pervasive occupational pride (Elizabeth Stamp's headstone noted: 'Mother of Oates Brothers, Saddlers, Leeds' – thus serving as an original advertising medium!). Such memorials tell of self-made folks (not a few of whom worshipped their maker), and sturdy independence (Samuel Smiles long worked in Leeds, though he was not buried in Beckett Street); but they also commemorate lives dedicated to civic munificence and Christian charity. And alongside such clashing but perhaps finally cohesive values, the cemetery's administrative and financial records afford further insights into the throbbing activities, growing pains, and tension points of the Victorian city: we encounter endless, niggling interdenominational conflicts being waged (Church v. Chapel, Consecrated v. Unconsecrated ground) within what was ostensibly an ecumenical civic amenity; we glimpse devotion to duty, but also scandals over perks and pensions; we see bureaucratic entrenchment and petty penny-pinching, but, occasionally, benefactors digging deep into their own pockets to cope with hard cases – these contradictions, these enigmas, of Victorian lives are captured by the author's tireless researches, intimate local expertise, witty pen and compassionate eye.

Victorian values have been much commended to us of late. As Sylvia Barnard herself emphasises, to endorse them would, however, mean reinstating an official face often stony, censorious, and sanctimonious. Blessed were the successful and the respectable. The cemetery's governing boards rarely flinched from what they saw as their duty of passing severe last judgements on fallen women and feckless labourers, dead or alive. Even employees who long and loyally served the cemetery itself were often denied a respectable resting place, replete with name and inscription. Yet one feature of life in industrialising Leeds, shining out from this study, could certainly bear emulation today. Burmantofts' burial books checked in the dead with dignity and a faith in records. Aldermen gave faithful and conscientious service; registrars, clerks and gravediggers performed their duties with punctilious pride. Overall, the Beckett Street enterprise exudes a sense of mission, which far transcends mere bureaucratic zeal or Benthamite efficiency, and which conveys a community of shared, public values and, ultimately, a sense of accountability beneath a common Maker.

Respect for the dead, that collective 'lest we forget', is perhaps the bedrock of civilisation and citizenship. It is certainly the hallmark of authentic history. Sylvia Barnard's remarkable and readable book is offered 'in loving memory' of those huddles of humanity who were the making of Victorian Leeds. At last, these individuals have arisen from their graves, and in the following pages, can be traced retreading those paths – rarely ones of glory – that finally led to Burmantofts.

Roy Porter
The Wellcome Institute for the History of Medicine, London

Acknowledgements

My greatest debts are to my husband, David Barnard, for his patient support and unstinting practical help; to Shirley Thorpe, for her tireless assistance in research and for the many useful suggestions her considerable local knowledge enabled her to make; and to Richard Freeman, for sharing the results of his intensive survey of the cemetery and its memorials.

At Leeds Central Public Library's Reference Department, Mrs Heap and the other members of staff answered my questions courteously and competently, and fetched me innumerable volumes and microfilms from their Aladdin's Cave. The officers of the Cemeteries Department of Leeds City Council have given me much help and hospitality. I am indebted also to Mr R. Remaynes of the Community Programme, to Mr I. Dewhirst of Keighley Public Library, to Dr B. Elliott of the Victorian Society, and to the staff of Leeds City Archives and of Cusworth Hall Museum, Doncaster.

The task of extracting information from the Burial Registers has been greatly eased by the work of the transcribing team; my thanks to my daughter and son Gillian and Nicholas Barnard, Louise Burns, Eileen Churchill, Brenda Green, Kay and Keith Gurney, my parents George and Mollie Hagedorn, Doreen Harris, Mary Jeffrey, the late Les Marks, Tonia Mason, Elizabeth Ogden, Beryl Pearce, José Roberts, Connie Samwell, Barbara Spencer, Shirley Thorpe, Charles Wallace and Barbara Worthington.

I am grateful for family information from Mr E. Baines, Mrs A. Broad and Mr A. Smith, Mrs E. Busch and other descendants of the Kidney family, Mrs E. L. Green, Mrs G. Hall, Mrs E. Janson, Mrs M. T. Mulart, Mrs C. Samwell and Mr and Mrs S. Temple. Mr E. J. Boys kindly allowed me to make use of his painstaking research on 'Chargers' and other soldiers of the Crimean War, and Mr F. Dalby, formerly of the 'Leeds Pals', gave me permission to use extracts from Private Pearson's verse memoirs. Mrs H. Irving advised on the selection of the illustrations. From T. E. Tilley Ltd., Stone Masons, I received help with memorial prices, and Mrs R. Evans translated the Welsh epitaph. The Harrogate Charge of the Light Brigade Society and the Humber Keel and Sloop Preservation Society also supplied information, and cemetery officials throughout England and Wales have taken much trouble over my enquiries.

Thanks are also due to the following for permission to use illustrations: Gordon Steadman, Doncaster [3]; Mr S. Temple [4]; Leeds City Libraries [6, 7, 16, 19, 30]; Mr T. Sinclair [11]; Mrs M. Morrell [12, 13]; St James's University Hospital, Leeds [14, 15]; Mr I. Dewhirst [17]; Mrs B. Green and Mr E. Pearce [20, 21]; Mrs M. Moss [22, 23]; Mr J. Whitmarsh Knight [24]; Wadsworth Atheneum Museum of Art, Hartford, CT. The Ella Gallup Sumner and Mary Catlin Sumner Collection Fund [25]; Mr A. Smith [27]; Mrs E. Janson [28]; and Mr and Mrs R. P. Freeman/Leeds Playhouse [31].

To the Leeds Town Councillors of 1842, who resolved to establish Beckett Street Cemetery, and to the Leeds City Councillors of 1985, who reversed the decision to clear it, my deepest thanks.

Chapter One

Decline and Fall

Be sure you lay me there he said
In that sweet lovely spot
And strew with flowers my grassy bed
To prove I'm not forgot.

Henry Parker, 1871

On 14 August 1845, a Thursday, a melancholy little group of people gathered behind a baby's tiny coffin in Joy's Fold, Leeds, at the meeting-place of Marsh Lane and the road to York. Half a century before, this had been the foldyard of a farm; now it was a collection of higgledy-piggledy, run-down cottages housing some of the less well-to-do working people of the town.

As they made their way northwards along the road called Burmantofts (named after the plots belonging to the burgesses or 'borough-men' of Leeds long ago), John and Hannah Hirst and their friends passed a few of the regimented brick rows of cramped terraced dwellings known as 'back-to-backs', where industrial Leeds was stretching greedy fingers out into the countryside. Yet there were still good large houses to be seen, standing in pleasant, tree-shaded gardens – Burmantofts Hall and Grove to the left, then Springfield House on the right, where Nippet Lane, dry and dusty, branched off towards the stream called Stoney Rock Beck. Passing the little wood down at the Accommodation Street crossroads, the road, now called Beckett Street, led straight on up the hill, where another short block of working-class homes stood on the left. To the north of Skinner Lane, down in the valley, the Hirsts could see the growing outcrop of housing known as 'Newtown', but along Beckett Street there was open country. True, the site for the new House of Recovery to replace the old fever hospital in Vicar Lane (which had been uncomfortably close to the most unhealthy area of the city) had been purchased, and in due course a dignified building costing £7,000 would rise behind the stone walls, but its completion was still, on that August day, a long way off.

The little procession was now moving along the powdery road past the brickfields which lay to left and right of Beckett Street. Clay had been dug and turned the previous winter so that bricks to fuel the Leeds housing boom could be moulded here, set out in rows to dry, and then taken to be baked in Mr Boothman's kiln, a little further on by the roadside. Beyond the brickfields, at the top of the hill, the end of their journey was in sight. It had taken barely twenty minutes to make the sad, slow passage from Joy's Fold out into the countryside.

Rising out of the fields on the right were the eight-foot high walls of the new Leeds Cemetery, the stones sparklingly clean in the summer air; this was the day of its opening, and the small group of mourners were bringing the body of nine-month-old Thomas Hirst for burial. The first set of heavy iron gates stood open beside the sexton's lodge, but the Hirsts and their little band went on to the further entrance, for they were Nonconformists, and the part of the cemetery nearer the town was for the use of Church of England members only. As they went in past the second lodge, the Dissenters' chapel stood before them, simple, heavy and buttressed, twin to the Anglican chapel which they could see over on the other side. All around was grass, as there had not yet been time for trees to grow or formal planting to become established; but the main avenues and walks had taken shape and the outline of grave plots had been measured and marked out. The grazing at the new cemetery had been let to Mr John Robson, of Thwaite Gate, whose sheep had helped ensure the grass would be trim for the arrival of the first clients.

John and Hannah were met by the Registrar, a Baptist minister in his thirties named Jabez Tunnicliff of whom the city, and indeed the nation, were to hear more. He was a kindly, bespectacled man with a Midlands accent, perhaps a little self-conscious on this, the first day of his new and unusual responsibility. The sexton, William Wright, had dug and prepared the grave, the very first in the cemetery, which lay towards the back, not far from the pebbly track known as Stoney Rock Lane. Of course, it was only a common grave; John earned a meagre living from the cloth industry as a 'stuff singer' and could not possibly have afforded a private grave and a permanent memorial. He had six other children to support, and this simple funeral, with the cheap hearse and small coffin and the various fees, had already taken a huge bite from his week's wages. The ceremony over, and a little bunch of wild flowers, gathered by the wayside, laid down to mark the newly dug grave, a feeling of desolation stole over the Hirsts at having to leave their baby all alone in this empty sixteen-acre field with scarcely any sound to be heard but the sighing of the breeze and the splashing of the neighbouring beck.

Another ten days were to go by before the grave was opened again for the body of six-year-old Mary Ann Atkinson, and yet more before the Anglican section received its first interment. Little did John Hirst think, on that sad day, that less than a year later the eightieth interment in the new cemetery would be of Hannah herself in a neighbouring grave to her son's.

J. & R. HARDWICK,

Most respectfully announce, that in addition to their business of

TAILORS AND DRAPERS,

They have commenced that of

UNDERTAKERS,

And pledge themselves that no exertion on their part shall be wanting to merit a continuance of that confidence they have so long enjoyed.

FUNERALS FURNISHED

ON THE

MOST REASONABLE TERMS.

THE

FUNERAL EQUIPAGE

Is Complete in every Department.

FAMILY MOURNING, GLOVES, &c.

The utmost Punctuality strictly observed.

49, Briggate, Leeds.

1. From Charlton & Archdeacon's Directory of Leeds, 1849.

It was a bold, yet necessary step the Leeds Town Council had taken in setting up this cemetery. In common with all other industrial areas, the city had seen a huge increase in population as births outnumbered deaths and as agricultural labourers abandoned the land in search of work in the new factories. In 1801 there were 53,270 people in the borough of Leeds; by the time of the 1841 census there were 152,054. The influx into towns with primitive water supply and sewerage systems, inadequate housing and very limited facilities in their few churchyards for disposal of the dead, brought with it appalling health problems. Many churchyards were in a dreadful state, raised high above ground level by layer upon layer of burials, with the effluvium from bodies seeping into the water supply of neighbouring dwellings, and with the poor remains frequently mangled and disturbed to make room for more. The example most often quoted is that of the scandalous Enon Chapel, opened in 1823 near the Strand, London, where it is said that 12,000 bodies, hacked about to save space, were stacked in the vault, separated by a simple wooden floor from the worshippers in the chapel above – who not infrequently had to be taken, fainting, into the fresh air.

In Leeds itself, the parish churchyard was said by Town Councillors 'to have induced relatives to commit atrocities that would disgrace the most barbarous people'.[1] An energetic and humanitarian surgeon and factory inspector named Robert Baker, who supplied a good deal of material from Leeds for Edwin Chadwick's great *Report on the Sanitary Condition of the Labouring Population of Great Britain,* wrote in 1842 that the burial-grounds of the Parish Church were overfull and in a disgusting state, and condemned unreservedly the unhealthy practice of interring the dead near the habitations of the living.[2] He later laid evidence before the Burial Grounds Committee, which was debating whether to order the final closure of the old churchyards:

> I was in the ground last Wednesday collecting information, and the sexton took me to a grave which they were then digging, for the interment of a female; two feet below the surface they took out the body of a child, which was said to be an illegitimate child, and it had been buried five years; below that and two feet six inches from the surface, were two coffins side by side, the father and the brother of the person who was then going to have the interment; the father was buried in 1831; the coffins were opened, the bones were in a state of freshness ... they were thrown on the surface, and at that time, the person came in who was going to have the interment; he spoke to me about

it, and made use of this expression, 'Look! These are the skulls of my Father and my Brother, and the bones of my relations, is not this a bad business? It cannot, I suppose, however, be helped; I must have a family grave.' He was very much shocked; he stayed there a short time, and then went away a little distance ... He knew they were the skulls of his Father and Brother, because it was a family grave; – the bottom part of the Coffin was chopped up and thrown on the surface, and I examined it. The residue was in an effervescent, putrescent state; after the bottom part of the Coffin had been taken out, a little soil was taken out again, and there were two other coffins side by side, containing the mother and grandmother of the same person. These coffins were broken up in my presence and thrown out, and then there was gravel underneath; all these bodies had been buried at the short distance of two feet six inches; and then, at a depth of one foot six inches more, lay others below them, on gravel, and they were thrown on to the grave side, in the way I have described to the Committee. I asked the sexton whether it was absolutely necessary that this should be, and his answer was, that it was quite impossible it should be otherwise; that it was not a single occurrence but was an every day occurrence, when they had to inter in that ground.[3]

Since the graveyards of the churches could no longer cope, it was clear that new and separate burial-grounds would have to be set up. Cemeteries (the name is taken from a Greek word meaning 'dormitory') had existed in Britain well before the nineteenth century. The Dissenters, who strongly objected to having to be buried in consecrated Anglican ground, had had their own cemetery in London, Bunhill Fields, as early as the seventeenth century; Edinburgh's citizens were buried from the eighteenth century in the cemetery on Calton Hill. In Norwich a far-sighted Nonconformist clergyman had established an undenominational cemetery, 'The Rosary', in 1821, which, however, was slow to capture custom.

Influential voices, particularly that of London barrister G.F. Carden, were raised during the 1820s and 1830s in support of the establishment of cemeteries, and their arguments quickly won support. There was a rush to promote joint-stock companies which would not only provide for the hygienic and acceptable disposal of the dead, but would also put healthy dividends into the pockets of the shareholders. The Liverpool Necropolis of 1825 was soon followed by the dramatic St James's Cemetery, also in Liverpool, scenically laid out in a disused quarry; Glasgow's Necropolis (1832) was high on a hill, and its commanding situation and splendid monuments earned the praise of Queen Victoria and Prince Albert when they visited the city. In London, Kensal Green Cemetery, also opened in 1832, and patronised by royalty, was the first of a string of great cemeteries which included Highgate, Nunhead and Abney Park. Leeds also had its private General Cemetery Company, which in 1835 laid out St George's Fields at Woodhouse with an imposing portico and a mortuary chapel in the Grecian style.

What did the early Victorians want of their last resting-places? Hygiene, aesthetics and security all played a part – well-drained soil, pleasingly land-scaped grounds (if possible on a sloping site which would give interest to the scene), safety from the feared body-snatcher, the dignity of a permanent memorial. The cemetery was considered an ideal place for a Sunday after-noon stroll, combining good views (especially in such places as Highgate, where one could see right across London, and Undercliffe, perched on an escarpment in Bradford) with an uplifting moral experience: 'And when you come my grave to see, Prepare yourselves to follow me' ... 'Praises on gravestones are but vainly spent; A life of goodness is a lasting monument' ... 'Pause! Reflect! Pass on!' Yet the majority of city-dwellers were in no finan-cial position to purchase fine private graves, nor was the idea of making a profit out of death wholly approved of, and it was not long before Acts of Parliament passed in the 1850s made it possible for parishes and towns to set up Burial Boards and establish municipal cemeteries. Appendix A dem-onstrates the enthusiasm with which local authorities grasped at this new solution to an old problem. From 1860, says Dr Curl in *A Celebration of Death*, 'most cemeteries in Britain were established by public authorities, and were utilitarian, hygienic, and for the most part uninteresting'.[4]

Several years before this legislation, however, Leeds Town Council, prod-ded by Robert Baker, had made its own far-sighted move. Although White's Directory of 1837 describes the new privately owned General Cemetery as 'for persons of all religious denominations', Baker did not agree: 'It is true that in Leeds we have a large and excellent cemetery, founded by a company of proprietors a few years ago, and situated out of the town; but it is only used by the Dissenters, no part of it having been consecrated for the use of the Church.' Clearly, Leeds needed burial-grounds which anyone would feel able to use, and which would accommodate the poor as well as the rich. The Leeds Burial Bill, passing through Parliament along with the public health reforms of the Leeds Improvement Bill, was commended by the *Leeds Mercury* on 11 July 1842 as an innovatory measure ('This is, we believe, the first bill that has passed in England conferring upon the Town

Councils the power of imposing rates for the purpose of the general interment of the dead'). On 2 July the same newspaper had emphasised both
the philanthropic and practical purposes of burial-grounds on the rates; 'a
certain source of revenue to the Town Council', the measure also formed
'a precedent for providing Burial Ground in all parts of the kingdom for
persons of all religious persuasions on equitable terms, protecting all just
rights, without inflicting injury on any denomination'. On 16 July 1842
the Council obtained its Act of Parliament 'for Providing Additional Burial
Grounds in the Parish of Leeds in the West Riding of the County of York',
and the way was open for new cemeteries to serve the townships of Leeds
and Hunslet. It took just over three years from the Act of Parliament to the
opening of those iron gates in Beckett Street.

The Burial Act Committee set up on 3 August 1842 consisted of seventeen aldermen and councillors, and their deliberations make fascinating
reading. The first task was, with the help of Mr Child, the Borough Surveyor,
to fix upon a suitable site. After several had been considered, tested and
rejected, they had what they wanted in two adjoining fields belonging to
the MP William Beckett Esq., one of eleven acres and one of five, the price
asked being some £210 per acre. On 22 September 1843 there was a site
visit to York Cemetery to get ideas on the layout, the buildings, the format
of the registers, the costs and charges, and soon advertisements were being
placed in the *Leeds Mercury* and *Leeds Intelligencer*, inviting firms to tender
for the various works.

Long and agonised arguments took place over what to us today would
seem relatively trivial matters. What, for instance, was to be done about the
mortuary chapels?[5] Since the burial ground was to consist of two separate
portions, one for Anglicans and one for Dissenters, there must be two chapels; but should they be separate buildings, or two chapels under one roof?
After changing their minds several times, the members of the Committee
opted for the former, commissioning Chantrell and Shaw as architects, and
although the buildings were identical, local custom referred to them (incor-
rectly) for ever after as 'the Church' and 'the Chapel'. The Bishop of Ripon,
whose ancient see included what had once been a tiny settlement by the
Aire and was now the major industrial city of Leeds, had to approve the
plans for laying out the Consecrated portions of the Leeds and Hunslet
grounds; in January 1844 a deputation of councillors waited upon him and
were 'much pleased with his Lordship's courtesy and urbanity', so much so
that they felt themselves able to agree to most of the small alterations which

2. Religious divisions: the site of the chapel of the Consecrated portion of Beckett Street (Burmantofts) Cemetery, demolished *c.*1960.

he proposed, such as the lengthening of the chapel windows – although 'in the opinion of this Committee the Act of Parliament does not provide for the expence of a Bell'![6] On 20 September 1844 Mr Jacob Verity was paid the sum of seven guineas for work which included 'setting boundary stones' between Consecrated and Unconsecrated portions.

Social divisions which make a modern reader feel slightly uncomfortable were also incorporated into the layout – first-class graves on top of the hill, fifth or lowest at each end. Fees were constantly revised before the cemetery opened, but show a wide range. The charge proposed on 6 December 1844 for a Nonconformist pauper, for instance, 'buried at the expense of the Township', was a mere 3*s* 6*d*, but an Anglican in a private grave in Ground 1 would pay £2 for the land and 16*s* for the interment – 50 per cent more for non-residents. Even between the tiny corpses of the stillborn there was discrimination – 5*s* in Ground 1, only 1*s* in Ground 5.

Contracts were prepared for the businesses which had offered acceptable tenders. After two firms were discovered to have made mistakes in estimating for the masonry work on lodges and chapels (such mistakes seem to have resulted in the Committee's immediately rescinding acceptance and taking the next firm's offer, even though it was higher than the corrected tender),[7] Mr Charles Drury received the contract at £1,330 15s. The job of erecting the outer walls, to be eight-feet high instead of seven at the Bishop of Ripon's request, was given to Mr John Walsh, who quoted 28s a rood (five and a half yards). However, this gentleman did not prove entirely satisfactory, for the minutes record on 26 July 1844 that 'this Committee having found that Mr. Walsh has been deviating from his Contract in not using Mortar in building certain portions of the boundary wall around the Leeds Burial Ground and although the Committee think the wall is not seriously injured by the deviation yet RESOLVED that the sum of £5.0.0. be deducted from the amount to be paid to Mr. Walsh to mark the displeasure of this Committee for his having done so'.

A good deal of thought went into the commissioning of the registers from Mr Henry Woodhead Walker – among them eight Royal Folio books, to be printed at the head of each page 'Register of Vaults and Graves in the Leeds Burial Ground', two Imperial Folio books headed 'Register of Burials in the Leeds Burial Ground', and two Imperial Folio books of certificates of grave purchase, all these bound in the best Russia leather, surmounted with brass at the top corners, and varying in price from £11–16 each.

It is unfortunate that an equal amount of care did not go into selecting employees who could write neatly and spell correctly, for while the first clerk of the Consecrated section kept well-written and orderly records, the corresponding Unconsecrated register is an untidy mess of illegible writing, erasures and corrections, with extraordinary orthography such as 'Sharlotte', 'soilder' and 'Cavielier Street'. We do not know for certain who was responsible for filling in the registers for, although the Burial Grounds Committee minutes seem to show clearly that it was originally the sexton's job, the handwriting does not always correspond with a change in this post; in the case of the Unconsecrated register, suspicion must fall on the Revd Tunnicliff, whose early education, as we shall see later, had been rather neglected. If the sextons were keeping the registers, they may perhaps have been overworked, for they seem to have combined the duties of clerk and gravedigger – which included all paperwork when the grave was ordered, receiving and accounting for the payments, making the graves (with assistance in digging where necessary), cleaning the chapel windows and cleaning and dusting the furniture, keeping the grass avenues and walks clear, and locking and unlocking the gates.[8] The slovenly keeping of the records evidently continued for many years, for a sub-committee of the Burial Grounds Committee had some astringent comments to make in 1881. The report on 'Registers of Burial' ran:

> These registers are kept by the Sextons, but inasmuch as the Burial Grounds Act, 5 and 6 Victoria, cap. 103, section 51, provides;–

> That all Burials in the *Consecrated part* of any such Burial Ground shall be registered by the CHAPLAIN of such Burial Ground *if a Chaplain shall be appointed thereto,*

> Your Sub-Committee would strongly urge the desirability of carrying this provision into effect. They do so for the following reasons, namely: – 1st. – The Registers would doubtless be more neatly kept than they now are, and would, at any rate, be free from the very defective spelling which at present mars their pages. 2nd. – They would then be the means of an additional check for the Borough Accountant in the Audit of the Burial Grounds Accounts, which at present they are not; as in some instances the registers are signed by the Chaplain a week after the interments have taken place, he merely taking the word of the Sexton that the Burials are correctly recorded. And 3rd. – It is desirable that the extracts from the Registers which are applied for from time to time, and for which the Registrar charges a fee of 3s. 7d, should be made by a person who can write a tolerably fair hand, and who can, at any rate, spell his words correctly.[9]

So bad did the situation become in the Consecrated portion that in 1885 a clerk, one Arthur Foster, was employed to correct the errors in the records. For several months he worked painstakingly on comparing the Burial and Grave Registers with each other and with the Rough Order Books, 'trying' in the grounds to see whether graves blank in the register were in fact occupied, and peering at the memorial cards of recent burials under their glass shades. In fact, he felt obliged to apologise to the Burial Grounds Committee at the end of his report for the length of time he had taken to set matters right, but his list of errors rectified (including no fewer than 528 graves in which one sexton, Sinclair, had made interments without entering any particulars in the Grave Registers) must have exculpated him. The incumbent sexton, William Bates, had made 1,065 mistakes in four years and two months of office, mostly by copying up the Grave Register from the Rough Order Book instead of from the more accurate Register of Burials. 'Found mistakes in spelling in a very many instances,' chided Mr Foster, 'and some of the pages in a somewhat blotted and dirty condition.'[10] Some years later the Committee wished to set in motion a similar exercise for the other half of the cemetery, but by then so many of the order books and other documents had gone missing that the task could not be attempted.

The Registrar and Clerk for the Unconsecrated section in 1845 were appointed by councillors' votes, Revd Jabez Tunnicliff having a clear lead with twelve votes over his nearest rival's nine for the position of Registrar;[11] his colleague on the other side was Revd Henry Pass Wright, and the two clerks were William Wright (Unconsecrated) and Richard Hodgson Pickard, the sexton from the Parish Church. It was the privilege of the Bishop of Ripon to approve the appointment of the staff of the Consecrated side, and there was a clear difference in management from the start, the Anglican Chaplain being non-resident, whilst sometimes the Registrars of the other side not only lived in the North Lodge, but even controlled the grave-digging side of the business.

As we have seen, the first burial took place in the Unconsecrated section on the day the cemetery opened, but things moved slowly at first. The Leeds annalist Mayhall comments:

> The new ground provided by the town council at Burmantofts was opened in August, 1845, for the burial of the dead, but owing to a dispute respecting the fees to be paid to the vicar and the clerk in orders but few interments took place therein, and the old ground continued to be used until the 30th of November, 1847, when the bishop of the diocese on the recommendation of the vicar, consented to the closing of those places.[12]

The Revd W.F. Hook, DD, Vicar of Leeds, was entitled, under the Burial Grounds Act, to a surplice fee of 1s for every Anglican burial in the cemetery, such as he received for interments in the parish churchyard; the Town Council, which paid an annual stipend of £80 to the chaplain appointed to the Consecrated portion, not unreasonably expected him to come to some accommodation with them over commutation. There was a major row between the redoubtable Vicar and the Burial Grounds Committee under its chairman Alderman Luccock, with letters, minutes and printed pamphlets flying back and forth like poisoned arrows. It seems to have been sparked off by the problems which gave rise to the following minute of the Committee on 10 February 1847: 'Resolved, that the Reverend the Vicar be informed that on the 26th January and several following days part of the Consecrated portion of the Leeds Burial Ground was in a very disgraceful condition, the sides and ends of several coffins being rendered visible, and the effluvium rising from the decomposition of the bodies apparent at a considerable distance.' The Vicar refuted any responsibility for the Consecrated section or its employees, but the dispute bared bones of contention. The Town Council had seen the institution of a municipal cemetery as a solution to the problem which had arisen when Dissenting ratepayers blocked the proposal to levy a rate for a new ecclesiastical burial-ground, but the extra charges were now penalising Anglicans. Furthermore, they resented reference to profit, which they claimed they would never be able to make, and to their privileges, which they described as 'that of being abused by yourself in words polite'![13] The Vicar, on the other hand, had a possible loss of income to bemoan, for he got nothing from the interments of Dissenters, who, had they been buried in the parish churchyard, would have had to pay his fees like everyone else.

The stalemate over burials continued until Councillor Joseph Richardson, a Methodist upholsterer and Liberal representative of the West Ward, dragged the question into the open by means of letters to the newspapers and debates in Council. While the parochial burial-grounds were still open, receiving 2,000 bodies annually, a mere 137 people had been buried at the new cemetery at a grossly unrealistic average cost to the ratepayer of over £5 8s 6d each. On 14 August 1847, when typhus or 'Irish Famine' fever was rife in the town, the *Leeds Times* reported a fierce argument in the council chamber, some attacking Dr Hook for his reluctance on a point of principle to close the churchyards, others blaming the Council itself for not having come to an accommodation with him over the contentious shilling. Mr Richardson related the prevalence of fever in the Kirkgate ward to the proximity of the parish churchyard, where, he claimed, nearly all the cases from the town's hospitals and institutions had been interred. Goulden's Buildings, Goulden's Square and Back York Street had been especially stricken. 'It is all through the accumulation of the Irish,' growled Councillor Bulmer, which was true, but not helpful, and earned him a sharp rebuke from Councillor Carr, who pointed out that the Irish were Christians and human beings like themselves. Alderman Gaunt thought the Bishop should have closed the churchyards even if the Vicar lost a hundred pounds a year thereby; was that a reason for destroying the lives of her Majesty's subjects? Polarised as they were on the question, the councillors eventually had to agree that their duty to the townsfolk must be paramount, and the Vicar was offered the sum of £30 in commutation of the surplice fees, so that he felt able to agree to petition the Bishop for the quid pro quo of closure.

This was not quite the end of the matter, since there were many relatives who insisted on the continued use of family vaults and graves. In 1851 the simmering pan of discontent boiled over once again with the prosecution of the Revd Samuel Kettlewell for illicitly burying William Wigglesworth at the Parish Church, the consequent declaration by the justices that the Council's closure notice was invalid, and the threat of further prosecutions unless the Bishop of Ripon finally agreed to end the use of the church-yards.[14] Despite the intervention of over forty Leeds medical men who signed a declaration that there could be nothing injurious to the public health in interment three feet below the surface in these private graves,[15] the Burial Grounds Committee finally managed to reach an agreement with the clergy which virtually eliminated further burials at the oldest Leeds churches. It had been a long haul.

Once the churchyard of St Peter's was closed, the two cemeteries (the Leeds General Cemetery Company's at Woodhouse and the Corporation's Leeds Cemetery at Beckett Street) were the major sites for burial in the town. The Unconsecrated part of Beckett Street Cemetery was consid-erably less popular than the Consecrated. On 11 August 1849 the *Leeds Intelligencer* had reported a Burial Grounds Committee meeting at which members had been informed that the income of the Unconsecrated portion was insufficient to defray expenses. (In fact, by the date of the meeting the Unconsecrated section had had 1,057 burials, compared with 1,883 on the other side.) The measure proposed to reduce expenditure seems extraor-dinary. William Wright, the clerk and sexton, was to be removed from his office, and Revd Tunnicliff, the registrar, was to occupy Wright's lodge – like him, free of rent, rates or other charges, and with coal, gas and water supplied – and to perform some of Wright's duties such as receiving orders and setting out and measuring graves. (Presumably he was not expected also to dig them.) The only charge which could be brought against Wright was that he had made headstones for other cemeteries in his spare time, which was causing complaints from local stonemasons of unfair competition, and that he had continued to do this despite an order from the Committee to desist. Alderman Luccock defended Wright, saying that 'the ground had got into its present good condition mainly through the zeal and ability of Mr. Wright. He had taken great pleasure in keeping his ground neat and in always having the graves dry, and he [Mr. Luccock] believed Mr. Wright had succeeded in giving universal satisfaction.' He pointed out, too, that 'with all respect for Mr. Tunnicliffe – and he had no doubt he had discharged his duties as registrar as well as anybody could possibly do – he was totally unfit to discharge the duties of clerk and gravedigger, and was as incompetent to set out a grave and to superintend the proper draining of the ground as he [Mr. Luccock] should be'. Councillor David Newton, backing the original motion, 'entered at some length into the history of the whole question', and ominously mentioned Mr Tunnicliff's claim that he had been so insulted by Wright that if the sexton were to stay he must resign his own office. Alderman Luccock had heard nothing about any insult to Mr Tunnicliff, and renewed his praise of Wright, stating that 'he was a man of warm temperament, but a better servant the town never had'. Tempers rose, or as the *Leeds Mercury* put it, 'a rather warm altercation ensued'! In the end this unfair expedient was not adopted, and the Committee - despite some foreboding as to how the parties concerned would be able to work together after this nasty episode – agreed to accept a deficiency of £200–300 a year on the Unconsecrated side, and to keep William Wright on at a reduced level of wages. Sadly, though, this was only a temporary respite, for on 5 March 1857 a minute of the Burial Grounds Committee records that Wright applied for a higher rate of remuneration and instead got the sack; so the Revd Tunnicliff was able to move into the North Lodge after all.

The Burial Grounds Committee continued to have many matters to deal with, large and small. In 1858 Messrs Crossland and Co. were mining the adjoining land, when they were accused of trespass because some of their headings were entering the cemetery. These headings were closed, but the Committee suspiciously ordered on 19 November that a shaft should be sunk inside the cemetery to see whether the coal or ironstone had been taken away. On 10 July 1862 it was resolved that urinals 'of a substantial and appropriate character' should be constructed in retired places in front of each chapel; apparently they had previously been sited against the chapel walls! Clearly the Committee must have been finding the whole business of satisfactorily managing cemeteries something of an effort, because at the same meeting a sub-committee was detailed to find out how the Woodhouse cemetery was kept 'in its present good order'. In 1863 there were already problems with neglected or damaged gravestones at the municipal cemeteries (which now included Holbeck), and the officers were instructed on 12 June that, where the owners declined or neglected to put stones into proper repair, those stones should be forthwith removed from the grounds; but by 1886 there was already considerable difficulty in tracing the owners of graves, for although the Superintendent sent out letters to those with defective grave-stones, the Committee heard on 30 July that 'nearly all [were] returned by the Post Office'. Unwanted trees caused difficulties, too; a minute of 2 May 1890 recorded that the tree growing on the grave owned by Mrs Beck was to be removed and that she would be charged with the cost thereof. Rewards were regularly offered for information leading to the conviction of people stealing flowers from the graves, or throwing stones into the cemetery. On 26 May 1893 the Councillors had occasion to rebuke the Chief Constable, one of whose policemen had refused admittance to a woman whom he considered to be improperly dressed: she had no bonnet on.

Human error was responsible for some unfortunate clashes. In 1881 there was a complaint by Mr Edwin Tesseyman that the grave in the Unconsecrated section in which he had interred 'several children' had, as he had reason to believe, bodies previously interred therein – a tricky situation, which was resolved by an investigation that showed the complaint to be unfounded.[16] Mr Thomas Beadles in 1884 employed a mason to cut an inscription for him, which by mistake was put upon the neighbouring stone belonging to Mr Boyle.[17] Even the chaplains sometimes offended; on 23 February 1885 the Visiting Sub-Committee dealt with a complaint from Mr D. Boothman that the Revd T.J. Hamerton had failed to turn up to conduct a funeral, despite having had proper notice. The reverend gentleman expressed his regret at the occurrence, which he stated was caused by his missing the 'Bus returning from Leeds'.

The story of the Sinclairs almost deserves a chapter to itself. Robert Sinclair was appointed to the position of Clerk and Gravedigger of the Consecrated portion on 28 December 1875, and it was not long before he was rebuked for incurring expenditure on his own authority. On 24 May 1877 a complaint was made against him by Mr Samuel Ellis for overcharging by 3s, and for using abusive language; in 1878 Mr Edward Jennins charged him on 17 January with neglecting his duty and with insolence, although on this occasion the Committee found that Sinclair was not to blame. Later that year, he was reprimanded for having charged for the use of the public water closets and for having cut flowers off the graves and cheekily offered them for sale at his lodge.[18] In 1879 he was in serious trouble. Mrs Edith Chapman accused Sinclair of not having constructed the vault for which she had paid him, and she also complained of insolence on the part of Mrs Sinclair. Rudeness the Committee might have been prepared to overlook, but financial irregularities, never. Sinclair was promptly called before the Committee and requested to resign within one month of that date, and we can read a good deal into the minute immediately following, which states that if he refused to do so, the Bishop of Ripon would be asked to dismiss him. Clearly Robert Sinclair was not prepared to go gracefully. As the date grew near, however, Sinclair sat down to compose a letter which must have softened the Committee's hearts, for he was allowed to remain.[19]

The stream of complaints continued. A Mrs Walton had become suspicious that all was not as it ought to be with the grave belonging to her, No. 3300, and she attempted to make enquiries, only to be truculently rebuffed by Mrs Sinclair, who seems to have been as unpleasant as her husband. A complaint was laid before the Committee, and Sinclair was ordered to open the grave so that Mrs Walton could inspect it, and afterwards to fill it up and replace the memorial over it, all at his own expense.[20] History unfortunately does not relate what Mrs Walton found. It was not only the public with whom Sinclair collided; the Anglican Chaplain, Revd William Studdert Kennedy of St Mary's, Quarry Hill, found his behaviour impossible. In an aggrieved letter on 27 August 1880 to the Committee, which had called him to order for lateness and non-attendance at funerals, he detailed several instances for which he laid the blame at Sinclair's door.

> Last Friday a special interment was arranged by him without my knowledge or consent and no notice was given to me although I was at the Cemetery every day, and when the funeral came at 12 o'clock and the mourners were in the chapel, the sexton went to my house to say a funeral was waiting, and my servant had to go through the Parish seeking me.

Finally, Robert Sinclair tripped himself up, and on 3 January 1881, following the discovery of 'discrepancies in the Accounts' and a most mysterious admission by another gravedigger, Thomas Scruton, that 'on or about the 3rd of June last at about 2 a.m. [!] he assisted Mr. Sinclair to open the grave No. 2638 belonging to E. Gaines and raised a coffin therein about two or three feet', he was compelled to resign his appointment.

The patience of the Committee with Mr Sinclair contrasts oddly with their callous behaviour towards Frederick Blackburn, his predecessor, who served them faithfully and without giving any trouble whatsoever for nearly thirty years, from 31 December 1847 to the end of 1875, and whose elegant headstone can still be seen near his former home. On 18 January 1877 the minutes record coldly: 'Mr. Frederick Blackburn late Clerk and Gravedigger at the Leeds Burial Ground waited upon the Committee, and applied for a gratuity or small allowance; – Resolved, that the Committee proceed to the next business.'

There was also trouble with the sextons on the other side of the cemetery. Mr Charles Hannam had been appointed in August 1865, but was suspended four years later for 'certain irregularities in the transaction of his business'.[21] Whilst suspended, he died, and his euphoniously-named widow Hannah was allowed to step into his shoes, being officially employed by the Committee as Clerk and Gravedigger, although the manual work was done by her son Thompson, who also lived at the Lodge with his wife and several children. There were no complaints about the Hannams until 1881, when offences 'with respect to the interment of stillborn children and the non-accounting for the moneys received for the same' came to light. Like Wright and Sinclair before her, Mrs Hannam had to go, and her son and his family with her.[22] It seems to have been hard indeed for an employee of the Burial Grounds Committee in Victorian days to resist the chance of pocketing a little of the money which must every day have passed in quantities through his or her hands.

The buildings, as well as the people, caused headaches for the Councillors of the Burial Grounds Committee. Both chapels and lodges suffered severely from damp. In a letter considered on 29 April 1881, the Revd Kennedy threatened the Committee quite rudely over the former: 'Is nothing to be done for our Chapel? If not I shall be obliged to ask the Bishop to close it for necessary repair. It is reeking with damp and the stench at times is intolerable.' The chapels were patched up with Roman Cement, wood cladding and ventilators, but the Borough Engineer could find no solution to the problem of the lodges other than, in 1880, to pull them down and rebuild them completely to the design of the architect Mr Braithwaite, at a cost of £600.[23]

Despite the occasional hiccoughs, however, Burmantofts Cemetery (as it was commonly called) was performing an extremely important function in the growing city of Leeds. From 220 burials in the first full year of its opening, the number rose steadily; already in the 1860s there were often fourteen, fifteen or sixteen burials in a day. The peak was reached in the 1880s and 1890s with around 3,000 interments every year. We can imagine

3. A funeral procession passing Christ Church, Doncaster, *c.*1910.

the frequent solemn processions along Beckett Street of black-panoplied, glass-sided hearses and crape-clad mourners, the noisy bustle of horse-drawn carts, vans and omnibuses respectfully stilled around them.

We are fortunate to have a lively picture of the cemetery in its heyday from Mr Stanley Temple, who was born in the North Lodge in 1904.[24] His father, Frederick, had come from York to be gardener at Waterloo Villa, the home in Garforth of ironworks owner Henry Berry. In the 1890s he took the job at Burmantofts Cemetery, and with his wife Clara and four young children (Ernest, Mary, Arthur and Cissie) moved into the North Lodge, where a further two children, Stanley and Ruth, were born. Frederick Temple, with an assistant, was responsible for all the gardening at the cemetery, and for the production of the bedding plants, which filled the three large greenhouses behind the South Lodge and overflowed into his own garden. Hundreds of

4. A rare moment of relaxation: Mrs Clara Temple outside the North Lodge, *c.*1920.

geraniums were raised each year, with bed edgings of lobelia and alyssum, and wallflowers for early summer, so that Beckett Street looked 'more like a park than a cemetery'. He also supervised the gang of gravediggers. When a funeral procession drove up to the cemetery, Mr Temple, in a black suit and highly polished black leggings, holding a black bowler hat in his hand, would meet the hearse with its etched glass sides and plumed black horses specially bred in Belgium, and would conduct the mourners to the chapel, where the coffin would lie in the mortuary separated from the congregation but visible through a large plate-glass window.

He was an extremely meticulous man, recording every incident in his diaries, and he was devoted to his job. Mrs Temple, too, was involved in his work. Young Stanley would be set to dust the cream-coloured pews while his mother scrubbed and scoured with calloused hands the stone floor of the chapel, and it was she who polished the black leather gaiters till they glowed. The elder sons grew up and left home – Ernest to become a lumberjack in Canada, and Arthur to join a troupe of Christy minstrels – and Stanley, at the tail-end of the family, had his own domestic tasks to perform. In the mornings, before setting off to Gipton School, the small boy chopped wood for the fire, and in the evenings, almost choked with the fumes, he helped his father to stoke the coke-fired boilers in the underground boiler-house which served the greenhouses. The boy was not allowed to go to the 'other side' (where Mr Joah Sheard, the Superintendent, lived in the South Lodge) except with his father, and he was not permitted to have any friends in unless he could convince his father that they were nice boys and would not get into mischief. His best friend was Jack Milthorp, son of one of the partners of the firm of monumental masons, Milthorp & Hodgson, who had their yard opposite the corner of Stanley Road and next to the Workhouse which was to become St James's Hospital. Stanley asked if he might set up a gymnasium in the toolshed with the ropes used for lowering buckets into the graves, and he and Jack spent many happy hours swinging and soaring on their home-made trapeze.

The years at the North Lodge were busy and contented ones for the Temple family. Discipline was strict; Mr Temple's brothers, one of whom was a moulder at the engineering firm of Fowler's, were both heavy drinkers, and Mr Temple himself, to set an example, would not have a drop of alcohol in the house. Only at Christmas was the rule relaxed, when a bottle of tonic wine would be bought to be offered to visitors! On Sundays all diversions would be put away – not just playing-cards, but even scissors and sewing equipment

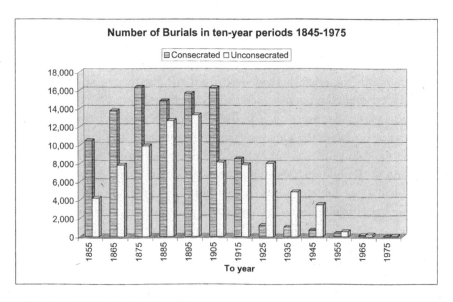

5. The rise and fall of Beckett Street Cemetery.

– and if Stanley and his pal Jack wanted something to do, they would go for a walk, usually to Roundhay Park. Arthur excelled at playing the banjo; when the family gathered round the fireside of an evening, Arthur would take out his banjo and begin to strum softly, and within minutes Mrs Temple would be asleep. Mr Temple had four days' holiday a year, which the family spent at Bridlington on the east coast, but there was also an occasional half-day trip. On one of these, in Whitby, he noticed a plant unknown to him growing in the old stone walls, and he brought a big bundle of it back to Beckett Street, where it was planted and throve. Not having had any formal training, he could not identify the plant, but referred to it for years as 'the Whitby seedling'; later, he would claim proudly that he had brought the first alyssum into Leeds. He was a talented amateur painter, and his other recreation was to go to the cinema, which he loved. This establishment was in Florence Street and was properly called 'The Western', but locally, and no doubt with reason, it was known as 'The Bug Hutch'!

In about 1927 Mr Temple reached retirement age and had to stop work and leave the lodge for a small back-to-back house in nearby Ashley Road, which the family felt to be very much a step down in the world. The decline thereafter of this gentle, fastidious old man parallels the decline of the cemetery he loved. As the older cemeteries filled up, new ones had been opened – Lawnswood (a showpiece, and later home of the first Leeds crematorium) in 1876, Roman Catholic Killingbeck in 1895, Harehills near Beckett Street in 1908, and several others. Burials at Beckett Street fell off after the end of the Victorian era, gradually at first, then steeply. By the time of the Great War there was little room left on the Consecrated side, and the rate of interment in the Unconsecrated section, which had always lagged well behind that in the Anglican part, at last overtook it. In the ten years from 1925, for instance, there were 5,000 burials in the Unconsecrated portion, five times as many as in the Consecrated; but this was but a ghost of the busy activity of former years. By the time Mr Temple was buried in the shadow of the chapel his wife had kept so well, in a plot which he had chosen with care as the best in the cemetery, Beckett Street was within a few months of its centenary. In its next fifty years it was to have only another 6,000 burials entered in its registers, to bring the total at the time of writing to just under 180,000.

Chapter Two

Down Those Mean Streets

Dangers stand thick through all the ground
To push us to the tomb,
And fierce diseases wait around
To harry mortals home.

John Tate, 1874

The grandeur of cemeteries such as Highgate and Kensal Green, full of splendid tombs and mausolea, is well known; Beckett Street Cemetery is an ordinary, largely working-class Victorian burial-ground. Its catchment area comprised the North, North-east and East wards of the town, the poor, dirty and ill-drained quarters where a flood of poverty-stricken Irish immigrants had arrived to join the indigent country-born labourers flocking to seek better-paid employment in the city. In the eighteenth century the centre of Leeds had been within easy reach of fields, and there was still adequate room for development in the gardens and innyards, and in the foldyards which in the second half of the century became the pockets of housing known as Joy's Fold, Ward's Fold, Blue Bell Fold and the like. With the trebling of the population in the first half of the nineteenth century, the city could no longer contain the influx within its Georgian limits, and Building Clubs and speculative builders ran up rows of cheap, sometimes shoddy houses to meet the new needs. Professor Beresford has demonstrated in his analyses of Leeds housing[25] how the typically long, narrow fields of Leeds, probably

35

created by enclosures in the later Middle Ages and often used as tenter fields for the drying of cloth, lent themselves to the construction of ribbons of the tiny, unhealthy dwellings known as 'back-to-backs'. ·

Manchester had them; Liverpool had them; in mid-century Nottingham they formed two-thirds of the housing stock. Back-to-back houses were condemned over and over again by the sanitary reformers during the Victorian age, and in these and other cities the further construction of such abominations was forbidden. Yet in Leeds the design maintained an extraordinarily persistent grip until well into the twentieth century. The cottages in these terraces were joined to their neighbours on each side and had a party or abutting wall at the back with the terrace in the next street, so that, with windows and door only at the front, there could be no through ventilation. Each house was about five yards square, with one room downstairs, one up, and perhaps a cellar underneath which could even be let as a separate dwelling. In order to pack more housing in on the land, the street might end up as a narrow courtyard enclosed by housing at the end, which further restricted what little light and air there might have been. There were even yards with housing at both ends, so that entrance was gained by a tunnel. Sanitary arrangements, of course, were minimal; Professor Beresford has also shown how the sale of small parcels of land led to a very piecemeal kind of development, in which streets came to a full stop against the blank end walls of houses or factories in other streets, and how difficult it was in these circumstances to achieve any kind of sensible pattern of drainage or sewerage.[26] The earliest back-to-backs date from the 1780s, and include such notorious names as Ebenezer Street, Georges Street and Union Street, which recur again and again in the Beckett Street Burial Registers. Building costs had to be kept low so that the rents were within the reach of the poor, and it can be imagined how squalid, how airless, dark and filthy were the conditions in these overcrowded dwellings.

By the year Beckett Street Cemetery was opened, there were large numbers of back-to-backs in the city, and Robert Baker wrote indignantly: 'Whole streets of houses have arisen in Leeds in an inconceivably short space of time, and in many instances evidently for the sole end of speculation, without regard to the absolute wants of the tenants.'[27] Baker drew up maps marking the distribution of fever cases, and showed these to be heavily concentrated in the crowded and insanitary areas. 'It seems clear,' he reasoned, 'that the rate of mortality in large towns diminishes in proportion to the means of ventilation and drainage.' But Baker was a prophet crying in

6. *Above*: 'The only wonder is
how persons can be got to live
in such holes' (*Leeds Mercury*,
1869). Garside's Court, 1901.

7. 'Hardly room in which to
turn oneself' (*Leeds Mercury*,
1869). Yards, Back High Street,
1901.

the wilderness as far as Leeds was concerned, and the speculators continued to cover the fields with a type of housing that few of them would have wished to live in. Not until the Leeds Improvement Act of 1866 (which conspicuously failed to prohibit the back-to-back) was there even a regulation which introduced a compulsory 'privy space' between each block of eight houses and required a reasonable minimum width of road; but it appears that even in these better developments there was a higher-than-average death rate. Yet the city clung obstinately to the design, claiming that more expensively constructed housing would be beyond the pockets of its workers; indeed, when the Housing and Town Planning Act of 1909 attempted to ban back-to-backs, Leeds Council petitioned against the clause, and by a quirk in the regulations they continued to be built until just before the Second World War.

It is worth looking in some detail at Robert Baker's 1842 report to Edwin Chadwick, for it gives a horrifying picture of the state of the area which, within three years, would be supplying the new cemetery at Burmantofts with the bulk of its clientele. He describes the discoloured waters of the River Aire and of the Timble Beck (which runs through the most populous ward) with the sewage of the town discharged into them and refuse left upon the side of the beck, which is 'so exhalant and noisome as to be offensive in the first degree'. The rubbish thrown into the Timble Beck has silted it up so that it is no longer capable of acting effectively as a drain, and sometimes overflows and inundates the houses nearby with filth. Only sixty-eight of the 586 streets in Leeds are paved by the local authority, and Baker condemns the custom of setting paving in ashes, which give a filthy dust in dry weather and foul puddles in wet. Everywhere there are posts, rails, steps, unprotected cellars, clothes-lines. Drains and sewers (wholly or partly absent in twenty-nine even of the Town Surveyor's sixty-eight streets) are lacking or choked, and 'stagnant water, and channels so offensive that they have been declared to be unbearable, lie under the doorways of the uncomplaining poor; and privies so laden with ashes and excrementitious matter, as to be unuseable, prevail, till the streets themselves become offensive from deposits of this description'. Three streets with a total population of 4–500 persons 'have not a single useable privy'. Indeed, in many cases there are no privies whatsoever, empty or full, and Baker quotes the answer of an old woman to the inevitable shocked enquiry: 'They do as they can, and make use of the street itself as the common receptacle.' A huge depot of street sweepings, being dried for use as manure, has been set up by a contractor to the Commissioners of Public Nuisances right in the centre of the crowded North-east ward and causes an 'insufferable stench'. There are offensive slaughter-houses, particularly in the Kirkgate and North wards, and an intolerable amount of smoke both from engine furnaces and, especially unbearable because emitted at low level, from dyeworks and tobacco-pipe manufactories. Baker writes, too, of the overcrowding and resultant moral aberrations; of the miserable condition of the dwellers for a rent of 1s a week in 'the dark and dank cellar, inhabited by Irish families, including pigs, with broken panes in every window-frame, and filth and vermin in every nook'; of the damage done to homes where the mother must be absent earning a meagre living, instead of being the true focus and guardian of domestic life; of the bitter, unavailing struggle against poverty and dirt.

Reports in the Leeds newspapers on local inquests cast a lurid glow over the lives of the poor. In 1856 an old man named Matthew Bedford was grazed and thrown by a cart, and died the same day. 'Deceased, an infirm man, resided in Wells Street, and gained a living by gathering bones and rags in the street ... ' Thomas Jackson fell dead in North Street, later in the same year. 'The deceased ... was a labourer of peculiar habits, living in a cellar dwelling in Brown's-yard, Ebenezer-street, the shutters of his abode not having been opened for fourteen years ... '

In August 1865 the local newspapers published the charge brought against Jane Brown by the Clerk to the Board of Guardians, who was supported by the evidence of two medical men, Mr Beardshaw and Mr Ruddock. Mrs Brown housed a woman and child in her living-room in Dufton Street; two young men and two young women slept in two beds in the bedchamber; while in the unventilated, windowless garret some fourteen feet square and seven feet high she had managed to cram three women and ten children, using a bed brought from Liverpool in which fever patients had been nursed. Her defence was that her sister and children had come unexpectedly from Sheffield and that she was unable to get a larger house within her means, which was very probably true.[28] Six months later Mr Swales, Inspector of Nuisances – who must have been a very busy man in mid-Victorian Leeds – summoned Michael McLachlan before the magistrates at the Town Hall for accommodating, in a three-roomed house in 'the notorious locality' known as Lloyd's Yard, his own family of eight and his sister's family of five.[29] The rooms averaged ten feet square. The two families were assailed by the virulent epidemic of typhus which scourged the town in the winter of 1865/6, and McLachlan's brother-in-law died, while six of the children were taken ill, three having to be sent to the House of Recovery. The dead body was coffined, and lay within two feet of the fire for three days before being removed for burial. When the sanitary officers got wind (an apt phrase) of conditions in the McLachlan household, they went to Lloyd's Yard and thoroughly cleansed and purified the house. 'The mattresses, &c., were in a most disgusting and filthy state from vermin and other causes,' reported the *Leeds Mercury* circumspectly, 'so bad, indeed, that the officers would not handle them, but conveyed them away on a large three-pronged fork, and had them burnt.' (This was all very well, but there must have been loud Irish curses and laments as the horrid objects were carried out, since the poverty-stricken inhabitants were left with nothing to sleep on but the bare boards.) In this case the excuse for the overcrowding was that the sister was being afforded an asylum from the ill-treatment of her husband – although he seems to have been living there with her when he died.

In an age when it was not customary to hurry the body off to an undertaker's Chapel of Rest, but to lay it out at home and take it directly from home to burial-place, the family with only one or two rooms would have to live, eat and sleep with the corpse until the funeral took place. Dr John Simon, London's first Medical Officer of Health, had written unhappily of this practice in 1852. 'The sides of a wooden coffin, often imperfectly joined, are at best all that divides the decomposition of the dead from the respiration of the living ...'[30] Various factors played their part in the long interval between death and funeral – tradition, reluctance to part with the loved one, the desire to make sure there was no possibility of burying the person alive. Michael McLachlan pleaded extreme poverty as his excuse for not burying his brother-in-law. Whatever the reason, we can be sure that, in many a Leeds back-to-back at this time, the living would have shared their accommodation with the dead.

The stark statistics of the Registrar-General show the results of the conditions described by reformers such as Robert Baker and John Simon. One child in every five born in Leeds at this time would die before it reached the end of its first year. The offspring of the middle and upper classes had a considerably better chance of survival; Baker's table, submitted to the Sanitary Commission in 1842, of the average age at death in Leeds, gives forty-four years for gentlemen and professional people and their families, 27 for tradesmen and farmers and their families, and only 19 for labourers and their families.[31] Because Beckett Street Cemetery served such poor districts, we must expect the number of child burials to be disproportionately high.

The infant mortality rate over the whole country was at its worst towards the end of the century, and did not begin to improve significantly until the last years of the Edwardian era.

In the dirty, crowded houses of the poor, any epidemic would rage like wildfire. There was an outbreak of the lice-born disease typhus (also known as 'gaol fever' or 'Irish famine fever') in 1847, in which several of the doctors at the House of Recovery died; a very malignant form was rife again, as we have seen, in 1865/6. Cholera and typhoid fever were both spread by contaminated water, and the former was particularly lethal, with large numbers of Leeds people dying in the 1849 epidemic. Smallpox was on the decline, but recurred periodically in vicious epidemics such as that of 1871/2; the Beckett Street Burial Registers record a number of dead from the hospital set up for smallpox victims in sheds belonging to the Board of Guardians and standing on land near the Workhouse. Today's minor childhood illnesses, such as measles, could easily sweep off an undernourished, sickly young child; whooping-cough and scarlet fever struck with particular savagery in the thickly populated towns. The industrial cities were smoke-ridden and often fog-bound, and respiratory disease was a major cause of death; of the 6,261 deaths in the borough of Leeds in 1867, no fewer than 1,177 were classified as due to disease of the lungs, including 815 deaths from bronchitis. Some of the more common causes of death affecting different age groups in that year are shown in Appendix C, Table 2. Add to this the toll of industrial accidents and occupational diseases to which so many workers were exposed in the mines, the flax mills, the wool-combing rooms and the tailors' sweatshops, and it seems almost a wonder that anybody lived to any age at all. The Burial Registers of Beckett Street Cemetery unfortunately do not give the cause of death, but we can well imagine the tuberculosis and asthma, the epidemics of diarrhoea and scarlet fever, the deformities and miseries encouraged by foul air, impure water and overcrowded conditions.

The most dramatic of the epidemic illnesses to which the Victorians were subjected was undoubtedly the Asiatic cholera, the first wave of which hit Britain in 1832. Sufferers lost so much fluid by diarrhoea and vomiting that their bodies became dehydrated and their vital functions were often damaged beyond recovery, the pulse and heartbeat weakening, the skin growing cold and wrinkled ('washerwoman's hands'), and the voice reduced to a whisper. The process of infection was not understood, there was no proven remedy, and the speed with which fit people succumbed to it was terrifying. In 1849 the dreaded disease appeared again. The first Leeds victims were two little boys aged nine and seven, John and Michael McCarthy, the sons of a poor Irish labourer living in Wheeler Street, Bank. The *Mercury* trusted that 'with prompt and proper care as to ventilation, regimen, and temperate habits', the outbreak of an epidemic might be avoided, and noted that the McCarthys' situation was most unfavourable to such care:

> This family were by their circumstances every way predisposed for the recep-
> tion of the disease. Besides those who have had the complaint, there are the
> husband and several children, who have hitherto escaped it; but all are located
> in a miserable cellar dwelling, with only a single bed for the living and the
> dead; and subsisting up to this time principally upon vegetable diet, not
> having the means of procuring more substantial food.

The McCarthy boys were buried at Beckett Street on 15 June; there were one or two other cases, then a lull for a week or two. At the end of July, the cholera struck at Smithies Street, 'one of the most unhealthy in the town'. The *Mercury* describes the house occupied by Hannah Grayshon, a widow of sixty, and her twenty-five-year-old son William, as 'situated in a sort of confined yard, sunk below the level of the street', and notes that there had been a fatal case in the same street the previous week. Mark Smith of Cavalier Court was buried on 3 August. His death occasioned some surprise, as his house was rented from Messrs Croisdale, whose cottage property was among the best in town; and Smith himself for most of the week lived at his place of employment, a paper maker's in Meanwood, where he enjoyed country air.

There could be no doubt by now that another major outbreak was gain-ing hold, cutting swathes through the population of the poorer districts. The Craven family was virtually wiped out. Ellen Craven of Cavalier Street, a delicate woman who had not been well for the previous three years, was attacked at three o'clock in the morning of 6 August and succumbed less than twelve hours later; at the inquest Mr Bearpark, the surgeon, described how she had looked when he visited her. 'He found Mrs Craven in bed, her countenance very much shrunk, her eyes sunk, her pulse very feeble, the surface of the body cold, with every other symptom of the worst state of cholera. She had no cramps at the time he saw her, but had excessive purging of a rice-water character.' Her husband John, a coal-miner, died early the following morning. The child who was sent for the doctor was the next victim, followed by Sarah Tempest, Mrs Craven's married sister, who had given evidence to the Coroner that Ellen had lent a sheet for the use

8. The central east–west path in Beckett Street Cemetery, showing the line of pencil-shaped marker stones dividing Anglicans (on the right) from Dissenters. (*See* p. 60.)

of Mark Smith. 'After his death she wrung it out, and she said she then got a bad smell.' John's brother Robert took in one of the orphaned children, who developed the disease, giving it to its uncle and aunt; all three died, as did a nineteen-year-old son or nephew. Again, the poor conditions of the family were emphasised. Mrs Tempest stated that her brother did not earn more than 10s a week. 'They had been badly off for years. They had not at times sufficient to eat. They would not get into debt, and did not apply to the parish to which they belonged, which was Rothwell.'

The rapidity of the course of the disease was frightening. Dorothy Shepherd, aged fifty-nine, who kept a cook-shop in a cellar near the Royal Hotel in Briggate, was taken ill in the afternoon of 22 August, and died at five o' clock the next morning. One young man fell victim whilst playing a cricket match at Hunslet, and expired before the game was over. The medical men did their best to preserve a calm front before the ravages of the sickness; the problem was that nobody understood how cholera was spread. It was thought to be passed on by personal contact, or through the air; the *Mercury* report on one of the 1849 cases even suggested that the victim had been pre-disposed to the disease by reason of her diet of boiled pork, new bread and cabbage![32] The response of the sanitary authorities was to burn bedding and to issue chloride of lime to wash down dwellings; nobody realised that the cholera vibrio was water-borne and that water supplies contaminated with sewage from previous victims were responsible for spreading the sickness, although it was widely recognised to be in some way connected with conditions of urban filth. Evidence given at the Craven inquest stated:

> There was a drain in a field belonging to Mr. Judson, and immediately in front of Ball's-buildings, where a collier's wife, of the name of Barber, had died. This drain received the refuse from 300 or 400 people located there, and it had no outlet whatever. It was an open drain, without outlet, and when full it ran over the adjoining land and fertilised it. This drain had not been cleaned out in any man's recollection ... from the appearance of it, for it was full of putrid matter, 18 inches to 2 ft. in depth.[33]

Nor was it known that the only possible successful treatment was to rehydrate the patient. Cholera is still endemic in the Ganges delta, but patients who are given replacement fluids (sometimes as much as twice their own weight) usually recover. In nineteenth-century Leeds the sufferers had to endure the well-meaning attentions of doctors whose treatment was largely guesswork. Baby George Wormald of Cavalier Street remarkably survived Dr Horton's management, which consisted of large doses of capsicum, small doses of calomel (a purgative!) and 'the assiduous application of blankets wrung out in boiling water, hot sandbags and mustard poultices'.[34] A correspondent to the *Mercury* of 30 September strongly recommended his own remedy, which had cured his son. 'Ten drops of tincture of opium, 15 drops of nitrous acid (not nitric), in one tablespoon of strong mint water. In a very bad case, hot flannels to be constantly applied to the heart and feet.' The Bishop of Ripon organised a Day of Humiliation on Wednesday 19 September, with places of business closed so that the frightened and afflicted citizens could take part through public worship and private devotion in requesting the Deity to cease His chastisements. Or one could simply put a bold face on things, as did George Breary of Lion Street, Newtown.

A man named Breary, who had been very active and useful in cholera cases at Newtown, died on Wednesday morning. The Sanitary Committee had voted him several sums of money as rewards for his services, and he had frequently boasted of his courage in going amongst those attacked with the disease. The scourge caught him, however, on Tuesday night, and he died after a few hours' illness.

Perhaps the most notorious case of the whole outbreak was that of a young woman called Susannah Brown. There was nothing unusual in her contracting the disease or dying of it, but the circumstances had more than a tinge of the Dickensian about them. Susannah was a married woman, aged about twenty-six or twenty-seven, who lodged in York Street and made a living from the manufacture of velvet purses, which she hawked about the town. She had suffered from 'purging' for a day or two before she made her fateful journey on Wednesday 22 August 1849. From the centre of Leeds she wandered north-west through the suburbs, out to the township of Horsforth and as far as Guiseley before turning south, down towards Bradford. By half-past three in the afternoon, when she reached Eccleshill, she had already covered at least fifteen miles, and it was then that she began to feel really ill. She had a glass of beer at a beerhouse, but was unable to keep it down. Assistance was summoned in the shape of Mr Newstead, surgeon, and Mr Baxter, overseer, who both arrived at the same time, to find Susannah sitting on a step outside the beerhouse. Mr Newstead examined her, ascertaining that she had

had violent purging and noting her thready pulse and cold hands, and in a trice the rumour was flying round Eccleshill that a woman from Leeds had brought the cholera into their midst.

Now Mr Newstead and Mr Baxter conferred as to what was to be done. There was a practical obstacle to keeping her in Eccleshill: nobody would have her. Indeed, people locked their doors and went to hide upstairs in order to avoid being required to take her in. The obvious course would have been to remove her to the workhouse, except that the expense of her care would then have fallen on the ratepayers of Eccleshill, which Mr Baxter, as their loyal servant, was no doubt anxious to avoid; in any case, the immediate problem here was that the Eccleshill Union Workhouse was not at Eccleshill but at Carlton, some five miles off to the north.

Since Susannah herself wanted to get home, the most sensible course seemed to Joseph Baxter to take her to Apperley Bridge Station on the Leeds and Bradford Railway, which was only a mile away, and to escort her back to Leeds by train and cab. Mr Newstead concurred in this decision; although he would not have given a guarantee that it was perfectly safe to remove her, he thought the case was unlikely to terminate fatally, and in fact he claimed later that he was never asked whether she was dangerously ill or not. They got her a glass of brandy at the Victoria public-house, and then Baxter took her in a spring cart to the station, where they arrived at about five o'clock. As they waited for the train, poor dazed Susannah gradually grew worse. The journey, at her own request (for she wanted to be where there was air) was in an open carriage, and they reached Leeds at twenty to six. There was only one cab at the station, and, not surprisingly, the driver took one look at Susannah and declared that he was already engaged. So, with Susannah leaning on Baxter's arm and he carrying the pathetic basket of velvet purses, they made their way towards York Street; but they never reached their destination. In Duncan Street, saying 'Oh master, I must sit down,' the sick woman sank upon the doorstep of Mr Heald's warehouse, and in no time a crowd had collected. She was got to Mr Bulmer's surgery, and the doctor was hastily summoned. 'She was in a state closely resembling death,' he described her later. 'She was dark-coloured, shrivelled, and pulseless. She was in a perfect state of collapse – in fact, I thought she was dying. The disease was malignant cholera, and it was a very bad case.' He sent for a spring cart and some blankets, and Susannah was conveyed on the last part of her miserable travels, this time to the poorhouse known as the Mendicity Office, where, next morning at half-past nine, her earthly journey ended.

She was buried at Beckett Street Cemetery later that day, in one of the mass graves of the cholera burial area.

Public opinion was revolted by the cruelty of treating a fatally ill woman in this way, and at the inquest the Leeds Borough Coroner, Mr Blackburn, had some harsh words on the case. He observed that it did not say much for the humanity of the people of Eccleshill, which was a very large place, that when a stranger was taken dangerously ill not a single human being in the township was to be found who would give accommodation to her. The witness, Mr Newstead, replied that there was no proposal to take her in by any person. 'No,' retorted Mr Blackburn sharply, 'the proposal seems to have been to get rid of her in the best and quickest way you could.' Mr Bulmer, the Leeds surgeon, while unwilling to shop a colleague, was clearly of the opinion that it had been very improper to remove the sick woman. He was anxious that the inquiry should take place, because this was not the only case of its kind:

> It had frequently occurred that poor persons seriously ill had been brought to Leeds from their townships in order to get rid of them, and to save expense. When the fever was raging people suffering from it were sent here from all parts. Two persons were sent by railway from Goole a few days ago who had been attacked with cholera; one of them died, and the other was ill in a house close by the house where the deceased, Susannah Brown, lodged. If the disease was infectious, which he considered it was, any person travelling in a railway carriage which had contained cholera patients might get the disease and not know how or where they had contracted it ... He did not blame the surgeon or the overseer, but still he thought there was a great want of humanity in removing her.

The Coroner, in summing up, felt that although the whole affair had been very unsatisfactory, Baxter had not had much choice.

> At the same time he thought it should be known to overseers that when persons were attacked in a similar way to the deceased they ought not to bring them to Leeds, but to use every exertion to obtain some place for them in their own township; because there was plenty of sickness in Leeds without increasing it and increasing the expense attending it.

So ended the sad case of Susannah Brown.

It was now, with this dreadful disease raging unabated, that the new cemetery really came into its own. At first cholera cases were buried with those who had died of other causes, but once the Burial Grounds Committee realised what they were dealing with, mass graves were dug at the back of the cemetery, and the victims were hastily interred in these unmarked resting-places. Burials shot up from three or four a day to thirty or forty. 'At the new cemetery in Beckett-street, Burmantofts,' stated the *Mercury* on 8 September, '40 burials took place on Wednesday and 53 on Thursday.' The toll on the officiating clergy was severe. 'The fearful mortality of the late visitation having happily abated,' wrote the Revd George Hills, Chaplain of the Consecrated Portion, to the Mayor in November that year,

> ... I am sure I need not remind you how arduous these duties have been the last three months. They have been quite beyond the power of any one man. Since January 1st of the present year there have been 2,000 funerals, of which 1,200 occurred in about six weeks. Some days there were as many as 42, 45, 47 or even 49. In all weathers and at all times from eight in the morning till near midnight have these three clergymen been in attendance with a cheerfulness and a readiness for which the town of Leeds I must think owes them a debt of gratitude. The labour and fatigue were such, that Mr. Bickerdike and Mr. Nowell each suffered a severe illness, and were for a while suspended from their work ...[35]

The Revd Tunnicliff, too, had had a trying time, with burials in his half of the cemetery between 26 March and 28 September reckoned at 396 (as compared with 184 during the same period in 1848 and 228 in 1850); on 16 November he requested 'remuneration for extraordinary service during the prevalence of the Cholera', but it is not recorded whether he received any.

We should remember, however, that even in the most distressed lives there must have been rays of sunshine – the 'tingalary man' or organ-grinder coming down the street, perhaps, or a Christmas festivity like the one for the children of the Leylands Ragged School, who in 1860, through the kindness of Mrs Whiting,

> were regaled with an excellent tea, in the dining room of the institution. After the repast, the party adjourned into the school room, where suitable and interesting addresses were delivered to them and the parents by Rev. W. Guest, Rev. S. Jackson, Mr. Whiting, and Mr. Godson. The gallery was reserved for ladies

and gentlemen, of whom a considerable number were present. During the evening, the children sang several hymns, and repeated with accuracy many passages of Scripture. The room was tastefully decorated, but the centre of attraction was the Christmas tree, profusely hung with books, fruit, toys &c., which were afterwards distributed to the children.[36]

Doctors and clergymen ignored the dangers of disease to bring comfort to the poor - and sometimes paid dearly for doing so. Other benefactors were working to improve education, to establish libraries, dispensaries, Working Men's Institutes and Temperance Hotels, and many of these public-spirited people will appear later in our pages.

Not all lives were short, sad ones. In Beckett Street Cemetery are buried several people who were noted in their time for the ages they achieved, such as Ann Wilkinson of Quarry Hill, affectionately known as 'Granny Wilkinson', who was ninety-three when she died in 1856; or Jane Coxon, of whom the *Supplement to the Biographia Leodiensis* records:

> On Saturday, Jan. 29th, 1848, a woman, named Jane Coxon, of Leeds, died in the 103rd year of her age. She was born on the 12th of March, in the memorable year of 1745, and was the widow of Thos. Coxon, a farm-labourer, who died in the year 1804. The old lady had borne ten children, and leaves four generations of children behind her. In early life she frequently worked as a labourer in the fields, but during her long existence was never known to have a day's illness, or to require medical aid, except at her confinements. She retained the use of her faculties to the last, and even on the day she died, she prepared her own last meal, consisting of a mutton-chop and tea. She partook of that repast, and seemed to enjoy it, about four o'clock, but began to complain of illness shortly afterwards, and died about six o'clock, at the house of her daughter, Jane Steel, No. 56, Ward's Fold, Mabgate, Leeds. There were then living of her offspring two daughters, twenty-six grand-children, forty-four great-grand-children, and five great-great-grand-children.[37]

In the slow course of time both national and local Acts of Parliament brought about improvements, although in many areas it seemed as if Leeds were fighting rearguard actions all the way. The Public Health Act of 1848 established a General Board of Health, and gave powers for the setting-up of local boards and the appointment of Medical Officers of Health, yet the people of Leeds waited twenty years for their first MOH. The water supply was ameliorated by the 1860s, as we shall see, but antique methods of sewage disposal persisted; when the Public Health Act of 1875 was passed, Leeds was still arguing for the right to retain the privy-and-ashpit system, not capitulating until 1899 to the notion that every new home should have a WC. Despite legislation, nothing much was done about slum clearance (which involved considerable expense in purchase, compensation and rehousing) until the Housing of the Working Classes Act in 1890, and the threat of a Tory resurgence spurred the Liberal council into the promises which led to the Insanitary Areas schemes of 1895–1914. At last the worst streets were torn down; some of the most notorious were photographed before they were obliterated, and can be seen pictured in Leeds Reference Library in the eloquent volumes of the Borough Engineer. Better housing, better diet, better working conditions, possibilities of recreation undreamed of by our great-grandfathers, have now all but wiped out the memory of Wellington Yard and Goulden's Buildings.

Young and old, rich and poor alike had to have provision made for them after death; the cost of burial is outlined in Appendix B, Table 1. A person of some means would be able to purchase a grave plot for the private use of his family, and perhaps erect a memorial over it. The price of the plot depended, as we have seen, on where it was situated, and the construction of a brick vault, if desired, was an additional cost. A fee was payable for the right to put up a memorial, besides the payment to the monumental mason for providing and carving the stone. Kelke's *Churchyard Manual* of 1851 gives some prices for headstone designs: carved crosses from £2 to £6, coped stones £10 to £12 'if not elaborately ornamented', chest tombs, 'the most costly of churchyard monuments', from £20 to £50. Sixty years later the 'richest and most durable of all granites, PETERHEAD RED', could be supplied as a plain headstone or cross for £11 or so, while ten feet of obelisk cost £19 10s, coped stones ranged from £23 to £27, and a good solid memorial eight-and-a-half feet high (including the surmounting draped urn) would set the bereaved back by a breathtaking £33 10s.[38] Lettering would be charged per dozen letters; in the case of Sarah Baines, we have the instructions for the inscription written out by her family, with the mason's scribbled calculation for 165 letters at 3d per letter, amounting to £2 1s 3d. At a time when the working-man's weekly wage was counted in shillings, it will be obvious that a private grave would be beyond the means of most, and that of those who managed to achieve one, only the comparatively well-off would be able to put a memorial on it.

Death itself, therefore, provided no escape from the crowded and promis-
cuous circumstances of the poor. In the first forty years of the cemetery's
operation, the overwhelming majority of burials were in common graves.
A grave was dug and unrelated dead of both sexes and all ages were put
into it over the course of a week or so, until it was full. There would be no
memorial, of course; and in fact many of the occupants were paupers buried
at the expense of the ratepayer, perhaps coming from the Workhouse which
from 1861 was conveniently situated on the other side of Beckett Street.
The fee paid to the Corporation in the early years was 3*s* 6*d* for an adult in
the cheapest part of the grounds; in 1880 it was 5*s*. Unbelievable numbers
of corpses were sometimes crammed into a single common grave. Take, for
instance, Grave 6631, in the Consecrated portion, which was opened on
5 July 1856 for the bodies of an adult named Ebenezer Kitchin from Fleece
Lane and sixteen-year-old Elizabeth Graham from the Infirmary. Five more
adults followed, and then a string of little ones – Alice Lord aged ten, Rachel
Schofield aged one-and-a-half days, Hannah Holt aged one-and-a-half
years, George Smith aged eleven months, Joseph Binns aged one month,
Sophia Penny aged six days, Joseph Malthouse aged seven weeks ... and so
on, and on, and on, until with seven-month-old Patrick McAnnallys on
14 August the pathetic list comes to an end. *Thirty-eight* people had been
buried in that one grave theoretically twelve-feet deep, thirty-one of them
babies and children. It was clearly to the advantage of the Corporation that
each grave should be fully used, providing maximum fees to offset the cost
of construction, and the Revd John Bell, Registrar, makes this plain when
in 1881 he proudly compares his figures for the first seven common graves
opened under his superintendency, with the last seven of his predecessors, the
Hannams: 'Mine hold 32 Adults and 55 Children yielding for fees £17.12.6.
Hannam's hold 19 Adults and 39 Children yielding for fees £11.11.6.'[39]

Even as early as 1842 there had been criticism of the practice of common
interment. Wilson and Levy, in *Burial Reform and Funeral Costs*, published
in 1938, quote the evidence to a Select Committee on the case of a pauper
whose body had had to be exhumed:

> The coroner inquired of the summoning officer the precise number of bodies
> interred in the same pit. The officer replied, 'to the best of his recollection,
> there were 26 bodies.' The coroner wished to be informed if they rammed
> them in with a rammer. The officer said that he 'was not aware that they
> resorted to such a process, but the bodies of the paupers were packed together

as closely as possible, in order to make the most of the space', to which the coroner observed that such a revolting system of burial was a disgrace on a Christian country.[40]

The same authors write of the evidence given to the Cohen Committee on Industrial Assurance in 1932 by a former Secretary of the British Undertakers' Association.

A common interment is a grave dug ten, fifteen or twenty feet deep and the bodies are put in one after another. There will be about eight adult persons in that grave, and they will finish off the top with a layer of four children so there may be twelve to sixteen people in one grave ... It is not nice to think you are put in a pit with a crowd of other people. If they can possibly afford a private grave they have it.[41]

Grimly, Wilson and Levy conclude that 'the pauper funeral is still an integral part of English social life, a source of shame to the families of those who cannot afford better and, what is perhaps worse, of apprehension and fear throughout their lives to millions of working people. It was, and still is, a legacy of the liberal doctrine of "self-help".' Nowadays the common grave is still dug, and in a busy cemetery like neighbouring Harehills interments in such graves may average two a week; but there will be only four bodies in each, and although common burial is still regarded with dislike and perhaps even shame, it can be nothing like as horrific and humiliating as in Victorian times. It is interesting to note (see Appendix B, Tables 2 and 3) that although growing prosperity led to a corresponding increase in the proportion of private graves at Beckett Street Cemetery, a substantial number of interments, as late as the Great War, were at the expense of the Guardians, in common graves.

In a much-quoted passage from her 1913 Fabian tract *Round about a Pound a Week*, Mrs Pember Reeves describes the funeral of a three-year-old child who had died of tuberculosis:

The funeral cortege consisted of one vehicle, in which the little coffin went under the driver's seat. The parents and a neighbour sat in the back part of the vehicle. They saw the child buried in a common grave with twelve other coffins of all sizes. 'We 'ad to keep a sharp eye out for Edie,' they said; 'she were so little she were almost 'id.'

The chapter is called 'A Horrible Problem', and lays bare the struggle which the poor had to pay for even the most simple funeral and burial in a common grave; a penny a week, scraped together with great difficulty for each child and paid into a Burial Club, would scarcely cover the expenses. Many could not manage even a penny. 'Insurance ... is always a gamble, and people on £1 a week cannot afford a gamble.' One child who had been insured (for 2d a week) was buried in a common grave in 1911. The list of expenses which Mrs Pember Reeves gives was hardly extravagant - £1 12s for the funeral, 1s 3d for the death certificate, customary tips to the gravediggers, hearse attendants and insurance agent, a woman to lay her out at 2s, sixpenny-worth of flowers, and a black tie for Father at 1s – yet the cost of the burial exceeded by 1s 9d the £2 received from the policy, which meant that the survivors had to go short of food for two weeks to make up the money.[42]

On 9 September 1856 Sarah Whiteley of Hunslet Lane, aged thirty-eight, was buried in Grave 3160. This is one of a group of four graves purchased by Revd Edward Jackson MA, incumbent of St James'. Some of the thirty-two people interred in them were obviously related to each other, most were not; a few came from the pauper institutions of the Workhouse and the Industrial School. The names are elegantly inscribed on the four head-stones, each with a Scriptural text. Who were these people, and what bound them together? We can only surmise that they may have been deserving parishioners, either fallen on hard times and dependent on the Revd Jackson's charity for their final resting-place, or insured with him in some kind of ecclesiastical Burial Club. More importantly, did the councillors of the Burial Grounds Committee become aware of Jackson's good deeds and take from him the inspiration for the most unusual – and in their way, the most moving – memorials of Beckett Street Cemetery, the famous 'Guinea Graves'? A resolution of the Committee dated 15 October 1863 reads: 'That for the future a Headstone and Curb be provided for Public Graves, the same to be lettered and charged equally to all parties interring in such Graves, but leaving it optional to such parties so interring, whether they will have the Stone or no.' Although it apparently took fifteen years to come to fruition, this decision was to provide a measure of consolation and hope for thousands of Leeds people, and to change radically the appearance of Beckett Street Cemetery.

The visitor to the cemetery today is struck immediately by the sight of row upon row of gaunt stones, upright, leaning, toppled, like survivors at

9. The guinea graves

the roll-call after some great battle. There are three or four basic shapes – the rounded, the pointed, the squared-off – but otherwise they are identical. Each side is closely covered with names, ages and dates of death. There are little groups of these stones, too, and even single specimens, sitting oddly between proud private memorials which have obviously cost a great deal of money. To come across these scattered specimens on a first visit is to wonder what catastrophe – a railway accident, maybe, or a colliery explosion – could have killed all these people within a few days of each other. Over the brow of the hill, however, the serried ranks become visible, and the visitor begins to reconsider. Not a disaster, then; perhaps, as a local newspaper surmised, 'victims of an epidemic at nearby St James's Hospital'?[43] Indeed not. These are the 'Guinea Graves', common graves in practice, yet distinguished by the brilliant and humanitarian concept of placing over each a headstone with minimal but adequate commemorative details. The absolutely penniless were still destined for the pauper's grave; but if a family could scrape together a pound or so, this would cover the cost of a guinea grave and a share of the stone, with up to thirty-six letters of inscription. One stone served for the graves lying to east and west of it – the ultimate development of the back-to-back? – and from the minute of 30 June 1879, we can appreciate that Leeds Corporation did not lose financially by the provision of what are properly known as 'Inscription Graves', for Mr Hodgson of Woodhouse Lane was prepared to supply and fix the stones and curbs at £2 10s each, every headstone carved with 'IN MEMORY OF', and with further lettering at 7d a dozen for three-quarter inch letters. Even though the size of the stone must have dictated a certain restriction on the number of commemorations, the bodies were still crammed in – nineteen, mostly babies and children, in the grave opened for little Harry Brook in 1902, and the same stone serving, of course, for the grave to the west of it, each of the occupants having had a guinea paid for him (under-sevens half price). Appendix B, Table 2, shows how, with the help of the guinea grave, the proportion of persons achieving the dignity of a private burial and/or commemoration at Beckett Street Cemetery rose from 15 per cent in 1851 to 78 per cent eighty years later, when Wilson and Levy were writing.

Those who were poor, but not destitute, were now saved in Leeds from the shame of the pauper's grave; but most would still have preferred a little more individuality. In 1882 a gentleman applied to be allowed to black the letters upon the headstone of the public grave in which his wife was interred, to make them stand out from the rest of the stone. The Committee dealt with this one neatly. 'Resolved, that Mr John Johnson be allowed to black the letters upon the headstone ... on condition that he black the whole of the letters thereon.'[44] Blackened, whitened or even gilded names can be seen on guinea graves today, with or without the permission of the Council: that of five-year-old Annie E. Lynn, for instance, buried in 1893 in Grave 11153. Very occasionally, and not before the twentieth century, additions were made. At the end of the list of unrelated names on the stone under which Emma Booth lies has been carved that of her son Benjamin '7th Yorkshire Regiment ... killed in action Dec. 31st 1916 aged 18 years. Interred Les Bduefs Guards Cemetery, France' (either Mr Booth or the stonemason was defeated by the unfamiliar vowel combinations of the military cemetery at Les Boeufs near the small town of Albert). A 1924 guinea grave headstone commemorates Mary Stephenson 'and her stillborn child'. It is most unusual for a stillborn baby to be remembered; they were mostly buried cheaply and unceremoniously, without a service (in the 1860s they were even laid out in the Lodge toolshed to await interment),[45] and it is a sad fact that if an infant were doomed to die, hard-up parents would be relieved if it never drew breath in the first place, for the burial of a child that had lived, however briefly, could cost considerably more. An Edwardian actor named Sydney Lester Howard ('Laddie') – clearly not a particularly successful actor, since he is buried in a guinea grave – has had an extra commemoration in the shape of a marble book fixed at the foot of the stone by his widow. Finally, if you did have the misfortune to die at a time when the family fortunes were at a low ebb, your loved ones might be able later to purchase the plot which lay next to your guinea grave, so that your name appeared on two stones side by side, like Hinda Marshall, who died in 1921 – buried in the guinea grave, commemorated also on the family's posh black shiny stone next door.

The guinea graves (the great mass of which date from between 1880 and 1930) have been pitiful casualties of an age which, by and large, is not interested in the earthly remains of the dead. To make mowing easier, large numbers of kerbs have been removed and used for edging paths; deprived of even this small amount of support, the headstones have listed every which way, and many have fallen flat. A scheme for removing guinea grave stones altogether seems to have been launched at some time, for whole sections form a mysteriously bare prairie, rolling up to the feet of the stones which remain. The concept of the inscription grave, so laudable in its time, is seen now as pinning on the deceased an irredeemable badge of poverty (so much for the thousands upon thousands who lie in Beckett Street without any memorial at all). A visitor, tracing her family history, decided to conceal from her father the discovery that she had found his grandparents buried, not only in the 'Unconsecrated' portion – shades of suicides and vampires! – but, horror of horrors, in guinea graves.

Despised as they now are, the guinea graves are still a valuable lesson in social history; in the context of their times, they were a marvellous achievement by the Burial Grounds Committee of the Leeds Town Council which deserves to be acknowledged and remembered.

Chapter Three

Saving Souls

He was for sixty years a follower of Christ,
for fifty-eight years a preacher of the Gospel,
And is now for ever a saint in glory.

Peter Marshall, 1872

It is not easy for us today to understand the strong passions and animosities
aroused in Victorian times by the conflicts within the Christian Church;
it does not seem to matter much now whether the Anglican and the
Dissenters' chapels at the cemetery should have been separate buildings or
under the same roof.

Yet in the early part of the nineteenth century religion permeated everything: daily life and death, charitable provision, education, even politics.
The countryfolk crowding into the towns had cut themselves off from
their village hierarchies, headed by Parson and Squire, and found themselves poorly provided for by the religious establishment, so that for many
of them the Church ceased to be of importance in their daily existence;
but the Anglican and Nonconformist congregations contained the cream
of intellectual, political and commercial life, and the moral values of these
influential people reached out to shape the secular lives of others. Yet the
bitter rivalry between Church and Dissent, and the struggle of the Dissenters
to dismantle the old privileges of the Church of England, led to increasing
secularisation as the years passed. In 1836, for instance, the Registration of

Births and Deaths Act removed the onerous necessity for a Nonconformist to be married in an Anglican church, and even permitted civil marriage in Registry Offices; compulsory church rates were abolished in 1868; in 1880 the Burial Laws Amendment Act allowed burial in Consecrated ground to take place without the rites of the Anglican church – or, indeed, any religious rites at all. Increasing material prosperity and new discoveries in the sciences contributed towards weakening the hold of the spiritual anchor. An era of great religious bigotry became also an era of increasing godlessness.

When Queen Victoria came to the throne, all shades of religious conviction were represented in Leeds. The life of the Church of England centred on the medieval Parish Church of St Peter's, with the Carolean St John's, the three eighteenth-century foundations of Holy Trinity, St Paul's and St James', and the new churches of Christ Church (Meadow Lane) and St Mary (Quarry Hill) which had been formed in 1826–7 under an Act of Parliament for the provision of extra churches in the cities. These all operated under the chapelry system, which meant that they were not independent parishes, but were in the charge of curates answerable to the Vicar of Leeds, although two new parishes had also been created in Woodhouse and Kirkstall. When the redoubtable Dr Hook took over as vicar in 1837, with responsibility for some 125,000 souls, he saw that the cumbersome chapelry system and the lack of sufficient Anglican churches were largely responsible for the strength of Dissent within Leeds. With the assistance of the Ripon Diocesan Church Building Society, Dr Hook promoted an energetic programme of church construction, while the Leeds Vicarage Act of 1844 created independent parishes out of the chapelries and provided for more as the new churches arose.

Dr Hook's brand of Anglicanism was moderately High Church, but his clergy ranged from one extreme to the other. The Oxford Movement, beginning in 1833, was directed at a rediscovery and reaffirmation of the Catholic principles of the Church; although it was intended to be a 'middle way', a number of prominent Anglicans eventually seceded to the Church of Rome. In some Anglican churches ritual was introduced which was abhorrent to Low Churchmen. Pusey, one of the leaders of the movement, donated to the working-class district of East Leeds a church named St Saviour's, where Edward Jackson (he of the scriptural graves) was among the first staff. There confessions were heard, the choir wore surplices and the clergy birettas, altar frontals and chalice veils draped the furniture, and kneeling amounted virtually to prostration.[46] This was too much for the lower end of the Anglican

Church, which countered with debates such as the lecture 'frequently and loudly applauded' in the Philosophical Hall in 1868, given by a clergyman from Bury St Edmunds and catchily entitled, 'Rome the misrepresentation of Christ, and Ritualism the mimicry of Rome'.[47]

Dissent was strong. There were long-standing Unitarian, Independent and Baptist congregations in the town; all numbered important and influential citizens among their members, as did the Quakers. The largest of the Nonconformist churches, however, was Methodism (although a tendency to schism among its followers meant that, by the time a census of church attendance was taken in the middle of the nineteenth century, there were five separate branches of Methodism in Leeds). Nigel Yates, in his essay on the religious life of the Victorian city in 'A History of Modern Leeds', quotes Dr Hook as writing from his new post, 'The de facto established religion is Methodism.'[48] From the 1840s, too, the Roman Catholic population was greatly swollen by the stream of Irish immigrants, escaping from the poverty and famine of rural Ireland to the dirt and misery of urban England.

On Sunday 30 March 1851, returns were made of adults attending the church services, and although we must bear in mind that many people attended, and were therefore counted, more than once, the Leeds figures do give some idea of the relative strength of the different sects at a time when the Church of England was experiencing a revival under Dr Hook, while support for the Methodists had declined, perhaps on account of their internal disagreements. At the sixteen Anglican places of worship in Leeds township (the historic administrative unit, some three by one-and-a-half miles in area, comprising the core of the town), there were just over 13,000 attendances; taking all the different branches of Methodism together, the nineteen chapels attracted nearly 15,000. There were 4,000 attendances at Independent chapels, 3,600 Roman Catholic attendances were recorded, and 2,000 General or Particular Baptists occupied sittings. Mr Yates comments on the surprisingly low figures, with less than half the sittings in Leeds churches being taken up at either the morning or the evening services. 'The best attended,' he says, 'were Leeds Parish Church, where some 350 people were customarily obliged to stand through the evening service and some people had even to be turned away on occasion, and St Patrick's Roman Catholic church, in the heart of the Irish quarter, which was full for three morning Masses and the evening service; even so this only represented less than 20 per cent of the known Irish population of Leeds in 1851.'[49]

Beckett Street Cemetery mirrors the religious life of Victorian Leeds, not least in its rigid division between the Established Church and Nonconformity. We have already seen Mr Jacob Verity busy in September 1844 with his task of digging holes and planting a line of boundary stones as indicated by the Borough Surveyor. The two halves were known officially as the 'Consecrated Portion' and the 'Unconsecrated Portion', although it is obvious from a minute of the Burial Grounds Committee that this is not how they were commonly described; on 7 December 1863, after a body was interred by mistake in the wrong section of Holbeck Cemetery, the Committee resolved that officers of all the grounds should 'ascertain directly from every person applying for a Grave, as to whether they intend to inter on the Church or Chapel side, and also that a plate be put upon the Doors of such Sexton's and Registrar's Dwellings respectively, stating the side "Church" or "Chapel" to which they belong.' (A few months later, this resolution was rescinded in favour of installing plates labelled with the official terminology.) The descriptions 'Consecrated' and 'Unconsecrated' were never much liked, carrying as the latter does a subtle undertone of the unhallowed and outcast, although its literal meaning is perfectly accurate in this case. By 1913, when Frederick Temple paid £3 for his carefully selected plot (plus 2s 6d for the parchment certificate), the receipts printed 'UNCONSECRATED' were being overstamped with the word 'GENERAL'.

During its first forty years, the two halves of the cemetery were administered differently. As we have seen, the appointment of a Chaplain to the Anglican side lay in the hands of the Vicar of Leeds, and the Chaplain never resided at the South Lodge, since he was also the incumbent of a parish and was provided with a parsonage there. If the Chaplain was absent when a funeral was expected, it was his responsibility to arrange for his curate or another clergyman to officiate. The appointment of the 'Clerk and Gravedigger', who lived at the Lodge, was also made by the ecclesiastical authority (although for a few years he was concurrently described as 'Gardener and General Manager', in which capacity he was appointed by the Committee). For the occupants of either of these positions – Chaplain or Gravedigger – to be got rid of required the sanction of the Bishop of Ripon. On the Unconsecrated side, however, a Registrar was appointed who ran the affairs of that section, took the burial service (unless a Catholic priest or a minister of another branch of religion were required) and who might be resident at the North Lodge, as was Jabez Tunnicliff after the

10. The South Lodge (rebuilt 1880), home and office of Superintendent Sheard from 1885 to 1923. Now sold off by Leeds City Council to a private company for rented accommodation.

sacking of sexton Wright. After Tunnicliff's death the arrangement had reverted to that of a Clerk and Gravedigger at the Lodge and a non-resident Registrar, but following the problems experienced with the Hannams, Revd John Bell was appointed to administer both the clerical and practical work of the Unconsecrated portion from the Lodge, as Tunnicliff had done. In 1885 the whole system was changed; Bell and the sexton Bates were removed from their lodges and a Superintendent was engaged with managerial responsibility for the whole cemetery. Mr Joah Sheard, who had previously been employed in Huddersfield, moved into the South Lodge, and the other was given over to the 'Head Gardener and Gravedigger', who, during these extremely busy years, had a team of gravediggers under him. So matters remained until, with the declining use of the cemetery, resident staff were no longer required, and by 1980 the lodges were occupied by Council tenants, while the affairs of Beckett Street Cemetery were administered from the office at Lawnswood Cemetery and Crematorium.

All varieties of religious opinion were taken to the grave at Beckett Street. A number of the Anglican clergymen whose signatures appear in the Burial Registers are themselves buried there. On 15 November 1856 the *Leeds Mercury* reported the jolly proceedings at the second anniversary of the building of St Stephen's Church, Burmantofts, when the Vicar, Revd Frederick Rowell, gave an account of the year's progress in church, parish and Sunday School, after which the churchwardens gave a satisfactory financial report, 'and in a humorous and forcible manner solicited the continued support and kindly interest of the friends of Burmantofts'. Speeches followed, then music, 'creditably sung by the choir conducted by Mr. Groves. Three times three cheers were heartily given for the worthy Vicar and his no less worthy lady. "God Save the Queen" was then sung, and the company separated at ten o'clock, all apparently much pleased with the interesting and gratifying proceedings of the evening.' A cohesive congregation formed, educational institutions established, minds improved, even a reasonable choir set going, all these a mere five years after the foundation of the parish and when the church that was its nucleus had been standing for only a year, argue an impressive degree of enthusiasm for the mid-century Anglican Church in Leeds.

The reverend gentleman followed the paths of duty wherever they led. Nine years later the *Leeds Intelligencer* deeply regretted to announce his death after an attack of typhus fever. He was on the Committee of the House of Recovery, and had almost certainly contracted the disease in visiting the sick there. 'We need scarcely say,' added the obituary, 'that Mr. Rowell was much respected, not only by his congregation, but throughout the town generally.' His coped tombstone on the south side of Anglican Walk bears the inscription:

IN LOVING MEMORY OF THE REV. FREDERICK THOMAS ROWELL M.A. CANTAB. FIRST VICAR OF BURMANTOFTS. BORN 27TH MARCH 1822. THROUGH HIS EXERTIONS WERE CREATED THE CHURCH SCHOOLS AND VICARAGE OF THIS PARISH IN WHICH FOR 14 YEARS HE LABOURED WITH UNWEARIED AND SELF-DENYING ZEAL FOR THE WELFARE OF HIS PEOPLE AND THE GLORY OF GOD. HIS LIFE BRIGHT AS AN EXAMPLE OF CHRISTIAN HOLINESS WAS TERMINATED BY A MALIGNANT FEVER WHICH HE CAUGHT IN THE FEARLESS AND FAITHFUL DISCHARGE OF HIS MINISTERIAL DUTY TO THE SICK. HIS DEVOTED LABOURS ON EARTH WERE EXCHANGED FOR THE REST AND REWARD OF HEAVEN 12TH OCTOBER 1865. RIGHT DEAR IN THE SIGHT OF THE LORD IS THE DEATH OF HIS SAINTS PSALM CXVI VI5.

Rowell's successor also rests in Beckett Street, but he seems to have followed a thornier path. The elegant lettering, picked out in red, on the memorial of the Revd Arthur Hastings Kelk (1835–1908) informs us that after his incumbency at St Stephen's he was 'missionary to the Jews in Jerusalem 1879 to 1901, in London 1901 to 1904 and in Leeds 1904 to 1908'.

Often the congregation would club together for a memorial to show their regard for the deceased; the worshippers of St Stephen's paid for John Lean's gravestone in 1888 'in appreciation of his 14 years service as verger'. The Sunday School of St Stephen's, too, is remembered on the headstone of Thomas John Hutton of Crowle (1868), a chemist and druggist who was for eight years a teacher and superintendent. A parishioner of All Saints, Charles Dickinson won the esteem of the Choir and of his fellow-workmen, who joined in erecting a memorial to him in 1898. The Parish Church is also represented, with its church keeper 'for upwards of 25 years' William Fothergill (1871), and even a choirboy – twelve-year-old William Henry Proctor, buried in 1856, 'late of the Parish Church choir'.

Some of the most resounding inscriptions belong to the Methodists, whose differences of opinion are all here – Primitive, New Connexion, Wesleyan Association ministers are represented. Our chapter opened with a quotation from the headstone shared by Peter Marshall and his son Ephraim, both of Norwich; Ephraim's epitaph reads:

HE WAS FOR UPWARDS OF ELEVEN YEARS THE CHAPLAIN OF THIS CEMETERY. HE TRUSTED EARLY, FULLY AND TO THE LAST, IN THE INFINITE SACRIFICE OF THE WORLD'S REDEEMER. AND AFTER A CAREER OF ACTIVE SERVICE IN PREACHING THE GOSPEL, VISITING THE SICK, AND IN THE ERECTION OF THE FREE METHODIST CHAPEL, BECKETT ST. HE FINISHED HIS EARTHLY JOURNEY IN EXTREME PAIN, AND NOW RESTS IN THE LAND WHERE SUFFERING IS NO MORE.

The Revd James Lynch, whose interest for us lies perhaps more in his work for the Wesleyan mission to India than in his work at home, nonetheless reveals an unusual religious progression: a native of the County of Derry, Ireland, 'he was trained in Romanism; But in early life, became truly converted to Protestantism and to God'! Two laymen, John Hall Rider and John Wormald, who taught the United Methodist Free Churches Sunday School at Cross Stamford Street, drowned together in 1873 when they foolishly took a rowing boat outside the harbour mouth at Hartlepool. Another long-standing Methodist was Helen, wife of William Pawson, but the choice of grave site is a little odd – 'a consistent Methodist for fifty-four years', why is she interred in the Church of England section?

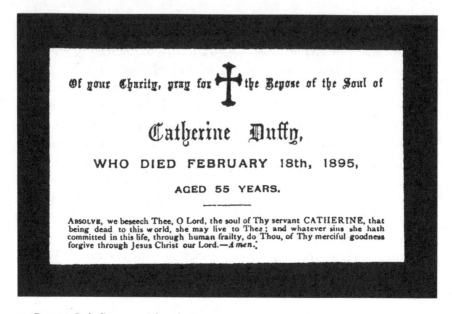

Of your Charity, pray for ✝ the Repose of the Soul of

Catherine Duffy,

WHO DIED FEBRUARY 18th, 1895,

AGED 55 YEARS.

ABSOLVE, we beseech Thee, O Lord, the soul of Thy servant CATHERINE, that being dead to this world, she may live to Thee; and whatever sins she hath committed in this life, through human frailty, do Thou, of Thy merciful goodness forgive through Jesus Christ our Lord.—*Amen.*

11. Roman Catholic memorial card, 1895.

The Congregationalists have John Anderson (died 1924), for forty-two years Pastor of Burmantofts Congregational Church; the Baptists Jabez Tunnicliff, Minister of Call Lane Chapel and Registrar of the cemetery. There are so many people connected with one or other Christian church that it would be impossible, and tedious, to list them all; and we shall conclude with one of the more curious inscriptions, with its distinct odour of violets and ectoplasm – that of Elizabeth Midgley, who in 1879 'entered the spirit world'.

Anyone who steps aside from Dissenters' Walk to look at the guinea graves, dating from the 1890s, in the aptly named Recusants' Row, will be struck by one feature which is missing from those on the other side of the main path. Carved at the foot of each roll of names are the letters R.I.P. – '*Requiescat in pace*'; it comes as no surprise that the great majority of the names above are Murphys and Rileys and Nolans and O'Mahoneys. Many of the private graves, too, carry the inscription: 'Of your charity pray for the soul of ...' When the Burial Grounds Committee succeeded in closing the overcrowded and unhygienic graveyards attached to the churches of the town, they also closed the burial-ground of St Patrick's Chapel, leaving the Roman Catholics nowhere of their own to inter their dead until the Catholic Burial Board was able to establish a sectarian ground at Killingbeck.

There are, however, fairly large numbers of Irish names in the registers of the Consecrated portion. Most of these presumably owed allegiance to the Church of Ireland rather than that of Rome, but in 1856 the disturbing case of Relieving Officer Robinson revealed that all was not as it seemed ...

'The poor are possessed of feelings as well as the wealthy,' thundered Mr Newton at a meeting of the Board of Guardians on Wednesday 10 December 1856, to cries of 'Hear, hear!' 'The poor have a right to demand that their religious scruples should be consulted' – 'Hear, hear!' – 'and they ought not to be "snubbed" and treated in the manner which I will show!' Mr Newton was a Dissenter, and the Revd Mr Tunnicliff had enlisted his help in curbing the cantankerous and unhelpful Mr Robinson, one of the Guardians' Relieving Officers or paid officials, who had been dealing with pauper applications for burial at Beckett Street Cemetery. When a poor person died and help was needed with burial expenses, the Relieving Officer would issue the relatives with a certificate which entitled the deceased to 'a coffin and dues', and the provisions of the Poor Law stipulated that the certificate should be made out for the Consecrated portion unless the family requested otherwise. But 'out of one hundred poor persons who applied for certificates,' declared Mr Middleton, another Guardian, 'ninety-nine believed that they could use them for either the consecrated or the unconsecrated side of the cemetery.' Difficulties had arisen when the applicant's wishes had not been ascertained and a certificate had been made out for the wrong section. Mr Hartley and Mr Bowser, the other two officers, had never made any trouble about altering certificates which were brought back to them, but there was no messing Mr Robinson about. Alter a certificate? He would do no such thing, he said tetchily, as he (the applicant) should have stated his wishes on the first application. He should always be altering certificates, and should never have done with such things, if people came for alterations in that way. So John Judge's wife was buried in the Consecrated portion, while her two daughters lay in the Unconsecrated; and since there had been complaints of similar harassment since 1854 and there was now a rash of such cases, the Dissenters of Leeds thought something should be done.

The three cases over which the Guardians argued during their meetings in December 1856[50] throw into relief some of the problems encountered by the poor in their dealings with officialdom, and incidentally cast a fascinating light upon the reasons for the choice of burial on one side of the cemetery rather than the other. The first discussed was that of Esther Judge of Shear Court, aged forty, who had been buried on 30 November. Mr Tunnicliff testified to the Board that when the certificate for the Consecrated portion was brought to him he had pointed out that he could not bury Mrs Judge in the Unconsecrated, and that he had written a note to ask Mr Robinson to alter the certificate, as the other Relieving Officers had often done. 'But after waiting for the corpse at the Cemetery for a long time,' as the *Mercury* reported, 'he at last discovered that the interment had taken place in the consecrated ground, and Judge told him that Mr. Robinson had refused to make the alteration.' After Mr Tunnicliff's declaration had been heard, Mr Robinson was despatched by the Guardians to fetch Mr Judge, a former Scripture reader, who was described as 'a good man, but poor'; however, he returned with a message that the man would not come unless paid for his time, which rather weakened the case until it was discovered later that 'Robinson had not fairly carried out the orders of the Guardians' – not surprisingly, he had failed to use his best endeavours to persuade Judge to come and testify against him! Mr Robinson denied having received any note from Mr Tunnicliff, but the plain facts were that the two Judge girls were buried on the Unconsecrated side and their mother elsewhere, and that seemed proof enough that the system was not working.

The second case was that of Ellen Chapple, who lived with her daughter Mary Oates at 12 Pleasant Row and appears to have been related to 'the gravedigger at the cemetery', referred to in the account of the case as Mary's brother. Mrs Chapple's religious convictions were clearly anything but firm. Although she had once been attended by Mr Bickerdike, incumbent of St Mary's and Anglican Chaplain of the cemetery, she had expressed a wish to be buried on the Unconsecrated side 'because she said it was better looking'! Mr Robinson admitted that Mary Oates had asked for a 'chapel-side' certificate but, aware that Mr Bickerdike had been once called to the deceased, he had decided to use his own judgement on where she should go. His attempts to persuade the daughter seem to have been most unacceptable. According to Mary Oates' testimony, 'He said "What do you want to bury there for? Should *you* like it?" I said "I don't know." He then said, "I shouldn't like to be buried there; for there are none but Catholics there." ' He thereupon issued her with a certificate for the Consecrated portion, saying that if her brother did not like it she could come back and change it. Since her mother had lived with her and not with her brother, she was indignant at this suggestion, and in any case a repeat visit was out of the question: 'I was waiting in the application office from half-past nine till half-past eleven before I could get an order, and I could not spare the time to go back again.' In the end Mr Tunnicliff had paid for the burial on the Unconsecrated side out of his own pocket. Actually, looking at the page of the Burial Register on which Mrs Chapple's interment is recorded, one must admit that there was something in Mr Robinson's claim, since the forty burials listed include those of John Kilroy, John McAvoy, Mary Burke, Margaret McGrath, Catherine Philbin, John Flynn, Mary Phene, Agnes Corcoran, John Cakanay, Edward Connelly and Ann Kelley!

Despite Mr Robinson's denials that he had made any such remarks about Catholics, and an insinuation by two of the Guardians that since Mary Oates was related to the gravedigger it was probably a 'made-up case', the uncooperative Relieving Officer was censured by the Board. Yet only a week later he was in hot water again, this time over the burial of Ann Pearson, aged twenty-four, of Green Road. Her mother applied to Mr Robinson for a certificate, and was given one for the Consecrated side. This time the intermediary was a Mr Simpson, class leader of the deceased at the Wesleyan church, who had kindly undertaken, out of respect for her memory, to have the order altered. At his suggestion Mrs Pearson returned to Mr Robinson with the certificate, but she was put through a regular catechism as to 'why she wanted an order for the Unconsecrated side; why she objected to the Consecrated side; and other remarks and questions which were highly improper'. Mrs Pearson herself apparently remarked that she did not think it was of much consequence on which side a person was buried, a sensible observation which did not find favour with the outspoken Dissenter Mr Newton of the Board of Guardians, who referred to the very strong desire expressed by the deceased before her death that she might be buried where her sister lay. ('Hear, hear!') The meeting then turned to other matters.

During Mr Tunnicliff's testimony in the case of Ellen Chapple, it became clear that Protestant Dissenters were not the only people who were being interred in the Consecrated portion against the will of their relatives. 'He had heard a great many complaints from the Roman Catholics, who had now no other place to bury their dead than in the unconsecrated portion of the cemetery. A priest had informed him that again and again wrong certificates had been given, and the application for an alteration refused.' One of the Guardians corroborated this. 'The Rev. Mr. O'Donnell, a Roman Catholic priest, had told him that he could make several statements similar to those of Mr. Tunnicliff, and that his people had been very much persecuted by Mr. Robinson. He also showed him an order for burial which he said he had himself paid for.' It seems, then, that some of the Irish names in the register of the Consecrated portion must have been those of Catholics who were the victims of the cussedness of Mr Robinson. It is to be hoped that the Guardians finally succeeded in making the obstinate Relieving Officer respect the religious convictions of the poor who were at his mercy.

With the Corporation cemetery at Burmantofts regarded perhaps as something of a poor relation to the burial-ground of the rich Dissenting merchants at St George's Fields, the Burial Grounds Committee was sensitive upon any question of dubious procedure. Complaints by relatives were immediately investigated, and often resulted in a magnanimous gesture by the Committee, such as a cost-free new grave for Mr Edmund Shaw in 1877 when his was found to be waterlogged.[51] In the case of complaints over religious matters, the Committee sometimes rushed in where angels feared to tread. On 15 December 1856 the following letter appeared in the *Mercury*:

GENTLEMEN,– Having occasion to visit the Leeds Municipal Cemetery yesterday, and passing over that portion of it termed the 'Consecrated side,' I observed the funeral of a little child; and in order that I might witness the last solemn rite performed, I took my stand near the grave. A man dressed in black was standing at the bottom of the 'narrow home', placing the coffin in a proper position, and to the best of my belief he had come with the parents of the child.

I noticed they were not in the best humour, on account of the officiating minister (whom I understood to be the Rev. Mr. Arthur, of St. Mary's Church) refusing to read the burial service over the child. The parents observed 'that they never knew anything like it in their lives,' and that they 'had had enough to do.' The child had been registered, and had had the united skill of two surgeons; and simply because it was so very ill, and could not be taken to the church to be baptised, the funeral service was refused to be read over it.

The body was taken into the chapel, and the clergyman finding that the child had not been baptised, refused to read over it *there*, and observed, 'It was not a Christian.' The parents enquired of him where they might take it to, and he answered, 'Where they liked'; but, happily, two elder children were to be laid in the same grave (though, I was informed by one of the relatives that one of these was not baptised), so that, under these circumstances, this little unfortunate one had performed over it some portion of the funeral ceremony.

The mother, almost unable, on account of her late sickness and her weak state of body, to be present, but having a great desire to see her child laid at rest, was not at all benefited by this unexpected conduct.

The parents themselves did not seem to think that this refusal of Christian burial would at all affect the child; but it materially added to their grief.

I think that this case should be made fully known, in order that those who, through neglect or choice, refuse to have their children baptised, may inter their deceased children where such scruples are not thought of, or such remarks made. Hoping you will insert this,

I remain, Gentlemen, yours respectfully,

AN OBSERVER.

The only entry in the register for 14 October which does not have against it the signature of the clergyman who performed the Burial Service is that of two-week-old Elizabeth Ward of Regent Street, placed with several other children in a common grave, 6560.

The Chairman, Alderman Richardson, reported to the Committee on this occasion that he had seen the Revd John Bickerdike, Chaplain of the Cemetery, who had satisfactorily explained the matter, and who was prepared in his turn to write to the *Mercury*. This he duly did. His letter appeared on 18 December, and made it clear that both the law of the Church and the law of the land forbade the use of the Office for the Burial of the Dead 'for any that die unbaptized'. He remarked cuttingly that 'the parents had had time to get the child registered, and to call in "the united skill of two surgeons", but not to send for a clergyman to baptize their child'. Further, he pointed out that it would not have been necessary to take the child to a church, for the clergy were bound to come privately to the home to baptise the sick, and *in extremis* even baptism by a layman would have been valid. One would hardly have expected the Committee, when a similar case arose twelve years later, to pass a strongly worded resolution censuring Mr Bickerdike, and the reverend gentleman was furious. His reply of 28 April 1868 is couched in sarcastic terms, referring to 'a Resolution purporting to come from the Committee', and scything down the Town Councillors with the observation, 'I can only suppose that the Resolution to which I refer was, if genuine, passed when but few Members of the Committee were present, and those few among the less informed and experienced' (!) 'A similar case occurred once before,' he continued, 'when Alderman Richardson, then Chairman of the Committee, wrote to me on the subject. I called on him and shewed him the law of the case, which he confessed he had not been aware of. He said of course when I knew the person had not been baptized, I could not have done otherwise.' The Committee, although clearly without a leg to stand on as regarded the legality of the refusal, stood on its dignity instead, and recorded that the members were of opinion that a reply in more courteous terms might have been expected; then they wrote a complaint to the Bishop of Ripon, whose dulcet mediation finally smoothed all annoyance away.

It is interesting that although Mr Bickerdike, with his rigid principles and his determination to stand up for himself, was evidently not a person to be crossed, the Committee spoke glowingly of his valuable services and 'the faithful and efficient manner in which his duties have been discharged' when, in 1879, he received preferment and finally resigned his chaplaincy.[52]

Another clergyman who had a stormy passage through the pages of the Committee's minutes was the Revd William Studdert Kennedy, whose famous son Geoffrey many will know as the charismatic 'Woodbine Willie', poet, parson, holder of the Military Cross and distributor of Bibles, cigarettes and comfort to the miserable men in the trenches of the Great War. The Revd William had come from Dublin with his wife and a family of four, pausing *en route* for a ministry in Lancashire, where he added another six children, and completing the houseful with a further five in Leeds. This philoprogenitive gentleman had an obsession with surplices, and bombarded the Committee with demands that it should be responsible for the washing of them. More seriously, he was not a good time-keeper. When Robert Sinclair was the sexton responsible for the Consecrated portion, Mr Kennedy was constantly having obstructions placed in his way and found Sinclair impossible to work with; but the problems continued after the sexton had been sacked. The crunch came when, on 25 September 1883, the Chaplain was sunning himself in Southport while four cortèges waited in vain at Burmantofts. Whether or not he had, as he claimed, made arrangements with a locum who had let him down, the disgrace to the cemetery was too much to be tolerated, and, despite receiving a grovelling letter of apology on 28 September, the Committee promptly instructed the Town Clerk to ask the Bishop of Ripon to remove him from the Chaplaincy. After a long hearing at the Palace, during which other matters were also brought up, such as failure to comply with the Committee's instructions on signing the Burial Registers, the Bishop gave judgement.[53] That there had been neglect of Mr Kennedy's obligations to the Corporation and a gross want of punctuality in conducting burial services was evident, and the Bishop was concerned, as the Committee was, over the harm these scandals would do in the public eye. 'The cases mentioned are most painful and calculated in the face of a population not always disposed in favor of the Church of England, to create a feeling against the Church which I am most desirous to prevent.' With the struggle the Church was having to maintain the Anglican position against Nonconformity, such behaviour was unacceptable, and the Revd Studdert Kennedy was forthwith removed from his position at the cemetery (although, of course, he continued as Vicar of St Mary's).

Sadly, the Committee had not heard the last of the outspoken Irishman, for after his dismissal he sent a stream of abusive letters to members and to the Town Clerk, who eventually had to send copies to the Bishop, holiday-ing in Bournemouth.[54] His Grace was horrified, and must have taken some action, for Mr Studdert Kennedy drops out of our pages. It is good to add that he did not bear Beckett Street Cemetery any ill will, for he and his wife are buried under ledger stones near the South Lodge, his bearing the simple inscription: 'WILLIAM STUDDERT KENNEDY, PRIEST. VICAR OF ST MARY'S, QUARRY HILL 1879–1914'.

The concern of the Anglican hierarchy to maintain the standing of their Church in the face of the threat from Nonconformity needs to be set against the fact that the vast mass of the labouring population was immune to reli-gion in any shape or form. While clergy were being sent forth to convert the heathen in Madras, it was possible for the following conversation with a woman of about seventy to take place in Leeds in 1838:

'Do you know who Jesus Christ is?'
'I cannot say that I do, and yet I think I have heard.'
'Do you know what he came into the world for?'
'No!'[55]

The irony of the situation did not go unnoticed, and in the third decade of the century the Town Mission movement, inspired by David Nasmith, 'the zealous and indefatigable Secretary of the British and Foreign Mission', began its work of leavening the lump of proletarian indifference. The Leeds Town Mission, following those set up in London, Glasgow, Dublin and four English provincial towns, was established on 1 December 1837 under the motto 'NOT TO PROSELYTIZE BUT TO EVANGELIZE', and its first annual report contains a ringing call to work: 'Shall we not embrace the opportunities afforded to us?

Shall we slumber when all around is calling us to awake? The fields are white unto the harvest – shall not the fruit be gathered in?'

The Mission, run by a Board of Managers and supported entirely by charitable subscriptions and donations, was divided into districts, each staffed by a Superintendent and an agent, members of one or other of the evangelical churches, without distinction of sect. The agent's business was 'to visit the inhabitants of the District assigned you, for the purpose of bringing them to an acquaintance with salvation through our Lord Jesus Christ, and of doing them good by every means in your power'. To effect this, he was to read or speak of the Scriptures wherever possible, particularly those portions which expounded the depravity of man and salvation through Christ, and to persuade his hearers to read them for themselves. He was to avoid directing them towards any particular church, and to keep away from any political discussion, since the Mission was to be non-controversial. Parents were to be instructed in their duties in bringing up their children; vice such as swearing, intemperance, or profanation of the Sabbath was to be prudently reproved; tracts and Bibles were to be supplied where they were lacking. House-to-house visiting and holding prayer-meetings were expected to take at least five or six hours a day, and in addition, the agent would need to set aside time for study, prayer and reflection on his own account. He was to keep a journal, which should be inspected by the Superintendent at a weekly interview. Where great poverty was encountered, he should recommend the case, if suitable, to the various charitable and medical institutions of the town. Humility, courtesy and affection he would need in large quantities – and his salary was to be not less than £50, and not more than £80 a year. 'Your work is awfully important,' he was admonished. 'You have to deal with immortal souls, many of whom may never hear the gospel but from you, and whose eternal happiness may depend on the message you deliver to them. Be faithful, be simple, keep the Lord Jesus continually before your own mind, and commend HIM and His great salvation to the people.'

The main thrust of the Mission was always channelled into house-to-house visiting. In 1875 the procedure was thus described:

Reading a few verses of Scripture, with a word of explanation or enforcement, and a prayer where it is desired, occupy from ten to fifteen minutes, and leave no time, if the Visitor has good tact, for irrelevant conversation or gossip. After repeated visits a good understanding is generally established between the Visitor and the visited – the work is put aside readily on his coming in

– the chair is offered, and the visit proceeds. In other cases, if the visit is obviously unwelcome, or ill-timed, the Missionary leaves a tract and retires, to call again on his next round. A churlish reception at the first visit is often followed by a more gracious one at the second or third, and, in cases of sickness, the Missionary is almost *always* kindly welcomed; the general complaint being that he comes too seldom.

Outdoor meetings were often held at feasts and fairs, 'special efforts being made by preaching, and giving away short tracts, to counteract the torrent of evil which is invariably set in motion on these occasions'. In addition, the Missionaries visited infirmaries and fever-hospitals, workhouses, barracks ('The Barrack room is not very favourable for religion, but there is no reason why a soldier should not be a Christian') and the gaol. Later, they added the cabmen's shelters, the railway stations and the factories to their rounds.

Among the surviving printed annual reports are the two earliest; from the second, dated 30 November 1839, we get a good idea of the nature of the work, and of the tremendous amount of effort which was being put in. During the preceding year, 14,134 hours had been spent visiting and holding meetings, and a total of 24,951 visits had been made, 5,060 of which were to the sick and dying. Nearly 7,000 families had been regularly visited; the missionaries had found 1,100 families 'destitute of Scriptures', of whom 600 were Irish Roman Catholics, and it was estimated that between a sixth and a third of the adult population were illiterate. The agents had distributed eighty-five Bibles and Testaments and 17,730 tracts. There had been over 36,000 attendances at the 1,493 meetings in cottages, in schoolrooms and in the open air. Twenty-two females had been rescued from the paths of vice, and two houses of ill fame had been given up by the persons who kept them. (Prostitution and drunkenness were both a cause and an effect of the misery of the urban poor and, in the minds of the missionaries, were strongly linked with a new and evil canker in society – the spread of Socialism. 'Domestic discord, and contempt of parental authority, are its natural fruits; adultery and every species of lewdness follow in its train ...')

Several of the Leeds Town Mission's Superintendents and agents, with their families, rest after these Herculean labours in Beckett Street Cemetery, including Adam Ewing of the Marsh Lane District, who died in 1850, and Samuel Barbour, Superintendent 1839–53, whose missionary career had begun in Glasgow. In a very unhappy context, we shall later on meet Christopher Dove, a most respected and charitable leather-merchant, whose murdered daughter-in-law is buried at Beckett Street; he was Superintendent of the Quarry Hill district in its early days, and his benevolence enabled the agent, William Logan, to relieve some cases of extreme distress and destitution. Mr Logan describes his district thus in his 1839 report:

> The prevailing vices are these, – adultery, fornication, drunkenness, swearing and gossipping. Since I came to the district, eleven children have died from burning; and to me it is no wonder, when I find so many houses left with the children, and the mothers '*throng*' gossiping with their neighbours. The Lord's Day is awfully profaned – washing, baking, and sleeping in the afternoon, and in the evening, drinking ...

A little table gives some interesting statistics for the Quarry Hill district of the Mission:

Visitable families	719
Who attend public worship	155
Without Scriptures	247
Places of worship	2
Sunday Schools	1 (attendance 850)
Day Schools	1 (attendance 610)
Gin shops, beer shops, inns	11
Houses of ill fame	3
Females reclaimed	10

The last figure seems amazingly high when one considers for how many women this must have been their only source of income; let us hope there were not too many backsliders among them.

How were the missionaries received as they went about their daily work?

> Another family of socialists. The mistress of the house wanted 'none of my bother'. Warned her to answer at the judgment-day, for calling the message of God's mercy *bother*.

> I called three times to see an old woman lying ill at the house of her daughter. The latter was always careless, and rather opposed. She is a woman of immoral

character. On Tuesday, I tapped at the door. When the daughter came, and knowing my objective, ordered me away angrily, 'I have called,' said I, 'to see your mother. How is the old woman?' 'My mother is in Hell! where you will be shortly; begone, you bloody Methodist, or I will let my dog at you.' In such treatment, I am consoled by the word of promise – 'I am with thee, and no man shall set on thee to hurt thee. Speak my word and be not afraid.'

A woman refused reading and conversation on religion. If any evil was done, it was sure to be done by a Methodist. 'I am not come to talk about Methodists, but to read about Jesus Christ.' Here a man selling coals came to the door, and the woman (thinking to get quit of me) set him to ask me to buy coals. 'Not wanting any at present, but will you buy of me?' 'What?' 'The truth.' 'What do you mean?' 'Do you know that you have ruined yourself by sin, and it is a faithful saying, that Jesus Christ came to save sinners.' The man turned away, and I looked again at the woman, who, in a passion, began turning her mangle at such a speed, as partly to upset it, and make her thankful for my assistance, in putting it to rights. Left a tract, and we parted friendly.

The agents, it must be admitted, were not above scoring a point now and then: 'A young man, a professed Socialist, began to talk of the contradictions of the Bible. I asked him to point out some. He tried to evade it. I pressed him – when he acknowledged *he could not read a syllable!'* However, their wholehearted and courageous response to the call ringing in their hearts commands our respect. In 1873 one of them, visiting the Fever Convalescent Hospital during an outbreak of smallpox, caught the disease and died. Apart from the ever-present danger of infection, the threat of violence must have shadowed many of their encounters. One cannot but admire the bravery of the missionary who in the same year admonished a carter in Thorner who was roundly abusing his boy for failing to grease the cart axles. Hearing the man swear 'They are as hot as hell!' the missionary turned round and said, 'Then you believe that hell is hot, do you? Isn't it strange that you are determined to go there as fast as you can?' Luckily for him, this miscreant was not yet a hardened sinner, for, instead of punching the missionary on the nose, 'he thanked me for my warning, and promised to swear no more'.

In our more secular day we would certainly attempt to secure food, clothing and shelter for the 'from twenty to thirty ragged and neglected boys and girls' sitting around at an 1889 open-air meeting and singing

'I am so glad that Jesus loves me,
Jesus loves even me,'

rather than offering them tracts and admonishments, but to these men the soul was more important than the body. They made a great contribution to the Temperance cause; in 1885 one described how, a fortnight previously, a young man had come up to him in the street and said:

Twelve months ago I was locked up for being drunk and riotous, and got fourteen days in Armley Gaol. Then I remembered your address in the cells, and resolved to lead a different life. When I came out I carried out my good resolutions, and to-day I and my wife and my two children are a happy family. When I left home this morning my wife said, 'John, you remember last year this time how very unhappy we were; now we are looking forward with a cheerful prospect of a pleasant Christmas and a happy New Year.'

There must have been great satisfaction in the hearts of the missionaries at successes like this, tempered with sadness at the failures and – sometimes – with weariness before the horrendous task facing them. Let us hope that Samuel Barbour, Adam Ewing and the others of that company now at Beckett Street felt as did William Logan, the missionary at Quarry Hill: 'Amid all the perplexities of the past year, I would not have missed the real pleasures I have enjoyed for 10,000 worlds ...'

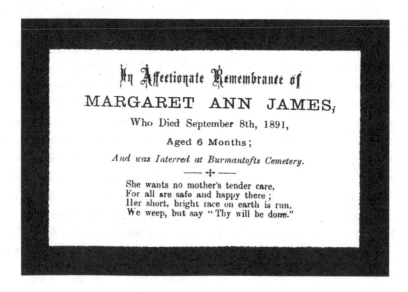

In Affectionate Remembrance of
MARGARET ANN JAMES,
Who Died September 8th, 1891,
Aged 6 Months;
And was Interred at Burmantofts Cemetery.

She wants no mother's tender care,
For all are safe and happy there;
Her short, bright race on earth is run,
We weep, but say "Thy will be done."

12. *Left*: Memorial card for Margaret Ann James.

13. *Above*: The reality of infant death: Margaret Ann James, born in March 1891, buried at Beckett Street Cemetery in September. Like so many other Leeds babies (220 in 1885), Margaret Ann died of acute bronchitis.

Chapter Four

A Chapter of Accidents

To part with our boy was a trial severe,
But ti's better he should be yonder than here.

John Henry Gallagher, 1876

The voyage of life starts, unfortunately, with some rather sharp and nasty reefs. Pregnancy itself was a dangerous state, as reflected in the *Leeds Mercury* on 30 October 1856:

FATAL ACCIDENT.– At the Leeds Court-house, on Tuesday, an inquest was held before J. Blackburn, Esq., on the body of Susannah Clarke, aged 24 (wife of Samuel Clarke, cloth-dresser, Rushforth-street, Newtown). On Monday night, after leaving work, she called upon her mother, in Cleveland-street, and was showing a kitten to a little boy in the room. By some means she fell backwards across a small rocking-chair, and ruptured an interior vessel. Deceased was six months gone in pregnancy. She bled profusely for twenty minutes, and then expired. Verdict: 'Accidental death'.

The chances of a baby born to an undernourished, frail, hardworking mother in Goulden's Buildings or Ebenezer Street were not very good. Stillbirths were frequent, but although the babies were given burial in the cemetery, they were treated in early and mid-Victorian days as non-persons, with no entry in the Burial Registers and no funeral service read over them; the only reason they were recorded at all was because of the shilling fee for the burial, which had to be collected by the sextons and delivered up to the Borough Accountant (and which caused the downfall of the Hannams, as we have seen). For a brief period in the 1870s, such burials were entered in the Unconsecrated register simply as 'Stillborn child', but on the other side they continued to be ignored. Due to the lucky survival of a few dirty, tattered pages of the Consecrated sexton's Rough Order Books of the same time, we can calculate just three yearly totals of these nameless babies. In 1872 there were 187 (6.3 per cent of total burials); in 1873, 204 (7.1 per cent); in 1874, 197 (6.2 per cent). In 1874 the Registration of Births and Deaths Act stipulated that no stillborn child could be buried without either a certificate from a registered medical practitioner who had attended the birth or examined the body, or else a declaration signed by some person who would, had the child been born alive, have notified the birth to the local registrar. Registers of Stillborn Children were accordingly commenced at Beckett Street Cemetery, but only one complete volume survives, the book for the Unconsecrated portion, beginning in 1922. Again, we fortunately have some ripped-out pages from earlier, lost registers, where we can read, for instance, two typical entries for the Unconsecrated portion in 1891:

October 10, Grave 25051: Board of Guardians for Annie Booth, Union Infirmary, Leeds; certificate 7 December, James Allan MD, Union Infirmary, Leeds; 1s.

December 10, Grave 24977: Mary O'Hara for Mrs Coghlan, 20 Little Lemon Street, Leeds; certificate 10 December, John O'Neil, surgeon, Marsh Lane, Leeds; 1s.

These babies were properly recorded and buried, but in those more censorious days there was a desperate problem for the young unmarried mother trying to conceal her shame from the eyes of the world. There is a trickle of sad little entries in the register of the Consecrated portion (where the religion was not known, the deceased was usually presumed to be C of E) for children who had been born alive but had died within minutes and had been secretly disposed of: 'newly born male child, found near piggeries, Forge Place, age 1 hour'; 'newly born female child, recovered from River Aire, age unknown'; 'newly born male child, found in lavatory at Holbeck Railway Station, age 5 minutes'. These burials took place in 1926, but there is no reason to suppose that such pathetic finds were not made also in the nineteenth century.

Often the baby did not die alone, for childbirth was a dangerous business for the mother. John Cooper, tailor, of St Mary's Lane, lost his eighteen-year-old wife Susannah on 12 July 1846, and his eleven-week-old son Alfred a fortnight later. On 1 January 1863 tiny Charles Foster was buried, aged one-and-a-half days, together with his twin sister Ann, who had lived just twice as long; and their father Robert, of 12 Beckett Street, saw the common grave reopened two weeks later to receive his wife Ann, aged thirty-seven. There are many cases like these, where it is reasonable to suppose that the mother never recovered from infections or complications which set in after the birth.

Charles and Ann Foster suffered an added disadvantage because they were twins. In the *Medical Times & Gazette*, 1862, Dr Arthur Mitchell gave his professional view: 'The whole history of twin births is exceptional, indicates imperfect development and feeble organization in the product, and leads us to regard twinning in the human species as a departure from the physiological rule, and injurious to all concerned.'[56] Dr Mitchell estimated one child in every forty-two born to be a twin. A count of babies two weeks old or less buried at Beckett Street over the three years 1857–9 reveals that, out of 358 children, there were five sets of twins:

Joseph and Benjamin Smith of 40 Burmantofts, aged three days;
John Henry and Joseph Goodison, sons of John, of Myrtle Street, aged two days;
James and Robert Waterhouse, sons of James, of 17 Dufton Yard, aged eight hours and seventeen hours;
Eli and Samuel Bailiffe, sons of William, of Sheepscar Green, aged two days;
Mary and Ann Hewison, daughters of William, weaver, of Red Bear Yard, aged one week and nine days.

There was also a set of triplets, buried on 13 October 1857: Thomas, Rosann and Harriot Hunter, aged one day, children of Thomas, labourer, of Kings Street. The number of twins in the sample may, of course, be larger, since we do not know which children are twins unless both die and are buried together (so that some of those who appear to be single children may be the non-survivors of multiple births). It should also be noted that, of the thirteen twins or triplets buried, nine were boys, male mortality being greater at every stage of life.

In some few cases we know the cause of death, even though it is virtually never stated in the Burial Registers. The cholera burials were in one
particular area, for instance; or there might be a helpful mention on the
memorial, if any. The only other source of information is the local newspaper, where accidents, sickness or suicide might be reported. These items,
although fascinating, give us a distorted picture of causes of death in the
nineteenth century, since only the more unusual or bizarre events, or things
which happened to relatively important people, are covered. It should also,
of course, be borne in mind that newspaper reports were often inaccurate
or biased, then as now; but they provide us with colourful, intriguing and
unforgettable glimpses into the lives of the Victorians, as seen by themselves
and by their contemporaries.

There are general summaries of causes of death for the whole of the city
in the annual reports of the Medical Officer of Health for Leeds, who was
appointed in 1866 and produced his first report the following year, summarising the 6,261 deaths of 1867 under the following headings:

Zymotic [infectious] disease:	1157
Disease of uncertain or variable seat:	208
Tubercular disease:	944
Disease of brain, spinal marrow &c.:	998
Disease of heart, blood vessels &c.:	233
Disease of lungs &c.:	1177
Disease of stomach, liver &c:	256
Disease of kidneys &c:	60
Childbirth, disease of uterus &c.:	28
Disease of skin, cellular tissue &c.:	35
Debility and atrophy:	500
Developmental disease:	187
Old age:	202
Sudden death [accident and suicide]:	251
Not specified:	25
Total	6261

During the year 168 people died from whooping-cough and 815 from
bronchitis; thirty-three babies died from 'teething'. For more detail on
the 'sudden deaths', we are dependent on the *Leeds Mercury* and the *Leeds*

Intelligencer, which are the main sources of information on the incidents described below.

Sarah, infant daughter of Martha Pheeney, a widow residing in Brick Street, 'died suddenly in bed', aged seven weeks, early in 1855. Perhaps this was what we nowadays call a 'cot death', made even sadder by the death of her three-year-old brother William three days later. Very small children were also at risk of suffocation, because they were usually put to sleep in the same bed as their parents; in 1849 five-week-old George Stamper was found dead in bed, suffocated, and the *Mercury* reported that 'the mother is said to be a woman of intemperate habits, and therefore in all probability she has overlain the child and so caused its death'.

A hazard which, like 'overlying', is now unheard of was the practice of drugging children with opium-based medicines, which caused a surprising number of the infant deaths recorded. A report by Dr H.J. Hunter in 1863[57] describes how mothers going to work in the fields would dope their children so that they would not give trouble to the old women or little girls paid a few pence to look after them; this must certainly also have been a widespread practice in the towns. Godfrey's Cordial, a soupy mixture of opium, treacle and infusion of sassafras, was a favourite; it was made up in different strengths by different suppliers, which could result in an inadvertent overdose, so that the surgeon summoned by the frightened 'nurse' might find 'half-a-dozen babies, some snoring, some squinting, all pallid and eye-sunken, lying about the room, all poisoned ...' Dr Hunter goes on to comment that cases of death from opium poisoning are 'supposed to be common'; when they were the subject of inquests, they were often wrongly recorded as cases of 'overlying' or 'debility from birth'. The parents of Sam May, aged ten months, put their faith in 'Holbeck Tincture':

> The child being cross on Saturday, the mother gave it twelve drops of Holbeck Tincture. No particular effect was produced, and the child was put to bed rather late. At nine o'clock on Sunday morning, however, when the mother awoke she found her child dead, the hands being clenched and lips discoloured. Mr. Hunt, of Upper Caroline-street, the druggist from whom the tincture was obtained, stated that the medicine was composed of aromatic spirits of ammonia, tincture of rhubarb, and laudanum. Verdict: 'Death from natural causes'.

Natural, indeed! Sometimes the medicine *was* exonerated, as in the case of an 1856 inquest by the surgeon William Nicholson Price (whom we shall meet again) on William Henry Coleman, son of a single woman living in Mill Street. Mr Price found that death was not due to the grain of calomel and sugar which his mother had obtained from the Dispensary, but to inflammation of the lungs. But there must have been large numbers of deaths for which (recognised or not) the dangerous nostrums easily obtained from dispensers were to blame.

The home was full of dangers; an inquest in June 1856 was held on Margaret Nolan, aged eighteen months, the daughter of James Nolan, of York Street. 'The child was playing in the house on Monday afternoon, and accidentally spilled a cup of boiling water that lay on the table upon her cheek and face, from the effects of which she died on Tuesday.'

Death from burns was sadly all too frequent in Victorian days, when open fires were the only means of heating and people wore voluminous clothes. We have already heard William Logan, the Quarry Hill missionary, comment that eleven children left alone in their homes had died from burning since he had begun his work in the district. In 1856 Samuel Cryer, aged four, was at home in Bread Street with an older boy, aged eight, roasting potatoes, when his pinafore caught fire. The report of the inquest on William Kelly, also in 1856, is actually headed: 'THE DANGER OF NEGLECTING CHILDREN'. 'On Saturday morning, about eight o'clock, a child two years old, named William Kelly, son of John Kelly, engine-man, was left by its grandmother in a room containing a fire, in Giles-buildings, while she went out to purchase a cake.' It was a cake bought at a dreadful cost, for during the few minutes she was away, William, who was wearing only his little nightshirt, began a game of poking a piece of paper into the lighted grate ... Older people were also vulnerable; in 1865 a sixteen-year-old, Mary Kirk, left home about seven o'clock on a grey March morning to look for work and, to warm herself for a moment, stood near a coffee-stall which had been set up outside the Robin Hood in East Street. She was too close to the glowing brazier; her ragged petticoats, perhaps, or the end of her woollen shawl, ignited, and her panic-stricken rush down the street created a gush of air which only made things worse. She lingered for a week in the Infirmary 'in great suffering' before she died.

From fire to water: for an inland city, Leeds had a surprisingly high number of drownings among the accident victims at Beckett Street. Of course, few people could swim; in his autobiography *A Life on the Humber*, Harry Fletcher, who was raised on a Humber keel from the age of two months, and whose father and grandfather spent their lives on working boats, comments:

'Neither my father nor my grandfather could swim. No more could I. Most of the keelmen I knew couldn't either, except my uncle Joe.'[58] 'Simply messing about in boats' brought death to two boys of seventeen and fourteen, Joseph White and John Cordingley. In May 1856 they climbed into a 'flat' or small boat owned by Mr Pashley of Water Lane, and foolishly unfastened the chain. The river was running strongly owing to recent heavy rain, and the boat was immediately carried out into the current, the boys, without oars or paddles, unable to stop it. Their shouts attracted the attention of the men on one of Crowther and Dixon's boats, opposite Ellershaw's Wharf, who threw them a rope, but when one of the boys caught it the flat was jerked to a halt and they were thrown out, losing hold of their lifeline. Both sank within minutes, and although the river was dragged repeatedly, the bodies were not recovered for several days, Joseph White's by a workman digging sand in the river at 'Jenny White's Hole' near Warehouse Hill.

A grotesque incident occurred a few months later, when a boy walking near Monk Suspension Bridge observed a hat, top upwards, floating in the river. Automatically he threw a stone at it, but to his excitement and horror he saw the skirt of a coat swirl to the surface. He rushed at once to the nearest building, which was Messrs Bell's ropeworks, and persuaded the men to drag the river. Soon the body was brought to shore, and proved to be that of a man of about fifty, wearing light-coloured cotton cord trousers, a brown jacket and Wellington boots. The hat was fixed firmly on the head, and it appeared that the corpse, bizarrely, had been floating upright in the water. There was nothing but a pair of spectacles in the man's pockets, and no means of identifying him. As no marks of violence were found, it was assumed that he had somehow accidentally fallen into the water, and an inquest verdict was duly recorded at the Wellington Hotel, whither he had been taken, of 'Found drowned – person unknown'. As usual with an unidentified body, he was buried in the Consecrated portion of the cemetery, and somebody, somewhere, was left wondering why he never came home ...

The *Mercury* reported with particular feeling on 17 February 1879 the drowning of David Hillyard and Frederick William Teale. A football match between the Leeds Parish Church Second Eleven and the Kirkstall team was in progress in a field near Crown Point Bridge, when the ball was kicked over the fence into the river.

> Hillyard, in endeavouring to secure it with a piece of wood, slipped, and fell into the water, which at this point (just at the back of a portion of Messrs.

Tennant's Flax Mill) is very deep. Teale, who was close by at the time, and who was an expert swimmer, courageously jumped into the water, with the object of saving the life of Hillyard, who could not swim. Hillyard, however, clutched the latter round the neck, and held him so tightly that he was unable to extricate himself, and both sank before assistance could be rendered ... Much sympathy is felt for the bereaved families, Hillyard's mother being an invalid, and Mrs Teale having, not long ago, buried her husband, the father of the young man who has been drowned.

Hillyard was fifteen years of age, Teale sixteen. Memorials to both survive; the Hillyard cross, to the south of Marshall Walk, is carved to look like wood and mounted on a base of rocks, with beautifully incised lettering on each smooth face. The cross from Teale's grave has gone, but the stepped base remains, with the inscription 'FREDERICK WILLIAM SENIOR TEALE WHO WAS DROWNED IN THE RIVER AIRE WHEN TRYING TO SAVE THE LIFE OF HIS FRIEND'.

Almost unbelievable to the reader under fifty or so will be the story of the young lovers who lie in one grave near the Stoney Rock Lane railings. The *Yorkshire Evening Post*, headlining 'A WEDDING THAT WILL NOT BE', tells the story of the sad night of 30 October 1897, when Walter Newbound, a lithographic printer aged twenty-six, set out from his home near the Dewsbury Road to meet his sweetheart, Ann Ellen Adkins, a twenty-year-old bookbinder from Hunslet. A highly respectable couple, well-liked in the neighbourhood, where Walter was described as 'a fine, handsome young man, regular in his habits' and Ann Ellen as equally popular and hard-working, they had been engaged for some time, and were due to be married at Christmas. For several weeks past they had been going into town on Saturday nights to choose furniture for their future home, and on the fatal day they met as usual despite the thick fog, did their shopping, and started on their return journey. 'The night was very dark, and the fog was so dense that they could not see a yard before them.' Time wore on; midnight came and went, and still they had not arrived home. The Newbounds had lost a son only a year before, and both families were extremely alarmed. Not until next morning was their dread confirmed by the identification of two bodies in the Millgarth Street police-station mortuary. They had been found by a boatman, Samuel Collitt, floating in the new Dock Basin at Chadwick Street. Despite the fog, the young people had attempted a short cut across the unpleasant open space between Clarence Road and Chadwick

Street, where the recent removal of some heaps of rubbish had altered the landmarks by which they could have navigated through the impenetrable 'peasouper'. 'Suddenly there was a cry and a splash, and the unhappy couple were struggling together for life in the cold inky water.' Miss Adkins' watch, found in Newbound's pocket where he had placed it for safety with his own, had stopped at five minutes past ten, marking their last moments. A fog caused by atmospheric conditions exacerbated by pollution, so dense that it could cause people to lose all sense of direction even in familiar territory, is hard to imagine now, but older people will understand exactly what Walter and Ann Ellen faced on their last walk home from Leeds.

A surprisingly large number of inquests held on people afterwards buried at Beckett Street Cemetery are the result of traffic − yes, traffic − accidents. John Whitling, a labourer employed by Mr Samuel Stawman, greengrocer at the Bank, was driving a donkey and cart to a market garden one day in 1856 to pick up a load of vegetables when the animal bolted in Accommodation Road, throwing Whitling, who was crushed by a wheel of the cart. Children, then as now, ran out into the street in the paths of vehicles. Henry Pearson Whitwam, who was five, died in St Peter's Square in 1879. A butcher named Edward Davis, standing nearby, saw the danger from the horse and cart bearing down on the child, and unfortunately Henry turned round at his warning shout, slipped, and fell under the wheels. But the strangest and most ironic fatality of all must have been the death of Mary Jane Duckworth in 1856. This eight-year-old was standing near her father's door at the corner of Cherry Street one Saturday afternoon when she suddenly dashed out into the road, just as a large vehicle loomed up, drawn by black horses being driven at a slow trot by coachman Henry Stewart. It was a mourning coach returning from a funeral at Burmantofts Cemetery ...

The railways too had their toll of fatalities. Two consecutive entries in the Burial Register on Boxing Day 1850 seemed unlikely to be coincidental:

Joseph Whittle Garrick, Railway Street, engine driver, aged 33.
Martin Tindall, Railway Street, engine stoker, aged 21.

It transpired that these men were working a passenger train on the York & North Midland Railway between Milford and Leeds, which was just being shunted out of a siding at Milford when nine breakaway wagons from a heavy goods train came careering down the main line from Garforth at 14 mph. 'The wagons dashed into the engine and tender, literally smashing them to pieces, and the engineer and stoker were also frightfully mutilated and killed on the spot.' The pointsman, too, lost his life, although mercifully the open carriages had not yet been manoeuvred on to the main line, and the two shrieking bonneted and shawled females who were the only passengers escaped injury. We must remember that in 1850 we are not talking about mighty engines of 70–100 tons, such as the still familiar 'Flying Scotsman' or 'Mallard', but of the early locomotives of less than a quarter of that weight, with their large driving wheels and tall funnels; the line itself, opened under the chairmanship of George Hudson of York ('The Railway King') was only ten years old. And yet 'the poor fellows belonging [to] the engine seem to have been literally torn limb from limb'.

John Rider's headstone gives us two interesting facts. During his life he had 'discharged his duty faithfully for twenty-six years as servant at the Board of Works for this Borough'; and he met his accidental end on 25 January 1855, aged seventy-four, in Bowling Tunnel on the Lancashire & Yorkshire Railway. His shockingly mangled remains were found by a platelayer within the tunnel, lying across the rails, and he could be identified only by 'a hairy cap, apparently made of dogskin, a hairy tobacco pouch, and a watch guard formed of hair'. With the simplistic brevity which characterised inquest verdicts of the time, the jury pronounced him 'Found dead'. It was not until after the inquest that his identity was established by his son, who testified that Rider had left his home in Newsome's Yard, Briggate, at three o'clock on Monday morning. 'No reason could be assigned for his doing so, except that the old man had for some time past manifested symptoms of dotage.' Poor old John.

Deaths by road and rail are nowadays all too familiar, but many fatalities resulting from accidents in the nineteenth century would be extremely unlikely in the advanced state of medicine today. In February 1855, for instance, the nineteen-year-old son of Mr Breasley, landlord of the White Swan, Ward's Fold, Mabgate, attended the Licensed Victuallers' dinner in his father's place. Arriving home at two o'clock in the morning – and one must assume that the alcohol consumed could have played some part in the events that followed – Benjamin, not wishing to disturb his parents, who had long since wiped away the spilt beer, emptied the spittoons, swept up the sawdust and retired to bed, climbed over the wall at the back of the house and attempted to get in through a window. He slipped and fell, breaking his thigh, and lay helpless, with no one to hear his moans, until a neighbour's night-watchman came by. The young man's parents were roused and a doctor was called, but although the fracture was reduced, Benjamin Breasley died two weeks later. In the days before antisepsis, any open wound was a risk, and even a fractured thumb could lead straight to heaven. Thrombosis, gangrene, shock, pneumonia were all potential killers.

Epilepsy, too, was a condition now controllable for which effective medicines did not then exist. Dr Frederick T. Roberts, in his 1873 textbook *The Theory and Practice of Medicine*, prescribes a suitable regime for the sufferer: a nutritious, but light and digestible diet; moderate daily exercise in the open air; proper hygienic conditions; the avoidance of mental work (which meant keeping children from school); cold or tepid sponging daily; the checking of any vicious habit such as intemperance or self-abuse; a sufficient amount of sleep, the head being well raised at night. 'Many epileptics require constant watching, and all need more or less supervision, above all, not being allowed to go into positions of danger from falling, or near a fire or water. Epileptics,' concluded Dr Roberts with vigour, 'decidedly ought not to marry.'[59] One wonders how many lives were blighted by such advice. However, few of the poor people struggling to make a living in the Victorian city would have been in a position to adopt the recommended lifestyle, and the knowledge that he was liable to fits did not prevent John Mounsey from following the trade of slater. It was in 1856 that, while engaged on the roof of a house being built in Caledonian Road, at the back of Springfield Place,

he suddenly jumped from his position and fell on his head to the ground, a distance of thirty feet. He was immediately conveyed to the Infirmary, where he expired in a few hours from concussion of the brain ... He was subject to fits, and it is supposed that he was seized by a fit when on the roof, thus causing his fall.

In the same year, Charles Denton Hulme, a house surgeon at the Leeds House of Recovery, was an unusually long time in the bath one day. 'The attendant [a nurse, Mary Edmonds] went to him, and was shocked to find him a corpse.' His head was under the water and his arms folded; Dr Chadwick, one of the physicians at the institution, came at once, but was not surprised, for he had frequently warned his colleague against taking warm baths. It was clear from evidence at the inquest that Mr Hulme, who became irritable and inarticulate before a seizure, had shown signs of the onset of this one, and it seems strange that he should have put himself in such a dangerous situation. The *Mercury* reporter recorded: 'Mr Hulme was a young man whose kindness and professional ability had endeared him to all with whom he came in contact, and his untimely end will be regretted, not only by the trustees, but also by those who are and have been inmates of the institution.'

Any disease manifesting itself in fits or 'abnormal' behaviour might be set down as insanity; and people were confined as lunatics who were not suffering from mental illness at all, or who were victims of mental conditions which today could be controlled in the community, or of mental handicap, often congenital, but sometimes resulting from an undiagnosed or mishandled problem. Dr Alfred Beaumont Maddock's textbook, *Affections of the Nervous System* (London, 1854), gives a series of vignettes of patients at his private Lunatic Asylum in Kent; they range from the usually quiet and dull fourteen-year-old girl now incessantly singing and pouring forth a flood of ideas, to the woman of twenty-three suffering from religious melancholia, so convinced of her damnation that she had attempted in an act of expiation to scoop out one of her own eyes; there is a young gentleman of twenty-two tormented with frightful dreams, palpitations of the heart, shortness of breath, feverish tongue, languid and feeble pulse, torpid bowels and a sinking sensation – all caused by 'sexual excess'; and a lady two weeks post-partum and terrified by imaginary black imps, evidently a severe case of 'baby blues'.

Dr Maddock seems to have been an amiable and thoughtful man, who believed that the bowels were the root of most of these problems, but who also advocated 'mental and moral treatment' of the sufferers, so that the rhubarb, calomel, brimstone and treacle were interspersed with warm baths, woollen clothing next the skin, and kind and friendly counsel. Let us hope that the staff in charge of the West Riding Pauper Lunatic Asylum, opened in 1818 at East Moor in Wakefield, shared his humane attitude, for a number of those interred at Beckett Street Cemetery had spent their last days in this institution, to which dangerous and violent patients were sent. White's 1837 Directory describes it as:

a very extensive and commodious building [which] from its external appearance, and internal management, is an ornament to the town, and an honour to the Riding ...The land, buildings, and furniture, with the recent additions, have cost upwards of £50,000, but this burthen on the Riding is greatly outweighed by the utility of the institution, which has now accommodations for nearly 400 patients;– the number of the unfortunate inmates being, in 1836, no fewer than 173 males, and 148 females, mostly paupers, sent hither by the warrants of magistrates under the provisions of the act, which requires that all pauper lunatics, and dangerous idiots, shall be sent to such institutions, and that the weekly payment of 6s. for the maintenance of each shall be paid out of the poor-rates of their respective parishes.

In 1853 the number of inmates had risen to 450. They came to Beckett Street, mostly to common graves, in increasing numbers from the mid-1850s, among them John Mitchell, a Leeds stuff-presser, who was confined in 1868 with suicidal tendencies attributable to his delusion that he had syphilis; apparently improving (although he told the medical attendant that it was 'only the same old story, sometimes better and sometimes worse'), he was allowed out of the wards on a working-party and, dashing into the slaughter-house, seized a knife and cut his throat. The Wakefield Asylum continued to be the main support of 'lunatic' patients from Leeds until into the twentieth century.

Drink contributed in many ways to the death statistics, as it still does, although only two of the 6,261 deaths in Leeds in 1867 were directly attributed to alcohol: one to 'excessive drinking', one to delirium tremens. Michael Murphy was a fifty-eight-year-old slack-riddler at Allerton Main Colliery, who in 1865, suffering from DTs and declaring to his gaffer, 'The curse of God upon the man who first brewed whisky', completed his self-imposed task of drinking himself to death; in the same year Joseph Jones, aged fifty-seven, a labourer for the Highway Surveyors, lapsed into a drunken stupor on the way back from Pontefract races, and tumbled off the hired bus on to his head. Drink fired the passions and led to many a domestic and street quarrel, sometimes with fatal results. A well-known phenomenon of the nineteenth century was the 'Irish Fight'; the papers were full of stories of people like Edward and Mary Kelly, a brother and sister who went to booze at the Boot & Shoe Inn in Richmond Road one night in 1856. The man was already drunk, and the landlady refused to serve him. 'An Irish row was commenced instantly, both in the house and outside ...'[60] John Burns, aged thirty, was the innocent victim of such an affray in the same year. Returning from the Lloyd's Arms with his brother to their lodgings in York Street, he was struck a totally unprovoked blow on the back of the head with a wooden stool by one Patrick Riley, who appears to have been in a half-frenzied state after being involved in a fight among a number of Irishmen. It says much for the physical toughness of Burns that he went harvesting next day with a fractured skull! However, his injury worsened, and in a few days he was dead, while Riley was on the run, never to be seen again.

It was a vintage year for the Irish Fight; let Robert Madden, the landlord of the Yorkshire Hussar, Union Street, describe the events in his pub one Saturday evening when two tailors employed by Messrs Smallpage, John Menzie and Patrick King, came in.

> They appeared to have had some beer, but were sober. Whilst in my house, they played at dominoes, and about half-past eleven they quarrelled over the game. The deceased got up and put himself into a fighting attitude. King did not seem disposed to fight, and deceased called him a coward. King replied, 'Well, I'll be a coward.' Mensey then sat down. They continued to have high words up to twelve o'clock, when I requested them to go. I followed them to the door, and when they got outside they began to fight. I requested some persons present to assist me in separating them. At that time they had fallen to the ground. We assisted them up, and immediately afterwards they fought again; but I cannot say who began it. They had then taken off their coats. Both again fell, and were again separated. King then went towards Vicar-lane, and Mensey went in the opposite direction towards his lodgings. The deceased and King were fresh, but able to walk. I had heard King say that he didn't want to fight, but he would not be 'put upon'. After they separated, I saw no more of them.

In fact the fighting continued as soon as both had arrived at the lodgings they shared in Lower Brunswick Street. Mrs Seaton, from whom the two Irishmen rented rooms, ran for a policeman, but by the time one came the fighting had stopped, for Menzie had had his neck broken and died two days later. Like Riley, King tried to make his escape, but was apprehended by the coroner's officer. At the inquest he said 'he was very sorry that it had happened, but Menzie began the fight'. Contrition was not, of course, enough to save him from being sent to York Assizes on a charge of manslaughter.

Deadlier poisons than alcohol were readily available, at least until the Pharmacy Act of 1868, over the counter of the Victorian druggist. Sometimes they were taken accidentally, sometimes administered with deliberate intent to heal or to harm. Nobody knows for sure why Sarah Ritchie, a depressed widow of fifty-one who made a living as a stay-stitcher and looked after her elderly bedridden father in Crescent Street, should have died in 1856 as a result of ingesting bichromate of potassium – 'a poison almost unknown to medical men as having been used to destroy human life,' stated the *Mercury*, 'and one of which scarcely one person in a thousand ever heard.' A verdict was returned to the effect that 'she had died from the poison bicarbonate of potash, but there was no evidence to show in what manner it was administered or the state of the deceased's mind at the time of her death'. Little John Jenkins woke up hungry at home in Napier Street one morning in 1865 and called to his father for some bread and butter, which was brought up to him by his elder brother; but Mr Jenkins, a warehouseman, had used the unwashed knife with which he had spread some bread with 'Battle's Vermin Killer' the previous night as bait for mice. Mr W.N. Price, surgeon, testified at the inquest that strychnine was an ingredient of this powder. Both strychnine and arsenic will feature later, in our chapter on CRIME.

The defective state of medical knowledge led to many strange inquest verdicts, although when thirteen-year-old George Henry Brown, walking to work with his father along Mabgate in March 1864, 'looked up at the church clock, remarked that they were late, then ran on ahead ten yards, suddenly reeled and fell down on the causeway', there could be little doubt as to the cause of death. Both Mr Nunneley and Mr Clayton, surgeons, had repeatedly told his mother since the attack of the scarlatina eight years before that the boy had an 'affection of the heart'. His schoolfellows, who had seen him healthy and lively at St John's Sunday School the day before, were greatly saddened, and most of them attended the funeral at St John's Church, after which the lad was interred at Burmantofts. To the modern ear, however, attuned as it is to the Welfare State, there is something positively cynical about the verdict returned in the case of William Keeley in 1849. This forty-year-old carrier had a miserable 5s a week to support a family of six persons, and as a consequence he was 'reduced to the brink of the grave by sheer starvation'. He set off one morning for a short walk, and a few minutes later was found lying on the ground at Woodhouse Carr. He was carried to Croft's beerhouse, but died five minutes later, worn-out, starved and exhausted. And the inquest verdict? 'DIED BY THE VISITATION OF GOD.'

John William Roper's fine memorial in Beckett Street Cemetery simply states that he was 'accidentally killed', but the headline in the *Mercury* of 26 January 1869 neatly sums up the story: 'THE FATAL RESULT OF VENTURESOMENESS'. What a marvellous pen-picture the reporter gives us of the fourteen-year-old boy: 'Deceased was a fine well-grown lad, and was of a bold and daring disposition.' The youth's father was the building contractor responsible for some houses going up in North Street, Sheepscar, and John William was employed to assist the workmen. The temptation to stray from his tasks was too great. 'On Friday he ventured into one of the attics by a way which would assuredly have been fatal to a person with less nerve.' The expedition did indeed prove fatal to young Roper, for, on being ordered away by the foreman, he tried to drop from the attic (the staircase not being completed) to a landing beneath, but misjudged the jump and instead crashed through several storeys to the basement, a fall which he could not survive.

The potentially disastrous effects of boys being boys are also demonstrated by the story of John William Dunning. From his gravestone we learn that the seven-year-old was killed by falling out of a fly-boat, but it is quite wrong to assume that he was on a river or canal trip, for the boat referred to was actually a swinging gondola at the twice-yearly Leeds Fair held in July 1873 at Smithfield, the cattle-market site in North Street. At the inquest, reported by the *Yorkshire Post* (the former *Leeds Intelligencer*), the 'evidence was to the effect that the deceased had overbalanced himself while endeavouring to reach the cap of a boy named Scholes, and fell to the ground, a distance of between eight and ten feet ... He was riding for the second time, and had been placed in the middle of the boat by two different men, but he persisted in going forward to the end seat.' The nearest medical aid was at the Public Dispensary, also in North Street, on a site now part of Vicar Lane. The Dispensary was a charitable foundation of which White's 1837 Directory comments that it afforded medical aid to some 3,000 poor and friendless persons a year, but adds wryly that 'it is to be regretted that its expenditure often exceeds its receipts'; it had been the first home of the Leeds School of Medicine, which we shall discuss later. The little boy, who had a crushed skull and several broken ribs, was carried to the Dispensary and immediately attended by the surgeons, but died shortly after his admission – a terrible end to a bit of childish mischief. The jury, returning a verdict of 'Accidental Death', recommended that children of such tender years should not be allowed to ride unaccompanied in these boats; but the problem of providing thrills without spills is, as shown by the spate of fairground accidents in the late 1980s, not an easy one to solve.

There was a certain fatalism about the Victorian attitude to death, as indeed there had to be when surroundings were unhygienic, medicine was unreliable, and life expectancy was a mere forty years or so. Our final report, appearing in the *Mercury* of 11 October 1856, concerns, not a poor ill-fed creature of the alleys drowning his sorrows in drink, but a respectable gentleman profiting by some home-spun culture at Mr Joy's Temperance Hotel, Briggate. 'While Mr. Thomas Burland was sat enjoying a discussion on literary topics with some friends he was in the habit of meeting there, he was suddenly seized with paralysis, about ten p.m., and in five hours after he breathed his last.' The item is headed: 'The Uncertainty of Life'.

Chapter Five

The Great and the Good

Still, in death he will be giving
A bright example to the living.

Thomas Newman, 1884

Through the clouds of tobacco smoke that fill the long low room, the visitor gradually becomes aware of the presence of one or two hundred wholly unoccupied males of every age between fifteen and ninety – strong and vicious men; men in all stages of recovery from debauch; weedy youths of weak intellect; old men too dirty or disreputable to be given special privileges, and sometimes, when there are no such privileges, even worthy old men; men subject to fits; occasional monstrosities or dwarfs; the feeble-minded of every kind; the respectable labourer prematurely invalided; the hardened, sodden loafer, and the temporarily unemployed man who has found no better refuge ...[61]

This description of a workhouse ward is from the Minority Report of the Royal Commission on the Poor Laws which was set up in 1905. There were many such accounts. In 1866 readers of the *Pall Mall Gazette* were horrified by the experiences of James Greenwood, brother of the editor, who had dressed up as a tramp and spent the night in a workhouse in order to be able to report on what it was really like. 'Every variety of cough that ever I heard was to be heard there,' he wrote, 'the hollow cough; the short cough; the hysterical cough; the bark that comes at regular intervals, like the quarter-chime of a clock, as if to mark off the progress of decay; cough-

97

ing from vast hollow chests, coughing from little narrow ones – now one, now another, now two or three together ...'[62] Such evidence, fortified by the growing social realism of nineteenth-century paintings and engravings such as Luke Fildes' magnificent *Houseless and Hungry* (1869), displaying to the magazine-reading middle classes the straggling line of human misery, cold and want which must have disgraced many a pavement outside the workhouses of Victorian Britain, brings home the utter terror of destitution – 'the daily fear', as a Manchester alderman put it in further evidence to the Commission, 'that the Workhouse must be the final refuge', a fear 'harder to bear than the pinch of hunger, the cold of insufficient clothing, or the poverty of their surroundings'.[63]

Until the early twentieth century, the only official relief of poverty was that which operated through the Poor Laws. Before 1834, money had been raised within each parish by a poor-rate, which was distributed to the needy by the local Overseers of the Poor, either in the form of out-relief (payments which enabled the old and long-term sick or distressed to stay in their own homes, or tided over temporary difficulties) or by supporting them in workhouses, where they were supposed to earn their keep. Naturally the rate was unpopular, and the Overseers spent no more than they had to; but at least they had personal knowledge of the cases with which they were dealing. In Leeds, as a large town, the situation was more complicated, with a Workhouse Board composed of Overseers appointed by the Magistrates (themselves representing the Corporation, which until the 1830s was mainly Tory and Anglican) and of Churchwardens and Trustees appointed by the Vestry (the ratepayers, who in fierce political battles often elected Dissenting Liberals).[64] With the New Poor Law of 1834 – only implemented in Leeds ten years later because of party controversy – parishes were grouped into Unions, each of which provided a workhouse, which now became the norm for the support of the pauper. The Unions were run by Boards of elected Guardians, worthy citizens usually several social strata above the poor with whom they were dealing, and very conscious that they were answerable to the ratepayers whose money they were spending. Attitudes to poverty hardened; it now came to seem almost the fault of the poor, something which they had brought about by their own lack of effort. E. Royston Pike refers to 'the belief, almost universal in 1834 and still very widely held seventy years later, that the able-bodied worker, if he really tried, should be able to find a job and earn sufficient to maintain himself and those dependent on him'.[65] It was now the policy to force the able-bodied pauper to strive to

14. Architect's drawing of the Moral & Industrial Training Schools, 1848. The first building of the Beckett Street Workhouse complex.

support himself by ensuring that the alternative, the workhouse, was unattractive enough to be his very last resort; almost a punishment, certainly a deterrent, and not a pleasant place.

Although the North of England continued to favour out-relief where possible, there were always those who, through no fault of their own, had to take shelter in the workhouse, and whom even the hardest of critics would recognise as needing help (see Appendix D, Part 1). There were the very old such as Jemima Dewse, widow of a cloth-dresser, who merited a mention in the *Mercury* in 1867 when she died of old age, at the advanced age of 100 years; and the very young, like pathetic five-month-old Albert Foundling, buried in March 1862. There were the imbecile and the chronically sick. They came to the cemetery from the Leeds Workhouse, once housed in an overcrowded, dirty building of 1629 in Lady Lane (with accommodation for tramps in the Mendicity Office in Grantham Street) but in 1861 transferred to handsome new buildings on a site adjacent to the Moral and Industrial Training School for pauper children in Beckett Street – handily across the road from the Corporation's burial ground.

Alongside this harsh and far from satisfactory official provision, there were swarms of public-spirited citizens doing what they could to improve the lot of the unfortunate. No doubt their motives were varied, like those of the do-gooders of any age – a genuine desire in most to help the suffering, a smug condescension in some towards social inferiors, or in others an arrogant joy in the exercise of power – but their efforts got results. Local politicians outfaced apathy, greed and self-interest to force through the provision of clean water, of sewerage, of parks and libraries and decent burial of the dead, and worked to raise the consciousness of the working classes and unite them in the struggle for better conditions. Doctors and clergymen moved through the teeming masses, trying to alleviate disease of the body and spirit; educators started Ragged Schools, gave free lectures, took Sunday School classes, founded Mechanics' and Working Men's Institutes; thrifty and thoughtful tradesmen served as secretaries to Friendly Societies, which would care for their paid-up members in time of trouble; teetotallers, men and women, exhorted young and old to cast off the mental and physical shackles of the bottle by signing the Pledge.

The spirit of the age was SELF-HELP; the best-seller of that name came in 1859 from the pen of Samuel Smiles, an expatriate Scot who was from 1838 to 1854 successively editor of the radical *Leeds Times* and secretary of the Leeds & Thirsk Railway before continuing his career in London. Smiles influenced millions of his fellow Victorians with wonderful examples of people who, under the watchwords of Energy, Cheerfulness, Prudence and Industry, had made themselves responsible for their own fate and had transformed their lives by their own efforts – like the later Professor of Linguistics born in a Scottish bothy, who had taught himself his letters by practising on an old wool-card with the end of a burnt heather stem. The existence of the labouring class was divinely ordained,

> but that this class should be otherwise than frugal, contented, intelligent and happy is not the design of Providence, but springs solely from the weakness, self-indulgence, and perverseness of man himself. The healthy spirit of self-help created amongst working people would more than any other measure serve to raise them as a class, not by pulling down others, but by levelling them up to a higher and still advancing standard of religion, intelligence and instruction.

Rather than being the passive recipients of charity, the poor should be given the means to work their own salvation – education, employment, and moral strength. Asa Briggs, in his introduction to *Self-Help*,[66] comments that in the mid-Victorian years 'little faith was placed in government and almost unlimited faith was placed in individuals'. Leeds Town Hall, opened on 18 September 1858, rings with this confidence in the ultimate value of personal effort: 'Industry overcomes all things', 'Honesty is the best policy',

'Forward!' Yet the large painted mottoes point also to those other sources of support for the Victorian citizen, private charity ('Goodwill towards men') and mutual assistance ('In union is strength').

A social reformer who shared many of Smiles' ideas was 'Mr Hole of Leeds', three of whose children were buried in Grave 7827 at Beckett Street Cemetery between 1854 and 1863. Born in London in 1820, James Hole came to Leeds in his twenties to take up a position as clerk to a firm of shippers, and stayed in the city for more than twenty years. He was a founder member of the Leeds Redemption Society, which established (in the same year that saw the opening of the Corporation's cemetery) a cooperative where Leeds workmen could produce goods such as cheese, butter, footwear and blackberry jam, selling them at the Society's store, a little shop above a stable in Trinity Street; the land which was offered to the Society happened to be in Wales, and the venture lasted some ten years with moderate success. This was 'producer cooperation'; 'consumer cooperation', where the members joined together to buy good quality produce at a reasonable price, led to the Leeds District Flour Mill Society of 1847, of which Hole was a committee member and later a director, and which in the 1850s broadened its scope to cover the supply of general groceries under the title of 'The Leeds and District Cooperative Flour and Provision Society'. Another of Hole's interests was cooperative housing; with the watchword 'As the Homes, so the People', the Leeds Society for the Erection of Improved Dwellings built working-men's houses which were sold at cost price to artisans who paid for them with the help of mortgages from the Leeds Permanent Building Society, of which Hole was a director.

Hole's most important field of activity, however, was the adult education movement – particularly the 'Mechanics' Institutes' set up to provide instruction for working men. It was at such an institute that Smiles gave the group of lectures which formed the basis for *Self-Help*. These organisations pursued a wide variety of aims and ideals: they might cater for the true artisan, or for the lower middle classes; they might provide scientific training, or education at any level, including basic literacy; they might set out to teach, or be content with providing mental relaxation of an enjoyable kind after a hard day's work. At a time when so few working-class people had the opportunity of education during their childhood, these evening classes for adults were especially valuable, and Hole, besides serving on the Committee of the Leeds Institute, was Honorary Secretary of the Yorkshire Union of Mechanics' Institutes, which J.F.C. Harrison describes as 'the most successful of all the efforts made before 1870 to organize adult education as a movement'.[67] In addition to his paid employment with the shipping firm and his involvement with other movements, Hole gave practical support to adult education by lecturing, taking classes, making speeches and chairing meetings; 'education,' he wrote, 'is not an affair of childhood and youth, it is the business of the whole life.' Yet another of his schemes, this one first dreamed up by Smiles but carried through by Hole, was the 'Village Library', which supplied boxes of books, fifty at a time and changed twice a year, to groups of twenty-five rural subscribers each paying 1d a week.

James Hole quitted Leeds for London in 1867 and died in 1895, leaving, among other bequests, £300 to the 'Village Library' scheme and £100 to the Society for the Prevention of Cruelty to Children. His work must have proved an inspiration to many Leeds citizens, such as Robert Garside, whose gravestone at Beckett Street Cemetery announces with delightful precision: 'of No. 8 (now 15) Harewood Street Leeds, Tailor and Draper. Born at Elland, Oct. 20th 1800, Died at Sheepscar March 18th 1878. He was one of the founders of the Working Men's Institute, of Hunslet.'

Among the institutions which were busily trying to equip the disadvantaged for a better life were two which were especially concerned with specific sections of the urban poor – the Moral and Industrial Training School, which cared for pauper children, and the Asylum run by the Guardian Society, which rescued fallen women. The latter was founded in 1821 at premises in St James's Street, and was described as 'a temporary Asylum for such women as, having deviated from the paths of virtue, are desirous to abandon their vicious practices; there they will have suitable employment and instruction, in order to the formation of those virtuous and industrious habits which will qualify them for a respectable station in life.'[68] Here we see the benefactors of the nineteenth century not prepared simply to dispense charity, but anxious to help the needy to help themselves; for the Committee of Ladies who ran the institution urged the public to make use of the industry of the fallen women in their care.

> Plain work of every description, and Laundry Work, including Washing, Ironing, Clear Starching, and Mangling, are executed in the Asylum with neatness and care, and on most reasonable terms. An ample supply of work is an object of the highest importance; for the attainment of which, the countenance of the Public is earnestly solicited. Habits of industry can be acquired

only by constant employment, which will prove the best preparation for future service, and at the same time form a source of permanent support to the Institution.

The rules were strict. No pregnant woman was admitted, and applicants had to undergo two months' probation before their penitence was accepted as genuine. Rising at six in summer and seven in winter, they shared domestic duties, worked at their sewing (a quarter of the profits from which they were allowed to keep), and were in bed at ten after a day of decent deportment and becoming silence. Lying, swearing, dishonesty or disobedience earned them public expulsion. A matron (preferably single or 'a widow unencumbered with children') oversaw the tidiness, cleanliness and respectability of the building and its inhabitants, her duties ranging from keeping the beds mended to inspecting all letters received or sent and offering the strayed sheep wholesome advice. After two years, or whatever time was judged suitable, the committee attempted to 'restore them to their friends' or to place them in service.

How successful was the attempt to rehabilitate prostitutes by means of the mangle and the darning needle? In 1845 the annual report described the results of the previous year. Of the seventeen women in the Asylum, five had gone out to service, one had been dismissed for improper conduct, and four had run away; three newcomers had brought the number of inhabitants back up to ten. Letters had been received from 'young women who found in this Asylum a safe shelter, in their fallen and forlorn condition, from the storms and blasts of a pitiless world'. Yet there must have been many failures where untutored vice, economic necessity or sheer desperation with the regime at the Asylum made prostitution a career to return to; and others must have suffered the sad fate of Jane Dawes from the Asylum, buried at Beckett Street on 23 April 1864 – a fallen woman only fifteen years old.

The Guardian Asylum was the product of the concern and generosity of private individuals; the Moral and Industrial Training School, on the other hand, was a burden shouldered by the ratepayer. The foundation stone was laid on 12 October 1846 by John Metcalfe, Chairman of the Board of Guardians, and the 'Elizabethan-style' building, 'pleasantly situated at Burmantofts, occupying an eligible and elevated site of six acres in extent, including the play-ground and garden', was opened two years later. Mayhall's *Annals*[69] describe the commanding appearance of the front (brick with stone facings), with its gables, bay and oriel windows, and octagonal stone turrets; the separate accommodation for boys, girls and infants; the covered colonnades to enable the children to take outdoor exercise in wet weather; the spacious dormitories, the fever wards, and the chapel with its imitation oak roof.

> The admission to the school is vested absolutely in the Board of Guardians, and the inmates generally consist of orphans or deserted children; but there are also a few who are children of deserving resident poor. They are received at an early age, and are immediately placed under the superintendence of the schoolmaster or schoolmistress to be taught industrial work. The building has accommodation for about 400 children and youths ...

The pupils certainly did start their life's training early; one cannot imagine that Henry Jowett from the Industrial School had much benefit from it, since when he was buried across the road in 1853 he was only ten months old! There are numbers of young children at Beckett Street Cemetery who came from the school, and at least one teacher, John Graffham, who died in 1857 at the early age of twenty-three.

In some respects the children's day in mid-century was not dissimilar to that of the fallen women at the Guardian Asylum, with its regimented rising and bedtimes, enforced silence at meals, and, for the girls, domestic duties and sewing. The boys learnt gardening, tailoring and shoemaking, and the young inmates also, of course, received an elementary education which they would probably not have had outside. The diet was simple and plain, featuring much suet, bread and porridge, but infinitely better than starving in the streets.

The School had been created partly as a way of avoiding the provision of a complete new workhouse, but with the praiseworthy aim of removing children from the workhouse environment. It had a chequered career, with episodes of staff problems, arson, brutal punishment and the like; and in 1879 the children were reported to be 'sickly, pale and dejected' in appearance, and to be suffering from a prevalence of diseases such as ophthalmia and rickets (which nowadays would suggest vitamin deficiency). From then on many of the orphans were boarded out in foster homes, and those left at the School were sent to local Board Schools in Cross Stamford Street and Beckett Street for their education. From 1888, children left on emigration schemes for Canada. Finally, at the beginning of the last century, a new Home was built at Roundhay for the eighty-seven remaining children, and the handsome

15. 'Able-bodied inmates'. An undated photograph from the Leeds Workhouse.

building of the Moral and Industrial Training School became part of the Workhouse, the first block of which had been its neighbour for forty years. Pamela M. Pennock comments on how the School may be said to have failed in its original aim: 'The Board of Guardians, doubtless with the best motives, had adequately housed, fed and clothed the children away from the workhouse, but never entirely away from its atmosphere.'[70]

When the leaves fall from the limes and sycamores in the cemetery, it is possible to stand by John Metcalfe's grave and see in the distance the Lincoln Wing of St James's Hospital, once the School of which he laid the first stone. Metcalfe was a maltster by trade, and he was clearly a busy and public-spirited citizen, holding many important offices, among them the Chairmanship of the Board of Guardians and a Directorship of the Leeds Waterworks Company. The Board, meeting to hear the melancholy news of his death in 1848, recorded his ability, intelligence and zeal, and spoke of the loss to the township at large of his 'deepest interest in the success of those good works which were calculated to elevate the moral and intellectual condition, or to alleviate the sufferings and distresses of the humbler classes'. It is unwise to believe all one reads in the newspapers or on gravestones, but John Metcalfe's epitaph has an appealing ring when, amidst the eulogy of the public figure, a little of the private man slips in: 'He was a kind husband, an indulgent parent, and a warm hearted and true friend.'

There must have been something about the aroma of hops which brought out public-spiritedness for, like Metcalfe, Richard Stead was a maltster. When he died in 1857 he had been Chairman of the Board of Guardians for nearly ten years, 'and on all occasions manifested a warm sympathy for the poor'. Certainly his humanitarian desire for the physical and mental well-being of the children in the Guardians' care is evident; as is his popularity among his colleagues who, six months before his death, voted that their warm approval of the conduct of their Chairman should be engrossed upon vellum, signed by each member of the Board who voted for it, framed and glazed, and placed in the Boardroom of the Workhouse. The finished product, executed free of charge by one of the Relieving Officers, Mr Chiesman, who was a dab hand with the pen, was displayed in the window of a Briggate shop, where (as the *Mercury* reports) 'the faultless style of the penmanship has elicited considerable remark and commendation'.[71] The account of Stead's funeral the following year is interesting.

> He was interred at the Burmantofts Cemetery, in the presence of between three and four hundred people of all political shades of opinion. At the cemetery an imposing scene was presented by the formation of a large circle around the grave, by the children of the Industrial Schools. To show the respect in which he was held in the ward that he represented in the town council, most of the shops in Kirkgate were closed on the day of the funeral.[72]

It is sad that the roll of his services should have almost entirely weathered away from the stone that marks his resting-place.

Near the crest of the hill, in the once-exclusive Ground 1 of the cemetery, now within a stone's throw of guinea graves of 1907 popped in to use up empty plots, is a dignified group of low coped and ledger stones, with their symmetry unbroken by any eye-catching and showy columns or obelisks. Among them is an imposing iron-railed double plot, and here lie members of the Price family, among them William Price and his son William Nicholson Price, who died in 1867 and 1888 respectively. In June 1831 Mr Price senior, formerly a naval surgeon, was invited to join a group of Leeds doctors who had decided that it was high time the dominance of London over medical training was ended. Previously, any aspiring English physician or surgeon had had to attend the courses of the Society of Apothecaries or the Royal College of Surgeons in London, and the expense and inconvenience of having to study so far from home were compounded, in the opinion of many, by the moral dangers to which innocent young men from the North were exposed in the wicked metropolis. Leeds followed Manchester, Birmingham and Sheffield in setting up its own Medical School, but the provincial cities had to struggle for recognition (particularly from the London surgeons), and it was 1858 before the examinations of the University of London were opened to external students.

The Leeds School of Medicine took rooms in a wing of the Public Dispensary, the expenses and the profits being shared between the founders. The latter were all engaged full-time in their own medical or surgical practices, as well as dividing amongst themselves the various topics to be taught at the Medical School; William Price's area was, naturally, 'Military Surgery'. At the inaugural lecture, as S. T. Anning tells us in the *History of the Leeds School of Medicine*, Mr Thomas Pridgin Teale, FRS, gave a solemn warning to the new students. 'You may be a blessing or a curse to thousands. Under divine Providence, you will often be the arbiters of life and death … Let there then be engraven on your mind, in characters too deep to be effaced, "Orphan – widow". Think of the ties your ignorance will dissever:– think of the blessings your honest industry may diffuse.'[73] The advice was no doubt heeded, and the School prospered; in 1884, the year when William Nicholson Price retired, the Medical School was amalgamated with the Yorkshire College of Science, which twenty years later became the University of Leeds. Some 250 men and women annually now qualify as doctors through the School of Medicine.

William Price was President of the School in 1837–8, as was his son in 1859–60 and also in 1881–2, when he had the honour of giving the presidential address at the half-centenary. During his second tenure of office, it was William Nicholson Price who had to smooth out a problem with the Burial Grounds Committee. Until 1832 the only source of bodies for the teaching of anatomy to medical students had been a limited number of corpses of executed criminals, plus such newly interred bodies as could be seized from the grave by the likes of Burke and Hare, the 'Resurrectionists' and murderers. In 1832 the much-resented Anatomy Act was passed, making it legal for the 'unclaimed' corpses of paupers from the workhouse to be sent to medical schools for dissection.[74] Fifty years later, in 1882, bodies were regularly being brought to Beckett Street Cemetery from this source: Esther Day, aged 47; Charles Reed, aged 46; William Hemmingway, aged 71; Patrick Gaffney, aged 36; James Ryan, aged 23 – all within the space of three months. However, something was evidently awry when bodies were arriving at the cemetery at odd hours and remaining (although it is hard to imagine where, unless in the chapels) unburied all night. The Committee resolved on 27 January that 'the authorities of the Medical School and other Institutions sending bodies for interment be requested to send the same during the hours allotted for interments instead of during the night'.

Throughout the years of the nineteenth century, the carriages of the Leeds medical men dashed around the city, bearing heavily whiskered and portentously named gentlemen on their errands of hope and mercy – William Petty Ruddock, Charles Wilson Scholefield, Henry Miles Atkinson, William Nicholson Price. At the cemetery are those also whose careers were cut off prematurely, like Charles Denton Hulme, house surgeon at the House of Recovery, who, as we saw, drowned in an epileptic fit. There are many, too, who are uncommemorated, like Mary Wright, a widow aged thirty-three, and Mary Haggitt, aged forty-nine, both nurses at the House of Recovery. Old Dr Clifford Allbutt, in 1909, remembered the nurses of his youth: 'They were great, powerful, red-faced women, who all ate a great deal of beef and drank a great deal of beer, and lifted the patients as you would lift puppy-dogs ...'[75] Yet they were not immortal. The two Marys died within a fortnight of each other in the month of June 1847 – when the 'Irish Famine Fever' was raging through the institution and the town.

Neighbouring the Price family grave is a stone simply carved with a plain cross and, in beautiful Gothic lettering, the name 'JOHN HOPE SHAW'. Here lies another man whose life and works touched on many of the areas of mid-Victorian concern which we have already examined. John Hope Shaw was a solicitor, head of a long-established firm, and at the top of his profession; he was also an eminent magistrate and a Trustee of Leeds Parish Church. He was a member, and seven times President, of the Leeds Philosophical and Literary Society, and the papers – mainly on legal and parliamentary institutions – which he delivered at its meetings were, as were his magisterial pronouncements, models of lucid reasoning, patient research and effective presentation. His support for organisations which would improve the mental and moral welfare of the working classes was always readily given, and he was President or Vice-President of the Leeds and Headingley Mechanics' Institutes, and of the Yorkshire Union of Mechanics' Institutes.[76] A Liberal, he was three times Mayor of Leeds, laying the foundation stone of the new Town Hall on 17 August 1853; and as a member of the Town Council, he was also concerned in the great question of the Leeds water supply.

16. John Hope Shaw (1793–1864), lawyer, public benefactor, and thrice Mayor of Leeds.

In the first half of Victoria's reign towns and cities were doing their own thing, often, as in Leeds, in a welter of political conflict. As Geoffrey Best points out in *Mid-Victorian Britain*, legislation originating from central government tended to be permissive rather than mandatory, and what was compulsory often could not be enforced.[77] Energetic towns could get themselves local Improvement Acts (as did Liverpool, which in 1847 appointed the first Medical Officer of Health in Britain) to carry out public health measures of their own devising; slothful ones could find ways of dragging their feet, even when directed to take action. The Report of the Royal Sanitary Commission in 1871 defined this principle: 'The theory is, that all, that can, should be done by local authority, and that public expenditure should be chiefly controlled by those who contribute to it ...'[78] Gradually the 'individualist' gave way to the 'collectivist' phase, and by the end of the century Parliament was taking a much firmer attitude. 'By 1914,' as B.J. Barber sums up the situation in Leeds, 'the corporation provided the gas, water and electricity supply, operated the tramways, was responsible for environmental health, had created parks, libraries, markets and other amenities, and was beginning to tackle the problems of the slums.'[79]

The provision of water and gas, the disposal of sewage and corpses, the cleaning and widening of streets, were among the matters left at first to local management or mismanagement. In Leeds, since the seventeenth-century waterworks could only supply a couple of thousand households, people got their water mainly from wells, boreholes and the filthy and contaminated becks. When the question of an improved system was raised in the 1830s, there ensued a long struggle between rival engineers (who disagreed on the siting of the reservoir at Eccup and on the route of the pipes), and another between the opposing camps which argued on the one hand for the Town Council to control the supply and on the other for a joint-stock company to raise the capital and receive the profits. A compromise was forced by the Earl of Harewood (whose land and water were required for the new works) and eventually resulted in the Leeds Water Works Act of 1837. George Leather & Son were to be the sole engineers, councillors would be represented on the joint-stock company's board, and the Council would have the power to purchase the works after twelve years had elapsed from the date of the Act. The new supply was in operation in 1843, but within ten years it was proving inadequate, and it was John Hope Shaw who, in written reports and in a two-hour speech to the Town Council based on both commercial and humanitarian arguments, persuaded the opponents of municipalisation that this was one public utility which should be under public control. Private management in other cities was demonstrably inefficient; public possession did not violate any principle of trade. 'He trusted that every member would think it desirable that they should maintain that Council in its present position of honour, and at the same time that they should obtain an abundant supply of one of the first necessaries of life for the use of this vast community, of whose interests they were the appointed guardians.'[80] In November 1852 the Leeds waterworks came into Leeds ownership for the sum of £227,417.

Shaw was a quiet, reserved man, warm only within his circle of family and friends, but courteous to all and tolerant of the opinions of others. 'In his character there was the most perfect honour,' recorded Mayhall, 'and in his manners an unassuming dignity.' At the opening of the 1849 Yorkshire Show, William Beckett MP (original owner of the fields which had become Beckett Street Cemetery) proposed a charming toast to him, reported on 4 August by the *Intelligencer*.

> He felt some little difficulty and hesitation, because he could not help recollecting that they had for two days been looking with agricultural eyes, and assigning money to nothing which was not very fat, and when he looked upon his friend's slender form (laughter) - he was only afraid that they would be disappointed at his toast, that it did not produce a good, fat, corpulent Lord Mayor (laughter, and hear, hear) – such a one as agriculturalists would always wish to see fill the gown of an alderman!

Both the Town Hall and the Parish Church bells were tolled at Shaw's funeral on 24 August 1864, and one cannot help feeling that, as a Headingley resident who might reasonably have been expected to opt for interment in the private Leeds General Cemetery or in a local churchyard, it was a statement of his beliefs that he should have purchased a grave in the Corporation's cemetery at Beckett Street.

In the year after John Hope Shaw died, a successful Leeds businessman was elected to the Town Council who has left, not merely a polished grey granite tombstone on the Unconsecrated side of the cemetery, but a number of other memorials around the city; he laid the foundation stone of the new Leeds Bridge in 1871, influenced the transformation of Boar Lane into a wide, handsome thoroughfare, erected the beautiful Moorish factory in St Paul's Street, and paid for the construction of the elegant domed drinking fountain – now, alas, waterless – in Roundhay Park. John Barran was born in Wandsworth, and when he came to Leeds he pursued the humble trade of pawnbroker; but his rise was rapid. He began his own business, diversified into clothing, and at once saw the shape of the future as a vista, stretching into infinity, of racks of wholesale ready-made suits. The great Leeds clothing trade was taking off! Barran was an entrepreneur, never slow to adopt a good idea; he pioneered the use of the newfangled sewing-machine, and when the Franco-Prussian War broke out in 1870, he was quick to turn his Batley woollen mill to the profitable production of blankets for the troops. From the work of municipal government his thoughts turned to higher things, and from 1876 to 1880 he was one of Leeds' three MPs; he was unexpectedly defeated in the 1885 contest for the newly devised Central Ward, but won Otley the following year. His philanthropic activities were considerable, and included the same concerns that we have met in other nineteenth-century public figures buried at Beckett Street Cemetery. He was President of the Leeds Working Men's Institute, Park Street, and a Life Governor of the Yorkshire College, which was later to blossom forth as the University of Leeds; the Infirmary likewise benefited from his interest.

The Victorian era was also the great age of the public park, beginning with Birkenhead in 1847, designed by Sir Joseph Paxton of Crystal Palace fame. Leeds was a latecomer on this scene. On 4 October 1871 at the Great Northern Railway Station Hotel, amidst tremendous public excitement, an auction of land took place. William Nicholson, the last owner of the large Roundhay estate to the north of the city, had died, and the daring proposal was afloat to purchase the park, with its woods and lakes, for the people of Leeds. John Barran, as Lord Mayor, was largely responsible for the initiative, firmly supported by Thomas Mosley, Councillor for the North-east ward. In the teeth of a Manchester speculator, Barran carried off the prize at a cost of over £100,000, and thereby secured what was to become one of the city's most popular amenities; although, oddly enough, Roundhay Park went through a period of being rudely known as 'Barran's White Elephant', since it was supposedly so far from central Leeds that many of the people whom it was intended to benefit could not reach it on foot and could not afford the cab fare. It was not until the first electric tramway in Britain was constructed in 1891, to run from Sheepscar to Roundhay, that full use could be made of this huge lung amidst the bricks and mortar, and today, as the bluebells carpet the valley in May, or the red, green and gold of fireworks explode and glitter in trails of stars across the dark sky above the Bonfire Night crowds, Barran and Mosley would have been proud of what they achieved. The citizens wished to erect a statue to Barran, but he declined, and instead was presented by William Beckett with a service of plate; in 1895 he was made a baronet. Roundhay Park is his greatest memorial; as he himself said, 'Future citizens will remember us with gratitude as they stroll along the pleasant walks and enjoy the ease and shade of the trees.'

Roundhay Park was officially opened by Prince Arthur, Duke of Connaught, third son of Queen Victoria, on 20 September 1872. Jubilant, shouting crowds lined his route from the Town Hall, but only ticket-holders were allowed on the platform specially built for the opening ceremony at the park. One of those who should have been on that platform was missing, kept away by the most final prior engagement of all. Only two months after the acquisition of the park, Councillor Mosley was dead. The *Mercury* reported that he had been seized with bronchitis three weeks previously, 'but his illness was not considered of a dangerous character. On Tuesday week he attended a meeting of the Council, which lasted seven hours, and it is supposed that his attendance at this meeting aggravated the symptoms under which he was suffering.' On the plinth of his toppled obelisk, deeply and proudly cut, the inscription reads: 'THIS MONUMENT HAS BEEN ERECTED BY A FEW FRIENDS AND ADMIRERS AS A MARK OF THEIR APPRECIATION OF HIS SERVICES IN ORIGINATING AND EARNESTLY ADVOCATING THE PURCHASE OF ROUNDHAY PARK FOR LEEDS AND FOR HIS PERSISTENT ADVOCACY OF THE PEOPLE'S CAUSE.'

Town Councillors who served on the Burial Grounds Committee, administering the affairs of Beckett Street, Hunslet and Holbeck Cemeteries, often ended up, like George Clay Cutler, in the grounds they must have known well. Cutler (another public figure from the beer trade!) struggled up from unprivileged beginnings to run first a grocer's shop and then the Saville Green Brewery, supplying his own beerhouse and others round about with pale and mild ales and stout, and becoming Conservative Councillor for the North-east ward. In 1884 he was serving on no fewer than five committees – Corporate Property, Recreation Grounds, Streets & Sewerage, Hackney Carriages and Burial Grounds. He must have been a punctilious and dutiful man, since a minute of the Committee for 14 March 1888, clearly a vile day, records that he was one of only three members who turned up at the Town Hall: 'This meeting was called for the purpose of visiting Leeds Ground but in consequence of the weather the visit was postponed.'

The Liberal and Tory parties were the long-established political groupings, but by the end of the century there was another fighting its way into the light. Under a small, humble stone in Beckett Street Cemetery bearing the date 1895 and the simple legend 'TOM MAGUIRE, SOCIALIST. BOLD, CAUTIOUS, TRUE, AND A LOVING COMRADE' lie the mortal remains of a pale, dark-haired young Leeds Irishman, intelligent and well-read, a man with a musical voice and a poetic tongue, who scraped a living as a photographer's retoucher. As a boy Maguire sang in the choir of the Roman

Catholic Cathedral, but later drifted into less orthodox thought, and when one day, at the age of eighteen, he picked up a *Christian Socialist* newspaper, his life's path was set out for him. 'Before long,' wrote his fellow Socialist Alf Mattison, 'he was out in the streets preaching the Cause.'[81] Mattison went on to point out that in those days Socialist ideas were looked on with horror, and to advocate them 'was to become almost an outcast; street meetings meant encounters with the police and scoffs and ridicule from the crowd'. Maguire disregarded the mockery. In London, William Morris had founded the Socialist League; Maguire started a branch in Leeds, and began to organise the unskilled workers who lacked the protection of unionisation. A surge of agitation and strikes followed – first the bricklayers' labourers, who under Maguire's direction formed a union and struck, successfully, in the summer of 1889 for an extra halfpenny an hour; then the seamstresses of Messrs Arthur's tailoring works, who rebelled in October at being charged the cost of the motive power for their machines, but whose strike collapsed after six weeks. Then in June 1890 came the Gas lock-out, when the Liberal Town Council tried to withdraw concessions already granted to the gas workers and found themselves, despite importing blacklegs and enlisting the protection of the dragoons, humiliated and forced to back down. 'The part that Tom Maguire played in this struggle,' declared Mattison, 'can hardly be over-estimated. He was the life and soul of it. Calm, thoughtful and practical all the time, the credit of its success rests mainly with him.'

At the beginning of 1893 Maguire's work came to fruition with the founding in Bradford of the Independent Labour Party under the chairmanship of Keir Hardie, which paved the way for the establishment of the Labour Party of today. Maguire himself was wanting in personal political ambition, and from then on his energies seemed to grow less. In March 1895, lacking food or heating, he collapsed with pneumonia, and within two or three days, refusing the services of a priest with the declaration that he would stand or fall on the last twelve years of his life and not on the last five minutes, he died. The *Mercury* wrote sympathetically:

He had long given much thought to matters affecting capital and labour, and as a public speaker was logical and lucid, holding his own in debate. Much of his spare time has been devoted to writing songs and poems ... His name as a Labour leader was known all over the North of England, and by his death the Labour movement has lost a keen sympathizer and an earnest champion.

Aged thirty, Mr. Maguire was not married, but he has left a widowed mother, who was dependent on him.

Over one thousand people watched the funeral, or followed the hearse in mourning-coaches or on foot; they included large contingents from the Social Democratic Federation and from the Independent Labour Party's branches in Leeds and other places. A brass band headed the procession, mournfully blaring the 'Marseillaise' turn and turn about with the Dead March in *Saul*; arrived at the cemetery, twelve leading local labour men, following the hearse in two relays of six, bore their departed comrade to his last resting-place.

There is a visible reminder of Maguire's work still, in the words carved high up on a building of dark red Leeds brick in Roseville Road: '(JEWISH) TAILORS', MACHINISTS' AND PRESSERS' TRADE UNION' ('Jewish' has been painted out). Built in 1910, this was the headquarters of the union which Maguire inspired in the heady autumn of 1889, and for which he wrote *The Song of the Sweater's Victim*:

Every worker in every trade,
In Britain and everywhere,
Whether he labour by needle or spade
Shall gather in his rightful share.

Another way in which people could band together for their mutual support and betterment was by joining a Friendly Society, of which, according to White's 1837 Directory, there were nearly 300 in Leeds and the surrounding villages. There had been Burial Clubs in Roman times, and there was an element of insurance in the medieval guilds, so the concept of an association into which members paid a subscription which could be called upon in time of need was not new. Friendly Societies grew up in the eighteenth century and became widespread in the nineteenth, when the large regional or national versions known as 'Orders' developed – the Oddfellows, Romans, Foresters and so on. Each of these was organised as a central body with a number of independent branches, usually known as 'lodges'. Their aims were the relief and maintenance of sick, old or infirm members and their dependents; provision for the expenses of birth and burial; benefit during unemployment; and the insurance of tools or other means of livelihood. They took something from Freemasonry in their rituals, ceremonies and secret oaths (and were therefore liable to be regarded with suspicion by outsiders). Their importance as insurance agencies is obvious, but they also fulfilled a useful function in their social and convivial gatherings, providing feasts and jaunts for working people who did not otherwise have much entertainment in their lives. Their rules were strict; applicants had to be in good health at entry, a minimum number of subscriptions were to be paid before benefit could be claimed, and illness resulting from misconduct, carelessness or intemperance was disqualified. Would-be cheats were thrown straight out. But there is no doubt that before the embrace of the State welfare system the Friendly Societies performed a most useful function, and White's Directory comments that 'they are the means of keeping many families from the workhouse, and of materially reducing the amount of human misery'.

All over Beckett Street Cemetery there are memorials erected by grateful comrades to the men who filled positions of authority in these organisations. There are several officials from the Ancient Order of Romans, like John Stead (1882), by trade a tailor and draper ('He was generous to a fault, had a strict sense of justice, and acted well up to it') and Joseph Hodgson, gentleman (1908), the esteemed Treasurer of the Order, and also of No. 76 Senate ('In life respected, in death lamented'). These are noble monuments indeed, with Roman Eagles standing guard on columns decorated with lictors' rods and proudly bearing the initials SPQR. The Oddfellows are also well represented, and include furniture dealer C.S. Nicholson of the Kingston Unity (1899), with the convoluted tribute: 'He was, but words are wanting to say what, That what a man should be, he was that.'

By the end of 1836 thirty-three Friendly Societies, eleven charitable societies and 5,019 individuals had deposited their savings with the Leeds and Skyrack Savings Bank, founded in 1818 and occupying a handsome building of 1835 in Bond Street which had been paid for, according to White, 'out of the surplus fund of this institution for the beneficial investment of the savings of the humbler classes of society' (shades of the palatial Bank and Building Society headquarters of today). Two successive secretaries of the Leeds Savings Bank ruled the last line under their lives' entries and were laid to rest in the Consecrated section: William Tanner, who died in 1860, and George Saville Carr, 'for twelve years secretary' (1872).

Through the records of Beckett Street Cemetery we have seen a different society from today's, a society where the individual was supposed to practise 'self-help' and to take responsibility for his own fate, where

17. A Temperance poster designed by G. Peake: 'The Tree of Misery & Death, with some of its roots laid bare'. Note the workhouse in the background!

private charities flourished and the State was not expected to provide more than the grudging minimum laid down by the Poor Laws, and where there was hostility, therefore, to the idea of provision by the local authority at ratepayers' expense of such amenities as pure water, education and open spaces for recreation, which today we consider our right. We have seen men banding together in Friendly Societies to arrange their own unemployment benefit and health insurance, in cooperatives to produce and consume on advantageous terms, and in trade unions to achieve better working conditions. We cannot close this chapter without a look at one of the most important areas of social reform, and at a man whose name is remembered by few, but whose work is known to millions.

In August 1847 Mrs Anne Jane Carlile, a Temperance worker from Ireland, spent some time campaigning in Leeds, and at the conclusion of her visit a Farewell Breakfast was given at the house of Mr James Hotham, a linen-draper, on the south side of Leeds Bridge. A Baptist minister, Jabez Tunnicliff, Registrar of Beckett Street Cemetery since its opening, was among those present.[82] Born in 1809 as one of twenty-two children of a Wolverhampton shoemaker, he had had only scanty schooling before being apprenticed to a japanner, and as a youth had fallen in with a bad set; his father had unsuccessfully tried to correct him and at last, with tears in his eyes, had admitted, 'Jabez, I have done beating you now, I see it does you no good; I can only commit you to God and leave you there'. The young man, however, was 'never happy in sin', and by the age of eighteen had begun to preach God to his workmates and in the villages around. Apart from his only surviving brother, a Methodist, the Tunnicliff family were Calvinists; his mother, unhinged by the dreadful doctrine of predestination, wandered from chapel to chapel, from preacher to preacher, crying 'I am not one of God's elect!' Jabez settled among the General Baptists, and became a minister in successive villages not far from his home town. Through an ill-advised early marriage he missed the chance of a proper training, although he was later able to attend Loughborough Baptist College for a year while continuing to work for a living. In 1842 he moved to Leeds where, devastated by his contact with a young man who had been a Sunday School teacher but had taken to drink on Sabbath outings and had brought himself, his wife and children to ruin, he signed the Temperance Pledge.

There is no doubt that drink, to some such a prosperous source of income, was a major social evil in Tunnicliff's time. 'Drink has done it all!' the Town Missionaries were able to demonstrate in case after case of lost

18. 'Mr Hotham's house', where, in 1847, the Band of Hope was founded. In 1888 Louis le Prince took the first moving picture with a single-lens camera here on Leeds Bridge.

employment, broken relationships, sickness and death. In 1874 a meeting of 'the women of Leeds, of all classes and denominations' was held in the presence of the Mayoress to organise a memorial to the magistrates, pleading for a reduction in the number of licensed premises in Leeds; there were 1,067 of these, and a watch kept on one of them during a Saturday from 7.30 a.m. to 11 p.m. had revealed an astounding total of 1,031 men, 947 women and 237 children entering its doors.[83] The adherents of Temperance (which really meant Abstinence) tried to persuade others to sign a pledge of commitment never to touch strong drink, and Mr Tunnicliff believed in catching them young. In the house by Leeds Bridge, that August morning, the idea of a Temperance organisation for children was put forward, and the suggested title was 'The Band of Hope'.

At the first meeting, in the schoolroom of South Parade Baptist Chapel, 200 children signed a simple promise to abstain from all intoxicating liquors; by the end of the year 1,000 had joined the movement. Tunnicliff, a kind, sympathetic and cheerful man, convincing and charismatic in his preaching to adults, understood how to win the hearts of children. 'Children are lost among great people ... We bring them together, and make them see that they are the sum total of this society. It is their society. They sing, speak, clap their hands, and form the band, and great folks have nothing to do with it, except to aid them.' With his musical talent, the minister enjoyed writing simple songs to catchy melodies. 'They soon learn the words, and go singing in companies in the schools, their houses, and in the streets. Thousands who never will listen to our speeches, hear our sentiments in the songs of our children, and are struck, convinced, and converted to our principles.' Sometimes the little ones brought their parents to him:

> Two children of the Band of Hope – one four or five years of age, and the other about nine – with their cards of membership about their necks, brought their father – a drunken, degraded man, whose appearance told the woeful tale of his dissipation – to me, the other night, to sign the pledge. While he was taking the pledge, his children looked on with an aspect of intense anxiety depicted on their countenances, evidently feeling the responsibility of the moment. When he took the pledge from my hand, and said he would keep it, they both sprang from him, the one out of his arms and the other from his side, and ran about the room up and down in a state of excitement that children only can manifest. The whole of this scene was worth anything to a benevolent mind.

19. Rev. Jabez Tunnicliff (1809–65), Registrar of the cemetery and Temperance campaigner.

S. JOHNSON,

LINEN DRAPER,

SILK MERCER, HOSIER,

GLOVER, & HABERDASHER;

IMPORTER OF FOREIGN GOODS,

SHAWLS, CLOAKS, MANTLES, JACKETS,

&c., &c., &c.

MILLINERY & DRESS MAKING,

168, BRIGGATE, LEEDS.

S. J. begs to inform the Public that her Stock is always large and well assorted, in all the different departments, both useful and of a light fancy character, and warranted of genuine manufacture.

S. J. gives especial attention to

The Family Mourning Department.

FAMILY, COMPLIMENTARY, AND SERVANTS' MOURNING,

May always be had to any extent, of the very best description, upon the shortest notice.

20. From White's Directory of Leeds, 1857.

122

The loving and caring character of Jabez Tunnicliff shines through this little story.

Once converted, some remained so throughout life, campaigners in the cause of Temperance even from the grave, like the Byroms of Arthur Street – Richard, a stonemason, who died in 1882, and his second wife Mary, who died in 1895 and is somewhat alarmingly described in the 1871 census as a 'Bible Woman'. 'HE WAS A TEETOTALER 42 YEARS' is his epitaph, capped by Mary's on the same stone: 'SHE WAS A TEETOTALER 56 YEARS'! Many joined for the sing-songs, the processions, the fun, and their resolve did not last. Tunnicliff's contemporaries, however, were convinced of the worth of the Band of Hope. When he died in 1865, worn out by his exertions, a tribute was paid to him in the Council chamber as the founder of 'an institution which probably more than any other in existence will be found able to grapple with our great national vice'. His funeral was attended by great crowds, including over a thousand temperance friends. 'Aged and infirm, as well as young people, were there; and as the coffin passed along, the almost dead silence which prevailed betokened the universal respect in which the deceased minister was held. Arrived at the last resting place of the dead, which is beautifully situated under a tree, on rising ground, the mourners took their places.' After the burial service had been read, an address delivered and a hymn sung, 'the vast assemblage, which could not have numbered less than 15,000, then gradually dispersed'.

On the house at Leeds Bridge, now restored after having been empty and boarded up for years, a commemorative plaque survives: 'IN 1847 AT A MEETING ON THESE PREMISES THE "BAND OF HOPE" MOVEMENT WAS FORMED ITS TITLE BEING SUGGESTED BY THE REVEREND JABEZ TUNNICLIFF A PROMINENT LEEDS TEMPERANCE WORKER.' Despite backsliders, mockery and indifference, many thousands of young lives were influenced by the work of a warm-hearted Staffordshire clergyman – one of the great band of Victorians who toiled for the betterment of others.

Chapter Six

Architect, Lawyer,
Left in the Lurch

For more than forty years a faithful servant of the Leeds Corporation.

John Binns, 1880

The impression left by those Victorians able to afford a memorial is that of a people confident of their taste, their values and their place in society; if they could pay for a huge ostentatious memorial they would have one, and they were not ashamed to shower praise on the departed or to mourn fiercely and publicly for him or her in words which would nowadays be considered distinctly over the top. They were proud of their trades and of their birth-place, paying the stonemason per letter to record them as 'late bootmaker of this city', or 'cab proprietor of this town'. One of the enjoyments which students of today's noncommittal gravestones will surely miss most will be such lapidary information on how the deceased saw his place in life.

In Beckett Street Cemetery the occupations of Victorian Leeds are everywhere to be seen. There are the ordinary everyday trades which were carried on throughout the country – butcher, brickmaker, corn miller – and there are those more specific to the locality, such as cloth-dresser or miner. Some jobs – shoemaker, saddler – have either been very much reduced or have had their nature changed by mechanisation; others no longer exist. A survey of 500 memorials[84] on which the occupation was stated gave a resounding superiority to the innkeepers, of whom there were 60 (White's 1853 Directory lists 309 inns and taverns and 312 beerhouses). It is only

necessary to walk along the sixth row east of the Consecrated chapel site to
see eight out of the first eleven surviving memorials bearing witness to the
prosperity of this trade in the middle years of the nineteenth century, with
the commemoration of the publicans (and their wives, mothers and daughters) of the Shoulder of Mutton, Marsh Lane; the Fleece, Accommodation
Street; the Woodman, Gower Street; a York Road beerhouse; the Horse &
Jockey, Commercial Street; the Palace Inn, East Street; the Wellington Arms,
Buslingthorpe Lane; and an unidentified inn in York Street. The yarn, cloth
and tailoring trades account for the next highest total (40); leather (including shoemaking) occupies 26. Masons, not surprisingly, have a high number
of the gravestones surveyed (26). The majority of the food purveyors are
in single figures, one exception being the butchers with 27 – despite the
almost meatless diet of the very poor. No fewer than 5 Inland Revenue
Officers appear, or 1 per cent of the total!

Sir Arthur Bowley in 1900 made tentative estimates of average wages in
the nineteenth century, setting down a provincial artisan's earnings in 1867
as 27*s* a week and those of a town labourer as 20*s* (the degree of prosperity these wages provided would, of course, be affected by the number of
dependents and by the amount earned by wives and children, also by the
regularity of employment).[85] Some incomes were much lower; the carrier
William Keeley, with five dependents, starved to death in 1849 on 5*s* a week.
At the end of the century Mr Temple, the Beckett Street gardener, who
earned relatively well since he had free accommodation and other benefits,
was given a rise in wages from 23*s* to 26*s* a week; but although he paid two
and a half weeks' earnings in 1913 for a private grave plot (£3, plus 2*s* 6*d* for
the parchment certificate), there was no gravestone for him when he died
thirty years later. At 21*s* or so, even a 'guinea grave' was beyond the ambition of many, so it will come as no surprise that the Burial Registers give a
quite different picture of the occupants of the cemetery from the impression imparted by the surviving gravestones of the better-off. The registers
were scantily kept, particularly on the Consecrated side; the early and mid-
century Unconsecrated registers are much more informative, usually giving
the occupation of deceased adult males and of the husbands or fathers of
females and children.

Five hundred occupations taken from these registers between 24 May and
18 December 1866 turn up only two innkeepers, compared with the 60 in
the survey of memorials. By far the largest category is that of the humble
unskilled labourer, of whom there are 124 – very nearly a quarter of the total.

ITALIAN AND BRITISH MARBLE AND STONE WORKS,

BY STEAM  POWER.

WOODHOUSE LANE,
LEEDS.

DENNIS LEE & WELSH,

SCULPTORS

AND

MARBLE MASONS,

Have always on view the most varied and extensive Stock in England of

MARBLE CHIMNEY PIECES,

In every variety of Italian and British Marble; together with every description of

Monuments, Mural Tablets,

AND TOMBS,

IN MARBLE, POLISHED GRANITE, AND STONE,

EXECUTED FROM THE CHOICEST DESIGNS.

BATHS in Marble and Enamelled Slate.

Hall Floors, Wash Tables, Chiffonier Tops,

AND ALL KINDS OF MARBLE WORK,

MANUFACTURED BY THE MOST IMPROVED MACHINERY.

Designs Given and Estimates Furnished for every description of Marble and Stone Work.

23·

21. From White's Directory of Leeds, 1857.

Sixty-two people are occupied in the cloth trades and in tailoring, thirty-seven work with leather (including thirty shoe- and bootmakers). Among the food trades, butchers again predominate; there are eight, including a pork butcher, but not more than two retailers of any other food. Mining is quite well represented, with nineteen miners and three coal dealers. Seventy people follow the basic trades such as blacksmith, bricklayer, plumber and painter, and there is a sprinkling of more unusual occupations – cow keeper, looking-glass manufacturer, picture-frame maker, cassimere printer, goldbeater, musician; there are only two people who describe themselves as 'gentleman'. The balance would have been very much altered had any female occupations been included; the 1861 census, for example, shows 12,488 Leeds women engaged in the textile trades in addition to the 15,823 men, and the small 'in service' category of our register survey (a butler, a groom, a waiter and four gardeners) would be considerably swollen by the appropriate proportion of the 8,458 females in domestic employment at this time.

In his *Historical Guide to Leeds* (1879), J. Dodgson careers breathlessly through the occupations of the town. Having mentioned the six to seven million pounds' worth of woollen goods annually turned out, and the ready-made clothing industry, he continues:

There are also extensive flax mills, linen thread, blankets, canvas, carpet, sacking and rope manufactories, and a limited trade in worsted goods. We have dye works, paper mills, paper hanging manufactories, iron foundries, machine and locomotive engine works, carriage and railway carriage builders, and boat builders; also steam saw mills, marble, glass, earthenware, and chemical works and breweries, very extensive tanneries, and glue works; besides numerous mills for grinding corn, mustard, and chicory, and also for seed crushing.[86]

Despite the inherent defects of both registers and memorials as guides to occupations in Victorian Leeds, a clear impression of Dodgson's thriving, busy, productive city comes through at Beckett Street Cemetery, and there are not a few surprises among the stones.

An industry of national importance was the production and distribution of food. The smaller the income, of course, the larger the proportion spent on this basic item; the Board of Trade's *Returns of Expenditure by Working Men* shows in 1889 that a family on an annual income of £28–40 would be likely to spend 87 per cent of that on food, while a family just below the income-tax net with £150 a year might spend a third.[87] Some items became cheaper in the course of the century, like tea and sugar, on which the tax was reduced; others became more expensive, like butcher's meat, which was severely affected by the 'cattle plague' which took up so many columns of the *Mercury* in the 1860s.[88] John Burnett, in his history of diet, *Plenty and Want*, reproduces information gathered in Manchester for the Statistical Society in 1841, where sample diets are described. An overlooker with five dependents, on £1 14s a week, spent 5s on rent, 1s 8d on coal and candles, and £1 0s 7d on food, and had a few shillings a week over for clothing, entertainment and emergencies. A family of seven, the father a mechanic's assistant earning 16s a week, spent 2s 8d on rent, 1s on coals, and 15s 8d on food, plunging the poor man further into debt every week. Needless to say, the lower the income, the less was spent on meat and the more on cheaper fillers like bread and potatoes. The same author quotes Engels, writing in 1844 in *The Condition of the Working Class in England*:

> Where wages are less, meat is used only two or three times a week, and the proportion of bread and potatoes increases. Descending gradually, we find the animal food reduced to a small piece of bacon cut up with the potatoes; lower still, even this disappears, and there remains only bread, cheese, porridge and potatoes, until, on the lowest round of the ladder, among the Irish, potatoes form the sole food.[89]

Where only a little meat could be afforded, it was given to the breadwinner, and the rest of the family went without.

The production of food was carried on both within the town and in nearby areas then still rural. Samuel Bickerdike, buried in 1867, kept cows in York Road. (In the same year the Town Council's sanitary officers decided to ban the keeping of pigs in sties closer than twenty yards to human dwellings; the inaugural meeting in the schoolroom of St Mary's, Quarry Hill, of the Leeds Working Men's Pig Protection Society, which immediately sprang up in response, attracted 300 people, with one of the porkers' defendants declaring that some of the sties condemned were so clean he would happily eat his dinner off the floor.)[90] Until his death in 1862, Timothy Allison was a market gardener in Snake Lane, Knostrop, described in White's 1853 Directory as a 'small but pleasant hamlet' with many neat villas, one-and-a-half miles from the town's main street of Briggate, but now chiefly occupied by light industry and a major sewage works. John Bolton of Orange Street, off York Street, regarded himself (according to the Burial Register) as a

farmer, and in confirmation his family erected a headstone in 1868 displaying a scratchy carving of a plough, although it is somewhat disillusioning to
find him described in the 1851 census as a 'dealer in milk' and in the 1861
census as an 'agricultural labourer'. At a later date (1902) we find William
Bickerdyke's memorial announcing 'late of Oak Tree Farm, Gipton'; this
was a spot also described by White in 1853 as 'a pleasant hamlet', now long
obliterated by streets of council housing with such nostalgic names as 'Oak
Tree Drive' and 'North Farm Road'.

The processing of food was also carried on within the city. On the
quaintly named Isle of Cinder, a strange agglomeration of mills, dye-houses,
print works and malt kilns south of Swinegate and cut off by water-
channels, weirs and mill-goits linking up with the Aire and crossed by pre-
carious wooden footbridges, the Dyson family had their empire. The family
stone mentions only Emily, four years old at her death in 1849, and daughter
of John, 'corn miller of this town'. The firm of Joseph Dyson & Sons ran the
unpleasantly named Flaycrow Mills, with Joseph himself, in 1837 a resident
of dingy Cavalier Street, well-off enough a few years later to own a country
residence in Wharfedale. The other son, Joseph junior, was responsible for
dealing in the firm's flour, while William Dyson, corn and flour dealer, was
milling in partnership with George Mason at the King's Mills, also on the
Isle of Cinder.

Brewing was another activity of great importance to the people of Leeds,
as we have seen from the involvement in public life of some of the brewers and from the sheer number of licensed premises. Most inns originally
brewed their own ale, sometimes in dangerous proximity to the passers-by.
In August 1866 Mr Woodson, landlord of the Anchor of Hope Inn, Leylands,
had caused the death of five-year-old Jane Ann Scatchard by his illegal pro-
cedures while engaged in brewing, for, as the *Mercury* reported, he had

> placed on the causeway a tub containing hot water wherewith to wash his
> barrels. The deceased, while passing, got hold of the tub, and springing her-
> self up, fell in head foremost, and died in four hours afterwards. The jury, in
> returning a verdict of 'Accidental death', severely censured Mr. Woodson for
> washing his barrels on the public footpath, a thing which Mr. Emsley [the
> borough coroner] said was against the law, and must not again be repeated.

The Beer House Act of 1830 allowed anyone to sell beer from their own
houses without a permit, and since these places seldom had the equipment

22. A military funeral, 1911: the cortège of John Strachan.

to make their own beer, the Act provided a great boost to the common brewers (i.e. those brewing for sale to others and not merely to provide beer for inns of their own), who had previously produced only a small proportion of the beer on sale. Gradually the inns ceased to make their own and began to buy from the breweries – the Saville Green Brewery, owned by George Clay Cutler, the councillor who sat on so many committees; the Brunswick Brewery where Thomas Naylor worked for thirty years, as his gravestone tells us, until his death in 1886; and, the giant of them all, Tetley's. In his history of the latter firm, *Quality Pays*, Clifford Lackey portrays the Tetleys as good employers, and certainly John Strachan, who was proud to have worked for them from boyhood for thirty-five years, must have agreed. Tetley's was among the organisations which established groups of volunteers after a war scare in 1859, to assist the defence of the country in the event of invasion or to help put down insurrection, and Mr Lackey interestingly claims that the need for time to drill was one of the factors which brought

23. Employees of Tetley's, artillerymen and onlookers crowd Beckett Street Cemetery for Strachan's burial. Officiating is the Revd John Anderson of Burmantofts Congregational Church.

about the reduction of the working week from six days to five-and-a-half.[91] Strachan reached the rank of Regimental Quartermaster-Sergeant among the artillerymen of Tetley's Own, his family recording both this fact and the length of his employment on his headstone. He was unfortunately retired from the Volunteer force (with rank and uniform) three years before his death in 1911, due to the reorganisation brought about by the Territorial & Reserve Forces Act of 1907, but at least he had a splendid military funeral, gold-frogged and shakoed comrades driving the team of horses which hauled the coffin on its gun-carriage through dense crowds from his home near Carlton Barracks to the cemetery.

There were numerous specialised outlets for the retailing of food. Agents were often experts dealing with one or two particular commodities, like Christopher Marshall, butter factor, who died in 1879, or Thomas Dawkins, bacon and cheese merchant (1855). The produce offered by Joseph Stenson (1862) bulked large in the Victorian diet; he was a 'potatoe' dealer of High Street. For those who resisted the blandishments of the taverns and did not have crates delivered by John Wilkinson in Boar Lane, 'wine and spirit merchant of this borough' (1852), there was always the Temperance Hotel (perhaps the one kept by John Thwaites until 1879) or the tea dealer – John

Haworth Harrison dealt in tea, according to his gravestone of 1859, but is confusingly entered as a coal proprietor in the Burial Register. Fruiterers and greengrocers are well represented, although there seem to be fewer bakers than one might expect, perhaps because so much more baking was done at home. Butchers, despite the poverty of many Leeds people, did well, as did fishmongers like David Gibson, whose family could afford a splendid angel with a harp to commemorate him in 1897.

In 1853 the category 'Shopkeepers' in White's Directory is subtitled 'Grocery, Flour etc. Dealers'; it includes Mary Strickland of 15 Mill Hill, buried at Beckett Street Cemetery, aged seventy, in 1869. Victorian shop-keepers worked their assistants mercilessly, since customers in those days selfishly expected the shops to be open for their own convenience. Already in 1866 an 'Early Closing Association' existed in Leeds, which attempted to coerce the shop-owners by getting the public to refuse to purchase goods from employers who kept their young men long hours. 'Short hours,' said Mr Sales, secretary to the Yorkshire Union of Mechanics' Institutes and chairman of a meeting held on 11 September, 'were really requisite for the proper development of the physical powers, and young men instead of being pent up for twelve or thirteen hours a day, should have ample opportunities of taking out-door exercise, and of joining in gymnastic games.'[92] And the Association's idea of 'short hours'? Not beyond 7 p.m. on weekdays and 10 p.m. on Saturdays!

Another way of purveying one's wares, more widespread then than now, was to hawk them from door to door. There are no gravestones to hawkers, but many appear in the Burial Registers, often with Irish or Scottish names like Hugh M'Larin, on whom an inquest was held in 1856 (the rather casual-sounding verdict was 'Died suddenly'; his largely outdoor trade, tough on the constitution, had not prevented his living to the age of seventy-five).

Tobacco is sometimes classed with food, and there were a sizeable number of cigar manufacturers and merchants (mostly at the turn of the century), tobacconists and tobacco pipe manufacturers. The long-stemmed, relatively fragile clay pipes bought by the Victorians were manufactured in their millions, using pairs of moulds to produce clay shapes, often with highly decorated bowls, which were fired in a kiln made of fireclay bricks. Frederick Strong, who died in 1895, was a manufacturer of clay pipes and is buried in the cemetery. His son, Corporal John Strong of the Royal Engineers, was awarded the Military Medal in 1917 'for gallantry and devotion to duty in action'. He had not followed his father's trade, for the *Yorkshire Evening*

Post, reporting the award,[93] says that before the war John was employed as a driver with the Times Laundry, York Road. Pipes were being made of wood, not clay, and that unrecognised time-bomb, the cigarette, was being puffed in preference. By the time of the Great War, the clay pipe industry was virtually finished.

In 1866 an unknown woman suffered a heart attack at a public bath in Princess Street. To assist identification the body was taken to the nearest inn, the Three Horseshoes, and was put on open display (where it so happened that a labourer named Fawcett, working nearby, joined the sensation-seeking throng and found himself looking down at the corpse of his wife Elizabeth) and a description of her clothes was circulated. The *Mercury* reported these as 'a black bonnet, grey shawl, and brown dress, with black flounces. There was a necklace of black jet beads around her neck and a wedding ring was upon her finger.' To supply this dreary attire (in which she must have looked an old lady, though at forty-five she was, by today's standards, in the prime of life), an army of workers had been beavering away. W.G. Rimmer's collation of statistics from the 1861 Leeds census shows 28,311 men and women, or 28.7 per cent of those in work, engaged in the production of textiles; 9,822, or 10 per cent, are occupied under the category 'dress'. These well outnumber the 5.8 per cent providing 'food, drink, tobacco and lodging'.[94] (Many textile producers and clothing establishments, of course, became increasingly involved with the supply of mourning attire in all its prescribed nuances of colour and material.) Our survey of occupations from the 1866 Burial Registers shows 1 hatter, 13 tailors and 36 boot- or shoemakers; there must also have been numbers of dressmakers and milliners among the women, whose employment is not specified, and many wives would have worked with their husbands, like John and Maria Ripley of Grantham Street, shoemaker and shoebinder in the 1861 census. The shoemakers at Beckett Street Cemetery range from the humble unknown to men like William Mabane (died 1853: 'PATIENT IN LIFE, TRIUMPHANT IN DEATH, AND WAITING A GLORIOUS RESURRECTION') who became household names in the city.

Although Leeds was, then as now, versatile in the tasks to which its people turned their hands, the cloth trades were the traditional strength of the city. In Tudor times, with sheep raised in their thousands on land once owned by the monasteries, plentiful supplies of pure, fast-flowing water to wash the wool and later to power the fulling mills, and abundant labour free from the throttling guild restrictions that afflicted older centres such as York, the West Riding had become an important cloth-producing area. Of the two types of cloth made from wool, Leeds concentrated on woollens rather than worsteds, made from the shorter fibres and felted by the fulling process into a warm, durable material. There were an amazing number of steps to go through before the cloth was ready for sale, and by the time Edward Baines issued his *Account of the Woollen Manufacture of England*[95] in 1870 many of them were mechanised. This account shows the tremendous importance of the trade to Yorkshire; of the 79,000 workers to whom it gave employment in twenty-two English counties, over half (43,000) were Yorkshire people.

According to Baines all Yorkshire cloth had been made, within living memory, from English wool, but by 1870 most wool was imported from Australia, the East Indies, South Africa or the Continent; the comparatively coarse English wool was out of favour, and working men were wearing finer cloth than gentleman had worn in days gone by. It was sorted into different qualities, scoured (using, until late in the nineteenth century, stale urine or 'weetings' as an alkali), washed and dried. The matted fibres were opened up by the processes of willying and teasing, and after it had been well sprinkled with olive oil (also, of course, imported) it passed through the wire brushes of the scribbling machine to draw out the fibres. The plucking machine mixed up the different qualities which still remained in the wool, and the carding machine, with its cards of wire pins, spread it out to a regular thickness and weight in slivers about three feet long. The frame known as a 'billey' slubbed it into a continuous yarn, after which it was spun and reeled. The warp, or set of threads through which the weaver would pass his shuttle crosswise to produce the weft, was prepared and stiffened with animal glue. The lengths of woven cloth were picked over by an army of women 'burlers' who teased out bits of dirt and irregular threads. At the fulling mill the cloth was pounded in warm soapy water by heavy hammers, so that it shrank and matted together, and after scouring to remove the soap it was dried. The tenter frames on which it had been stretched, in those long-ago times when 'Tenter Lane' got its name, were no longer to be seen when Baines wrote; there were steam-powered machines to do the job. The nap of the cloth was raised by the rudimentary but effective use of teasels, and next came the skilled labour of the cloth-dressers, whose huge and cumbersome cropping shears had been replaced by the inventions of men like William Lewis, designer of cutters almost universally used in Yorkshire. The cloth was then boiled to give it a permanent 'face', brushed, pressed in hydraulic presses between sheets of paper, and shorn a second time. The cloth-drawer would examine it carefully and repair any small faults which might be visible. A second pressing; perhaps a steaming process, to make the cloth more damp-resistant; folding; and at last the cloth was ready for the purchaser.

In 1858 Baines had collected from a Leeds woollen factory statistics of the wages paid for the different operations, which give a good idea of the aristocracy of labour in the woollen trade. Of the adult men engaged, excluding the overlookers and supervisors, the highest rates went to the cloth-drawers and the press-setters, who could earn as much as 40s a week. The lowest-paid men were the handloom weavers, on a mere 15s; by this time the handloom weaver was a rare bird indeed, for the power-loom, first used for cotton, had been sufficiently adapted to cope with the comparatively weak woollen yarn. Women could earn 12s a week as warpers, or 6s as burlers; young children could be set to work as 'billey piecers' for 2s a week, part-time. Andrew Ure, the author of a *Dictionary of Arts, Manufactures and Mines*,[96] strongly approved of the development of machinery, pointing out how it could 'render the cheap and tractable labour of children a substitute for the high-priced and often refractory exertions of workmen too prone to capricious combination'. He would not have got on very well with the Leeds cloth-dressers, who went on strike in 1866, claiming that their average wage was only 18s a week, and that subject to fines for damages of up to 3s a week (which was rebutted by a letter in the *Mercury* on 24 August, giving the figures for the Lewis machine men as 19s 10d per fifty-four-hour week, with an average of three-eighths of a penny damages per man per week). The cloth-dressers had come down in the world since their skilled handiwork had been turned over to the machines, and this no doubt contributed to their resentment; with attempts at trade unionism in their infancy, their strike weapon was limited in its power, and while some employers gave in and raised wages, others sat it out until the crumbling of the revolt.

All the better-paid branches of the woollen cloth industry are represented in the gravestones at Beckett Street Cemetery, from the woolsorter at the beginning of the process (Eli Taylor of Chadwick Court, buried in 1861, who was also a local preacher) to the woollen cloth merchant at the end (George Clay of Vance & Co., living grandly in Blenheim Square till his death in 1874). Cloth-dressers abound, and there are no fewer than 22 of them in the survey of 500 trades.

Surprisingly, Dodgson informs us that 'the flax manufactories turn out more work than any town in the United Kingdom, with the exception of Belfast'. The easy-to-grow plant was gathered and 'retted' in pools to decompose the outer covering (a smelly business). Flax-dressers like Joseph Fawcett of Mabgate (who died in 1850) broke and scutched (or beat) the bundles to remove the straw, and heckled them through combs to align the long fibres or 'line' while removing the short 'tow'. Marshall's New Mill, built in the Egyptian style to the design of Bonomi and fortunately still with us, was one of the wonders of Leeds. In the 1870s it was employing 2,500 hands and producing an incredible 70 million yards of linen yarn *daily*. Fine linen for good clothes, coarser linen for sheets, canvas for sailcloth and cap linings, tow for grain bags, sacks, and clothes for the poor ...

At some point during its production, most cloth would undergo the dyeing processes, and as a sidelight on what the great industrial city did to its environment it is instructive to listen to Stephen Todd Holroyd giving evidence in November 1866 before a Royal Commission on the pollution of rivers.[97] The members of the Commission had already heard from Henry Oxley, Mayor of Leeds, that as a boy he had caught fish in the Sheepscar Beck where now, if one were to dip a handkerchief in, it would emerge dyed blue. Stephen Holroyd, whose family headstone in Beckett Street Cemetery is edged with an unusual design of animal masks like some Romanesque church doorway, had an axe to grind, for he was a partner in the Sheepscar Dyeworks, situated at the junction of Gipton and Sheepscar Becks, and employing 130 hands in the dyeing of 3,000 pieces of heavy stuff each week for furniture goods. 200,000 gallons of water a day were drawn from the Gipton Beck, all of which was pure, since there were no industries sited higher up which would have made the water unusable at Sheepscar. The principal colours involved were crimson and green (how delightfully this brings the Victorian drawing-room to life!), produced by cochineal and indigo, dyes made respectively from South American insects and from plants, including British woad; fustic and logwood, both woods from the Americas, were used for yellow and black, producing an annual 120 tons of waste, which was turned, with all other refuse, into the Sheepscar Beck. The water was not much discoloured, added Mr Holroyd hopefully, and he did not think that anything his firm turned into the beck was prejudicial to the health of the residents in the vicinity. After all, the firm paid 2*d* a load to have the four tons of ashes daily produced from twenty tons of coal carted away, and even had removed to their own farm the soil from the privies of their workpeople. And – surely the clinching excuse for a bit of dirty water in the Sheepscar Beck – the Sheepscar Dyeworks received stuffs sent for dyeing from Bradford, partly because of the better water 'and partly, perhaps, because of the superior skill and management at Leeds'. It is rather disappointing to discover from Dr Eric Sigsworth's research that dyeing in Leeds had, in fact, already passed its peak and was yielding ground to the rival city.[98]

Leather, too, was a major Leeds industry; Dodgson claimed that it was larger than that of any other town or city, not excepting even the metropolis. Attributing this success to the city's lucky geographical situation and ready supply of hides, water and oak bark for tanning, W.G. Rimmer estimates that in 1870–1 there were twenty-three tanners preparing the hides, sixty curriers making the leather ready for use, and 800 shoemakers and shoe manufacturers, not to mention the makers of gloves, suitcases, saddles and numerous other objects.[99] (So proud was Elizabeth Stamp of her sons and their saddlery business in Lower Headrow that her 1874 memorial defines her place in society as 'Mother of Oates Brothers, Saddlers, Leeds'!) Stead and Simpson went on from Leeds to become household names; others, like Thomas Brogden, currier and leatherseller of Lady Lane in 1870, have sunk, but for a lichened headstone, into oblivion.

When the first settlement grew up by the River Aire, its inhabitants could not have realised what a very fortunate spot they had chosen. They had settled on the northern boundary of a vast and rich coalfield – 'with the never-failing accompaniment of very valuable beds of fireclay and ironstone', as Dodgson puts it – and in Victoria's days these resources were being exploited to the full. Men were sweating underground to keep the furnaces blazing and the tall chimneys sighing out black smoke above. The Waterloo Colliery, working the Beeston seam, produced some of the best house coal in the district, large quantities being sent to London and the Eastern Counties, but in Yorkshire, as all over the country, a heavy price was paid in lives for the coal brought out. Falls of the roof or sides of mines were the greatest cause of death, but accidents in the process of lowering or raising men or materials, mishaps above ground, explosions of methane, also contributed to the fatalities reported annually by the Inspectorate of Mines which had been established in 1850; in Mr Wardell's Yorkshire and Lincolnshire district there were, for example, 107 lives lost in 1877, or one per 153,000 tons of mineral raised.[100]

Methane gas, or 'firedamp' as the miners called it, was still a deadly hazard, bleeding away an average of sixteen lives a year in Mr Wardell's area between 1868 and 1891; carelessness and/or bad ventilation were usually the cause.

Several years earlier Joseph Keighley had fatally ignored regulations at the Waterloo Colliery. With William Charlesworth and eighteen other men and boys he had gone down into the 'Pasture Pit' at 6.15 a.m. on 23 July 1849. Neither Keighley nor Charlesworth was using a safety lamp, although both were in their fifties and had had at least twenty years' experience of work in the mine. Suddenly there was a loud report, and after the alarm had been conveyed to the top and the remaining men and boys immediately drawn up and found to be uninjured, search was made for the two missing men, who were brought out dead at 10.30. One of the bottom stewards was able to account for the accident:

> The deceased had left a quantity of coals which they had got on Saturday last lying on a heap, and by so doing had stopped a current of fresh air which flowed through that particular part of the mine. This had caused the inflammable air to accumulate, and on the deceased going to the working with their naked candles an explosion would ensue ... It was proved that lamps were provided for all the colliers, and that they had been cautioned against neglecting to use them; also that the two unfortunate sufferers had been threatened with dismissal if they left coals lying in the manner above described.

Sir Humphrey Davy's life-saving invention had been in use since 1816, well before the start of Keighley's twenty-five years down the pit; but what could be done when a man contravened the regulations because he found a stub of candle less bother than a safety lamp, except to pass the verdict 'Accidental Death'?

From 1818 coal had been put to a new use in the town with the establishment of the Leeds Gas Light Company, which supplied gas mainly by contract (at specified times and for a specified number of hours) for street lighting, to private houses, and, increasingly, to industrial works.[101] In 1848, for instance, the Burial Grounds Committee settled a bill with this company for supply of gas to the two chapels and the two lodges at Beckett Street Cemetery for the half-year ending 30 June; the amount invoiced was £1 2s. A rival concern, the Oil Gas Company, attempted to achieve commercial success with gas manufactured from oil, but failed. From its ashes arose the Leeds New Gas Company, which bought up its pipes, mains and premises for the production of coal gas, but competition with the Gas Light Company was always more in name than in fact; as the *Mercury* said in 1868, 'those who were connected with the lamps committee would know very well that the price charged by one company was exactly what was charged by the other'.[102] Leeds Town Council had already bought up the water supply company, as we have seen, and it could sniff healthy profits in the nasty smell from the gasworks in York Street. In 1869 the two gas companies were purchased for £763,245, and the financial results did not disappoint – although the quality of the gas itself was inferior, since the Council adopted a policy of selling cheap gas made from cheap coal (with highly profitable by-products of coke, tar and ammonia). Charles Smith, 'gas engineer of this town', had joined the senior company as a young man, fourteen years after its foundation, and had remained with it through the change of ownership till his death in 1875: 'He was for forty-three years the faithful servant of the Leeds Gas Light Company and the Leeds Corporation.' Thomas Butler, aged fifty-eight and a 'Gas House Man', had only a common grave in 1868.

Also quarried from the ground were the clays for bricks, firebricks, tiles and the handsome products of the Burmantofts and Leeds Potteries. We have already seen how the cemetery, at its opening, was surrounded by brickfields and kilns. As in every other industry, the protection of the Factory Acts could not always prevail against sadism and exploitation by individual employers and foremen. The anonymous hero of *The Unfortunate Genius* (1853) was obliged to work in a Yorkshire brickyard as a child during his father's illness, and was unlucky enough to encounter such a monster.

> In setting the under part of a kiln, I and the other boys had to carry the bricks to him in our hands, two at a time. The distance we had to fetch them, varied from about 30 to 50 yards. His conduct was always cruel, even when it bore the semblance of sport; but when he was glumpish, which was generally the case, – if he had to wait a single moment for bricks, no matter what the cause, he would strike us with a 'clapper', nip our hands, or bite our shoulders with his teeth. For the purpose of gratifying this brutal propensity, he would work both himself and us almost to death; he striving to have to wait on us, that he might have an excuse to punish, and we running at the top of our speed to avoid it.[103]

Poor little boys! The Unfortunate Genius escaped by emigrating to America, but let us hope that not all of those left behind were so unhappy. It was possible to do well enough to afford a very respectable memorial after death, like Lawrence Milner, 'bricklayer of Leeds, who departed this life Sepr. 16th. 1849, aged 29 years. FAREWELL MY FRIENDS, MY GLASS IS RUN. THE WILL OF GOD IT MUST BE DONE; THEREFORE PREPARE TO FOLLOW ME, WITH CHRIST, IN HEAVEN, I HOPE TO BE.' Not far away is the pink granite block which commemorates the Boyle family, owners of the prosperous Burmantofts brickworks in the second half of the century.

In the Unconsecrated portion two local builders' families (Lax and Swallow) lie side by side, an impish angel peering from the 1874 shrine tomb of little Harriet Ann Lax. Harriet has gone 'where the silver stars are shining', and her surname is no longer writ large on hoardings round Leeds building sites. By the middle of the nineteenth century Leeds was the fifth largest town in England, following London, Liverpool, Manchester and Birmingham, and the population of Leeds borough stood at 172,270. Numbers increased steadily at an average annual rate of between 1.3 and 2.3 per cent to total 428,968 at the end of the reign, and the need for accommodation led, as elsewhere, to massive construction of workers' homes and to the steady development of the suburbs. The 1890 Ordnance Survey map shows the cemetery area on the fringe of a dense blur of housing, mainly tight-packed terraces of back-to-backs, although the brickfields – of necessity – still survive. There were new churches and chapels, schools, commercial and industrial premises. Building was a boom industry, with 4,000 men employed in 1851, rising to nearly 15,000 at the turn of the century. The register of fatal accidents at work ground on. Let Joseph Wainwright, a nineteen-year-old slater's labourer at work on a new factory for a machine-making firm, stand for the thousands untimely dead:

> Deceased was employed by Messrs. Leach & Co., Canal Wharf, and on Wednesday last, while ascending a ladder at the new building erecting in Victoria-road, for Messrs. Burnley & Nichols, the scaffolding gave way, and the ladder falling, deceased was precipitated to the ground from a height of about 33 feet. He was conveyed to the Leeds Infirmary, but died about ten minutes afterwards from the injuries he had received. Verdict: 'Accidental Death'.

The raw materials readily available, the geographical situation of the city, and the supply of labour to hand, ensured that engineering would be one of the most important trades of Leeds. Throughout the nineteenth century more and more local people derived their livelihood from engineering: 7,000 men in 1851; 18,000 in 1881; 27,000 at the end of Victoria's reign. There are fitters, forgemen, moulders, blacksmiths, grinders, enginemen. Robson English, who died in 1860, was an agricultural 'impliment' maker; John Gay and his son John Robert (1851 and 1868) manufactured surgical instruments in Briggate. The Pollard dynasty produced Joseph ('spindle and flyer maker', died 1853) and George ('spindle and flyer maker of this city', died 1896), while Thomas advertised grandly in an 1853 directory: 'Manufacturer of every description of SPINNING SPINDLES, and FLYERS, For Worsted, Cotton, Silk, Flax, Tow &c.' Men of calibre were responsible for running the works; John Thyne came from Scotland to take charge of the Smithfield Iron Works in North Street (a Grade 2 listed building which survived him by just over 100 years, to be demolished in 1988), while Samuel Lawson of the Hope Foundry (still on its Mabgate site) earned praise in Mayhall's *Annals* (13 December 1866) for his work on Poor Law administration and for his presentation full-length portrait – his managerial abilities not being mentioned.

The ordinary workmen toiled away in factory and foundry under conditions that would have made a modern Health and Safety inspector blench. Sometimes they exposed themselves to danger through their own folly, like twenty-four-year-old James Smith, who in 1856 was renting a room and power in the Byron Street flax mills to carry on his trade of file-cutter; the strap having slipped from the drum, he injudiciously fetched a ladder and attempted to replace it while the machinery was still in motion, with horrid results. The boiler which blew up at the Frogland Mungo Works in Dewsbury Road in 1866, killing its 'tenter' Samuel Pearson, aged fifty-four, and another man, and injuring twenty workmates, was only about five years old; but it had been housed out-of-doors, with a covering of flagstones from which rainwater had dripped its deadly way down the iron, corroding it in some places to less than one-sixteenth of an inch. The coroner called two experts, Mr Manning of the Boyne Engine Works (a member of the Institute of Mechanical Engineers) and Mr Waller, engineer to the Midland Steam Boiler Association, with twenty-two years' experience of boilers; with models, plans and photographs the two gentlemen were able to attribute the tragedy to the corrosion and weakening of the iron plates. Mr Manning 'considered it desirable that a periodical inspection of all boilers should be made, but he did not wish the jury to suppose there had been any special neglect in this case. Such examinations were the exception rather than the rule.' Mr Shann, the owner of the works, praised Pearson as a particularly clever engine-man who had evinced considerable practical talent, and then made the revelation that the boiler *had* been insured until about a twelvemonth previously, and had been subjected to regular checks by the insurance company; alas, 'he only ceased insuring it at the suggestion of his own men (including Pearson), who had great confidence in the boiler, and thought it perfectly safe'.

Others were killed or injured by the shoddy materials or poor workmanship of the machinery upon which they were employed. A crane was being used by moulder Benjamin Wilkinson and four others in making a steam hammer standard at the New Soho Foundry, Meadow Lane, in the same year. The crane chain 'had been bought by Mr. Kennion, the proprietor of the works, as a fifteen ton chain, but from some defect in its construction, it snapped with the weight of about 6 tons, and the deceased was crushed to death'. The almost casual tone of the *Mercury*'s report is a world away from the frenzied search for scapegoats and rush to litigation of our own age. The maker of the chain was not blamed; Mr Kennion was in no way responsible; the State had no duty to ensure Wilkinson's safety or to support the bereaved family. It was just 'accidental death' again …

Vast quantities of materials and people had to be moved from place to place in consequence of all the frenetic activity of the Victorian city, and the century saw road transport progress from the stage of the horse and cart to that of the combustion engine. White's 1853 Directory lists twelve horse dealers, twenty-nine livery stables hiring out hackney coaches and gigs, twenty-two saddlers and eleven coach builders. In Beckett Street Cemetery lie men whose trades were vitally important in their time, but cater now for a minority pastime: Joseph Williamson, horse dealer of this town (1854); Robert Barber, farrier (1884); Herbert Clayton, shoeing smith, with his wife Emily (1900); Benjamin Binns, hay dealer of this town (1884); Francis McEvoy, saddler, late of Leeds (1849). There are cab proprietors, coach proprietors, waggonette proprietors. Looking after the horses could be a chancy business: 'The Coroner held an inquest upon the body of George Broughton, aged thirty-four, lately employed [1865] as an ostler at Mr. Stevenson's stables, North-street. Broughton received a severe kick on the head from a horse about a week ago, and died in the Leeds Infirmary on Thursday from the injury he then received.'

If you did not wish to hire a cab or a gig, you could travel by horse bus, perhaps from the firm of John and William Atkinson. These brothers from Northumberland, who lived unassumingly adjacent to their stables in Harrison Street, ran cabs and buses in Leeds from the 1820s for forty years, with bus routes between the town centre and the suburbs and outlying villages – Hunslet a mile and a half to the south, Headingley (a sixpenny fare from Upper Headrow) two miles to the north-west. In those days of fierce competition, when proprietors were capable of behaving like bandits and racing to get to prospective passengers first – and even forcing them on board! – the Atkinsons kept within the bounds of civilised behaviour. John was buried at Beckett Street in 1860, and for a time William carried on alone before the business was ceded to a creditor. The public omnibus was not always an enticing experience; two letters of 1857 to the *Mercury*, quoted by J. Soper in *Leeds Transport*,[104] suggest reasons why. 'Perambulator' complains:

> I have had the misfortune to ride with people half drunk, three quarters drunk, quite drunk, noisy drunk, sleepy drunk, dead drunk. The omnibus, unfortunately for some of us, passes two or three places of resort in Briggate and elsewhere, where men in respectable positions congregate of an evening to talk and tipple, then ride home in a public conveyance to the disgust of all decent people. Could not a tippler's omnibus be started for these should-be-gentlemen? I am not a teetotaller, but I hate to sit in a small compartment of about 4 feet wide by 6 feet long, with two, perhaps three redolent gentlemen trying to talk without stuttering, but none of whom could pronounce intelligibly the word 'statistics', if it were to save his life.

'Viator' was exercised by the difficulty of getting out from the middle seat of these cramped conveyances; to squeeze past a crinolined lady meant carrying with him 'almost an acre of petticoat', but to climb out on the side furthest from the pavement might mean having to wade through sludge and then leap a miniature mountain of roadside mud.

Horse buses were less profitable than the later horse trams, pioneered in London and Liverpool and copied in Leeds from the early 1870s; on the smooth rails twice as many passengers could be pulled by the same amount of horse-power as on the roads. One of many transport 'firsts' for Leeds was the electric tramway, constructed by a private company in 1891 but bought by the Corporation in 1894, which ran out to Roundhay and which, as we have seen, at last enabled ordinary people to make full use of 'Barran's White Elephant', Roundhay Park. Elegant even in their rust and dereliction, the poles for the overhead electric lines can still be seen at Roundhay terminus. Men like William Henry White were proud to be connected with the service by graven epitaph for evermore: 'late chief inspector city tramways' (1930).

We cannot leave the subject of road transport without mentioning that most distinctively Victorian of horse-drawn vehicles, the hearse, and the commissary who provided it. Funerals were big business; between the first census of Victoria's reign in 1841 and that taken in the year of her death, the population of Leeds borough almost trebled from 152,054 to 428,968, but over the same period the number of undertakers substantial enough to pay for a listing in Leeds directories increased tenfold from ten in 1842 to 101 in 1901. The undertaker coordinated the services of joiners, upholsterers, metalworkers, coachbuilders, textile workers, tailors, drivers, grooms, bearers, clergymen, sextons, stationers, florists, caterers and monumental masons. The big names in the trade were men like John Wales Smith, whose family firm had begun with Edward Wales in Briggate before 1820 (developing, like many others, as an offshoot of tailoring or linendrapery) and remained in business until 1956, delivering many customers to Beckett Street Cemetery over the years. In the 1880s and 1890s John Wales Smith & Sons were burying the comfortably off tradesmen of Leeds in their pitch pine coffins or Patent Metallic Airtight Shells, mainly at the 'better-class' cemeteries of Lawnswood and Woodhouse or in the suburban churchyards, charging one guinea for the personal attendance of the head of the firm. Not only hearses were involved, but also trains; part of the job was receiving home-coming bodies at the Great Northern Station, and speeding deceased non-Leodiensians on their way to Ilkley, Manchester or Scarborough. The bill for the funeral of a moderately well-to-do Leeds maltster in 1889 is reproduced in Appendix B, Table 4, and is contrasted with the cost of the pauper burial which was the lot of many other citizens. In 1926, by which time the Great Victorian Funeral was entering its terminal decline and a Glasgow undertaker had been convicted of a speeding offence in a motor-hearse (33mph., fine £3), Bertram Puckle was writing snootily:

> According to what you are prepared, or can be induced, to spend, so you will get more or less of the 'Dismal Trader's' sable horrors, plumes, palls, pinkings and furnishings, with anything from two to six of his flat-flanked Belgian apologies for horse flesh, whose crimpy manes and swaying tails are so dear to his ghoul-like heart.[105]

For travel between towns and out to the sea, waterways natural and man-made had long been in use; the Romans had used a network of navigations in East Anglia. The Aire & Calder Navigation, promoted by the merchants of the West Riding at the beginning of the eighteenth century, linked Leeds by river with the North Sea, and brought the stubby, square-rigged Humber keels to their mooring-places by Leeds Bridge. The bold initiative of the extremely rich Duke of Bridgewater in having an artificial water-way constructed in 1761 to carry coal from his Lancashire collieries led rapidly to the development of the system of canals which once covered the country; some are dried up, filled in, or the depositories for old prams, bottles, cans, plastic bags and obsolete household goods, while others, like the late-comer Leeds & Liverpool Canal of 1774, still witness the passage of pleasure boats, although they have long since said farewell to their last load of coal or timber. Two of the gravestones at Beckett Street bear representations of the Humber keel and tell sad stories which will be heard in a later chapter.

Leeds, with its superb focal situation between east and west, north and south, hill and plain, was as quickly gripped by 'railway mania' in the 1830s and 1840s as anywhere else in the country. The Middleton Colliery, to the south of the town, had provided another 'first' by using steam loco-motives (from 1812). Commercial interests promoted Leeds' first line for goods and passengers, opened in 1834, but the influence of George Hudson, the 'Railway King', assured the position of premier railway town to York. As lines were opened all over Britain, speculators went mad, hoping for a speedy fortune, and ill-considered, unviable projects crashed everywhere or were taken over by more judicious competitors. Thomas Walker, resident engineer of the Leeds & Thirsk Railway Company during Samuel Smiles' secretaryship and buried in Beckett Street Cemetery at the early age of thirty-four, was evidently a fine character:

THIS MONUMENT HAS BEEN ERECTED BY HIS SURVIVING FRIENDS EMPLOYED IN SUPERINTENDING AND CONSTRUCTING THE LEEDS & THIRSK RAILWAY, WHO ADMIRED HIS KIND AND GENEROUS DISPOSITION, HIS UNSWERVING INTEGRITY, HIS INDUSTRY AND PERSEVERANCE, AND THE SUPERIOR SKILL WHICH HE DISPLAYED IN THE ERECTION OF RAILWAY WORKS OF GREAT MAGNITUDE.

The railway he engineered, incorporated in 1845, had by 1851 already become part of the Leeds Northern Railway, which itself was taken three years later into the North Eastern Railway, a grouping that survived until the reorganisation of 1922 and the birth of the LNER.

If the worst came to the worst and the fare-money was lacking (or if you were just tired of hearing your neighbours talk about 'shtatishticsh'), you could convey yourself on the products of one of those hundreds of makers of boots and shoes, perhaps using the heel-tip design registered in 1886 by Thomas Johnson of Swinegate, whose brother John, also a shoemaker, rests in a guinea grave.

A scattering of professional men lie among the thousands of labouring folk, like George Pape (1856) 'of Burmantofts, for many years the assistant surveyor of this town ... He was held in respect and affection by all who knew him'; or William Ainsley (1866), whose setsquare and compasses proclaim him 'architect of this town'; or George Leather, the civil engineer whose two bridges still span the River Aire – the plain stone eighty-foot span of the Victoria Bridge (1839), decorated only with a cartouche on each side displaying the monarch's name, and the glorious 120-foot cast-iron trellis of Crown Point Bridge (1840), now soullessly disfigured by the attachment of a dreadful modern pipe. (Mr Leather, who was embroiled in the waterworks tussle already described, was the tenant of the Jacobean Knostrop Hall, long since pulled down; at his death in 1870 he was succeeded there by the painter Atkinson Grimshaw.) The uses to which the leisure time of the public-spirited Victorian could be put are well demonstrated on Mr Leather's impressive memorial with its multitude of capital letters. Besides attaining a high position in his profession and serving for thirty-five years as Land Steward to the Ingram Estate, he was Patron of the Parish Church and a Trustee of Potter's Almshouses and of the Pious Uses Property of the Grammar School Estate.

Doctors and clergymen there are aplenty, as we have seen, and an occasional teacher, although before Forster's 1870 Elementary Education Act schooling was very much a matter of patchwork provision to those willing to receive it and able to pay for it if necessary. Sunday Schools and Ragged Schools were run by churches and charities, dame schools took care of the children and drummed a few facts into them for a penny or so a week, grammar and public schools catered for the middle and upper classes. The 1870 Act enabled School Boards to be set up by local councils to plug these terrible gaps, although attendance was not free – nor, until the Mundella Act ten years later, was it compulsory. Every city in the land soon had (and still has) children coming day by day to those large, solid, now century-old buildings with the local School Board monogram proudly wreathed above the doors. However, the School Board teachers were not the ones who left the expensive memorials at Beckett Street Cemetery; they are the legacy of men such as John Bailey, 1775–1846: 'for upwards of Thirty Years as Schoolmaster at Knottingley and Ferrybridge he obtained the highest mead he could receive in his laborious duties, the lasting gratitude alike of Parents and of Pupils.'

In death, as in life, there is no escaping the tax inspector. The memorials of Inland Revenue officers survive in some numbers from as early as 1856; one of them, Harry Bumby (1895), provokes a wry smile with the choice of epitaph: 'BLESSED ARE THE PURE IN HEART'.

Among the profusion of innkeepers, shoemakers and cloth-finishers there are occupations which now sound an archaic note. In the days when cattle and swine were kept in the heart of the city it was perhaps not so strange to find a 'cow doctor' (John Walker) practising in Lower Headrow, one of the quadrangle of main streets. William Pawson, who died in 1890, was a 'handbell founder of this town'. Robert Child, buried in 1867 and described in the Burial Register as a 'medical galvanist', practised a form of medicine which involved 'treating' the patient with electric currents; in Charlton & Anderson's Leeds Directory, three years earlier, a Mr Bellhouse was advertising Medical Galvanic Apparatus in French Polished Case, the versions at three guineas and upwards containing the 'Primary, Secondary, and combined currents' (desperate times, desperate measures). George Hick, aged forty-two, lived alone in one room of a house near High Street, and obtained a livelihood in that manner so typical of a Victorian factory town, by 'calling up' mill-hands from their beds. One dawn in 1866 the sound of his footsteps on the cobbles and the tap of his pole on the windows were missed:

At four o'clock a woman named Wood, on looking through the window of his room, saw him knelt down by the side of his bed. The door being unfastened, and the key on the outside, Mrs. Wood opened the door and called out 'George'. Not receiving a reply, she went up to him, and found that he was quite dead and cold. He had all his clothes and his hat on, as though he had fallen on his knees by the bedside the moment he had entered the room.

Turning the tables, Death had 'called up' George.

Chapter Seven

Better Dead than Red

The Brand and the Ball had passed him by,
And he came to his native land to die.

Farrier Sergeant John Riddell RHA, 1869

'I shall name it to no one for I am ashamed to think of it,' wrote the heart-broken mother of William Robertson, a new recruit to the British Army in 1877. 'I would rather Bury you than see you in a red coat.'[106] James Turner of Halifax confided to his journal in 1881, 'My sister Jessie received a letter from Aunt Caroline saying that her son Charlie had enlisted for a soldier. I am surprised that he has enlisted as he was such a good lad.'[107] Frank Richards, the author of *Old-Soldier Sahib*, was working in the Welsh mines when the Boer War broke out and soldiers became heroes, but before that 'it was commonly believed in the village that any young man who joined the Army did so either because he was too lazy to work or else because he had got a girl in the family way. Hardly anybody had a good word for a soldier.'[108]

During the second half of the nineteenth century one million men enlisted in the British Army. Many of them no doubt joined up for the reasons given by Frank Richards; some, like John Leaf, buried in 1915 in Beckett Street Cemetery, who is said to have run away from home to become a drummer boy in the Crimea at the age of twelve when his mother died, were probably escaping from unhappy family circumstances. At times of high unemployment 'empty pockets and hungry stomachs', as one young soldier put it, 'are the most eloquent and persuasive of recruiting sergeants'.[109] Before the recruiters were banned in 1867 from setting up their headquarters in inns, other men were trapped by drink; plied with beer by the friendly redcoats (who received a bounty for each man recruited), many a young man would sober up in the morning to find to his surprise and, possibly, dismay that he had joined the army. There were also, of course, restless spirits, prepared to ignore the poor pay and bad conditions, who enlisted for adventure, for comradeship, for the joy of fighting, and for the excitement of seeing the world.

During the long-running dispute with the Vicar of Leeds, the nearby Cavalry Barracks did its part towards filling some of the graves in the much under-used Beckett Street Cemetery, contributing twelve of the first 270 burials. Many others were to follow. We shall be considering the reasons why these young men, fed, clothed, housed, in regular employment and presumably strong and fit, should so often figure among the entries in the Burial Registers.

The oldest military memorial in the cemetery is the crooked, lichened headstone of Samuel Cook, who enlisted in Armagh, Ireland, on 8 February 1826. At that time enlistment was for life unless a discharge was granted for medical reasons, and Cook was still a serving soldier when he died twenty-one years later after some seven weeks in the regimental hospital. In 1847, the year of his death, the system was changed, so that a cavalryman joined up for twenty-four years, an infantryman for twenty-one – still a longer term than the entire life expectancy of a city labourer. The Army Enlistment Act of 1870 was intended to improve on this by introducing 'short service' of twelve years, half with the colours and half with the reserve, with the option of extending the period to twenty-one years as before. Each regiment recruited at its own headquarters; every city and large town also formed the hub of a recruiting district staffed by army pensioners and seconded serving soldiers, like Staff Sergeant William Patterson 'of the Leeds Recruiting District, late 17th Foot Regt., who died 28th October 1864 aged 40 years. PREPARE TO MEET THY GOD.' The would-be soldier was given the King's (or Queen's) Shilling in token of the contract, and was taken before a magistrate and attested; from then on there was no escape, for deserters, if recaptured, could be branded with the letter 'D'. Such was the difficulty of attracting enough young men that physical standards had constantly to be lowered; from 5 feet 8 inches in 1861, the minimum height slid slowly down until in 1900 it was a mere 5 feet 3 inches, although it was far

24. A Victorian cavalryman: John Barnard (1822–1901), a Troop Sergeant-Major of the 18th Hussars, with his son George, born in 1855. John was stationed at Leeds Cavalry Barracks in 1858–9.

from unknown for the rules to be bent and even smaller, lighter or younger men to be taken on.

Pay was poor, comparable only with the lowest-paid of civilian occupations; many humble 'ag. labs.' earned more. For seventy years from the end of the eighteenth century, the wage of a private soldier in the infantry was 1s a day, plus a penny for beer. The cavalryman's rate was slightly higher, and of course pay went up with rank. A certain amount extra (one penny per badge per day) could be earned by 'Good Conduct Badges', awarded every five years to a maximum of five (from 1860, eight) badges. Cardwell's reforms in 1867 increased the daily rate of pay, but ignored one of the main grievances of the soldier – the iniquitous system of 'stoppages'; food, clothing, laundry, hair-cutting, medical treatment all had to be paid for before the soldier saw anything of his supposed 'shilling a day'. Disciplinary fines, barrack-room damages for unspecified items, and fiddles by cheating paymasters could all subtract yet further sums, so that, as Alan Ramsay Skelley says in *The Victorian Army at Home*, 'for years after 1856 even experienced men were lucky to see 3d a day', and indeed, if it had not been for a regulation stipulating a minimum 1d a day, many men would have received nothing at all.[110]

Promotion from private to corporal and from corporal to sergeant meant better pay and status, but it was virtually unknown for a man to rise from the ranks, William Robertson (whose mother, as we have seen, would rather have had him dead than red) being one illustrious exception, for he began his career a private soldier and ended it a Field Marshal. Even for those with ability and education, the jump from NCO rank into the snobbish ostracism of the officer corps was hardly feasible, and would never have entered the minds of the vast majority of men.

Pensions, like pay, were usually inadequate. A man who had served at least fourteen years with the colours and who had been invalided out received a permanent disability pension; a long service pension was given to those who had completed the maximum length of service of twenty-one or twenty-four years. Many received less or nothing, and for ageing men without skills and with dependents to support, even the full pension, starting at 8d a day, could be insufficient. When the pensioner died, so did his pension; his widow and children got nothing. Ex-soldiers could be seen begging in the streets or, as in Thomas Faed's evocative picture of 1879 'From Hand to Mouth', grimly turning out their ragged pockets for the last copper to pay for their meagre purchases of food for the children, while a dour shopkeeper glowered behind the counter. Often they were forced to depend on charity or on their small insurances; it was the Leeds Discharged Soldiers' Aid Society which in 1891 saved Maurice White, a Crimean War veteran, from the stigma of pauperism by paying for his burial in a guinea grave.

The image of the army suffered severely in 1819 at 'Peterloo' and in the 1831 Reform Riots at Bristol, where mounted men rode down helpless civilians. Dragoons were brought in to protect the blacklegs in the Leeds gas lock-out of 1890 from the angry crowds. Although White's Directory of 1837 approves of the layout of the Cavalry Barracks at Leeds, it is clear that they cast a long shadow over the town:

> The Cavalry Barracks, near Buslingthorpe, just within the northern bound-ary of Leeds township, were built at the cost of about £28,000, granted by Government, in 1819 and 1820, for the purpose of keeping in awe the popu-lous clothing district, then supposed to be on the verge of insurrection. The barracks for the officers and men, and the stables, are built of brick, on a commodious plan, and with the spacious parade ground, occupy more than eleven acres of land, in a pleasant and salubrious situation.

The situation may have been salubrious, but it is doubtful whether the bar-racks were. A response to the inconvenience and unpopularity of billeting in inns and private houses (the common method of accommodating the soldiery until the Napoleonic Wars), large numbers of such buildings were put up, often badly designed, poorly ventilated, overcrowded and lacking proper sanitary facilities. In the dormitories stood huge tubs for urine, which were emptied in the morning and then used for washing; the Army Sanitary Commission which reported in 1857 received evidence from one NCO that, on going into the men's room, he had often 'retired to the passage, and called to the orderly man to open the windows'![111] The Commission recommended changes, but little improvement was made, and it took an obstinate outbreak of enteric fever in Dublin in 1879 to renew interest in barrack hygiene. The handsome Leeds Cavalry Barracks, built to strike fear into the hearts of unruly citizens, survived another century before falling in 1988 to the demolition men, victim of vandals and of authorities careless of the city's heritage.

Infectious and contagious diseases were rampant; venereal disease was a permanent problem, with sometimes as much as a quarter of the entire force affected at any one time. A Royal Commission of 1857 discovered that the mortality rate in the army, which might be supposed to consist of healthy, well-cared-for young men, 'was considerably greater than that of (a) the civilian male population of approximately the same age, and (b) the more strenuous civilian occupations, mining included'.[112] Clothing was not designed for health or happiness; in the first half of the century the men were forced to wear heavy helmets, chafing leather stocks around their necks, and smart, tight-fitting, uncomfortable uniforms (dyed scarlet, which must sometimes have made them feel like sitting ducks). The Marquess of Anglesey, in his *History of the British Cavalry*, describes an action against Basuto cavalry in 1852 in which several unhorsed men of the 12th Lancers were killed because their overalls were too tight to permit them to remount without help.[113] Equipment was heavy, an infantryman's kit in 1851 weighing more than 68lbs. The barrack diet was appalling, consisting in the first half of the century of a basic ration per day of one pound of a blackish bread called 'Tommy', and three-quarters of a pound of meat of indeterminate quality, cooked in a large boiler which was afterwards used to brew the greasy tea. Any vegetables, butter, condiments or tea had to be paid for as extras; the result, for the improvident or badly-off, was a diet of bread and tea for breakfast, meat and potatoes for lunch, and bread and tea for supper. If they survived the poor nourishment, the disease-ridden environment and the dangers of death or disablement in battle, soldiers could always fall foul of the regulations and be condemned to the firing squad for mutiny or severely flogged (very occasionally with fatal results) for minor crimes.

Four of the first twelve soldiers to be buried at Beckett Street Cemetery were married, but this seems an unusually high proportion, for until late in the century only six men in every hundred were officially allowed to take a wife; 'married quarters' in most cases consisted of a blanket strung up across a corner of the barrack-room to shield the matrimonial bed from the other soldiers, probably all single, who slept in the same room. Here children were born, and in these circumstances young girls grew up. Small wonder that the census returns for Leeds show so many army families (helped perhaps by the lodging allowance available to a very few of them) clustered in the streets of little rented houses outside the barracks, often sharing their cramped accommodation, like thirty-one-year-old Christopher Monck from Wexford and John Lapping, aged forty-one and also an Irishman, who with their wives and a total of seven children were squashed in at 13 Cambridge Terrace in 1871. If the regiment was sent overseas (often for many years at a time), only a small number of the wives 'on the strength' would be allowed to accompany their husbands, and Lord Anglesey tells the heartrending story of one young Scottish wife, who in 1814 'walked from Edinburgh to

Folkestone only to draw the "to be left" ticket. She and her newborn child died before her husband embarked. He had no time even to bury them.'[114] Wives not 'on the strength' had nothing at all, not even the chance to go with the regiment, unless they could smuggle themselves aboard. They lived outside the barracks, coping as best they could, abandoned to charity, the workhouse, or other men if the regiment was posted abroad. 'Legitimate' or 'illegitimate' alike, many were left husbandless and near-destitute, like poor Bridget Foley, the subject of an inquest reported in the *Mercury* in 1868. She had been receiving half-a-crown a week from the Patriotic Fund since her husband's death in the Crimea, but 'as the money came to hand she had spent it in drink, and had led a very unsettled life'; going one day into a house in Kirkgate 'where her presence was not wanted', she would have been turned out had she not suddenly been taken ill. Two days later she was dead of 'want, accelerated by exposure and intemperance'.

The tedium of army routine could be relieved by alcohol and whoring, and in 1876 there were nearly 50,000 fines for drunkenness throughout the service.[115] Valiant attempts were made to distract the men into better paths by educating and training them, the Council of Military Education, set up in 1857, having discovered that one man in five was totally illiterate, while large numbers could only 'read and write a little' and less than 5 per cent could be described as 'having a superior education'.[116] Army schools, which had existed for a very long time without apparently achieving a great deal, were in 1856 teaching the three Rs, history and geography, with the aid of trained enlisted schoolmasters such as Richard Bennett of the 33rd Foot. Poorly paid and hard worked (for the army schoolmaster was expected to spend time on lessons for the soldiers' offspring as well as instructing their fathers), Bennett was evidently proud of his post, since, although he is entered in the Burial Registers on 1 December 1861 as 'miller', his gravestone prefers to record him as 'late School Master Sergeant of the 33rd Regiment'. During Victoria's reign, army education fluctuated between voluntary and compulsory attendance, although in 1861 the three grades of 'army certificate of education' were introduced, making it necessary to take tests of varying severity before being considered for promotion. In step with Forster's Education Act of 1870, the army too brought in compulsory education, and added a lower certificate for a minimum level of attainment, which was too meaninglessly simple to be of much use. However, helped by the introduction of libraries (where it was found that the most popular books were fiction, adventure and travel stories, and Smiles' *Self-Help*), and with the aid of programmes of talks and lectures and magic lantern shows, not to mention the establishment of tea and coffee rooms, something was slowly achieved towards increasing literacy, solving the problem of boredom and combating the lure of drink.

The regiment best represented at Beckett Street Cemetery comes from among the army's heavy cavalry. The 5th Dragoon Guards were frequent visitors to Leeds and, as we have seen, gave us in 1847 our earliest military gravestone, that of Samuel Cook. They were quartered at the Cavalry Barracks in 1871, and again in 1881, so that it is possible to discover details of the composition of the regiment from the decennial census returns (see Appendix D, Part 2). On the first of these visits the coffins of two of their sergeants were borne within three months of each other out of the Barracks, past the terraces, smoking mills and pungent maltkilns of Chapeltown Road (for there was no direct path over the open fields between barracks and burial-ground), along Skinner Lane and Accommodation Street, up Beckett Street and through the iron gates of the cemetery; and when they moved on after their next stay, they left behind their retired quartermaster, William Lemmon, who was not long to enjoy the benefits of his pension.

The census shows that soldiers might be recruited anywhere, but in every regiment there was a heavy reliance upon Ireland to part with her workless, hungry sons. Two of our four 5th Dragoon Guardsmen in Beckett Street – James Regan and Samuel Cook – had enlisted in Ireland. Of the 276 unmarried privates in the barracks on census night 1871,[117] 59 were Irishmen. (Four hailed from more exotic lands – Canada, the Ionian Islands and Trinidad – but it is a fair bet that they were the children of soldier fathers who had been stationed overseas.) Wherever they started out, it is remarkable how often they seem to have been content to settle down in the town where they took their discharge when their time expired; Quartermaster Lemmon originated from Norwich, while Maurice White, James Cunningham, Frederick Short and Richard Worger – four Crimean veterans from other regiments – enlisted respectively at Cahir, Dublin, Windsor and Woolwich, and were all buried in Leeds. It is unlikely that, after twenty-four years or so, there would still be anything to fear from embittered debtors, angry fathers of girls got into trouble, or vengeful victims of street fights, so we must assume that most soldiers had some more positive reason for not returning to their places of origin; perhaps they had been put in the way of obtaining employment where they were discharged, or perhaps their wives were local women.

The 5th Dragoon Guards' muster rolls for early 1871[118] show that a number of troopers had earned Good Conduct Badges; Private Murphy received 4*d* extra a day for his four, and he needed it, since he had a wife, Ann, and offspring aged ten, eight, six, four and three. There were also those whose Conduct was Bad. James Lawler was still paying off a £1 fine for drunkenness, imposed by court martial, at 4*d* a day during the three-month period of the muster; thirty-nine others were fined for the same offence, five men were imprisoned in civil gaols, and 184 days were spent in the guardroom. Police Constable Kaye had been able to do himself a bit of good by apprehending a deserter, James O'Reilly, for which he received £1, duly entered in the regimental accounts. The improvers persevered. Schoolmaster Perkins and schoolmistress Sarah Davidson doubtless earned their salaries of £20 5*s* and £6 for the quarter, although Perkins had four soldier assistants and Miss Davidson had the help of 'acting schoolmistress' Jane Reilly at £1 10*s*, probably the literate wife of Private Reilly, eking out his pay by teaching the little children their pothooks and helping the older girls with their seams and hems. The men were encouraged to save; Sergeant George Horne, once a porter in Bristol, who had enlisted in 1848 and who died in Leeds in 1870, had left £56 11*s* 7*d* balance in the regimental Savings Bank, which was rather a pity, since he had no wife or children to benefit. The accounts of the Paymaster feature an allowance in aid of the Library and Reading Room, and on several occasions the men and their families were entertained to magic lantern slides, fetched over from York.

Whatever the shortcomings of the army, many soldiers loved the life and were anxious to record for posterity their membership of some proud regiment, or their hour of febrile glory in battle. There is a touching sense of comradeship in the many military memorials which have been paid for by the subscriptions of the friends and companions of the departed; in most cases, of course, there would have been no other way for the poorly paid soldier to have escaped the unmarked common grave. Private Thomas Robinson, of the 21st Hussars, died in 1886, aged only twenty-two, and must have been a young man of considerable character to have received a tribute in stone from the officers as well as from the NCOs and men of H Troop, 'a token of their esteem'. Sergeant William Notley, of the 13th Hussars, was a survivor of the Crimean War; picked out in black paint, with the initials in red, the lettering on his stone reads: 'Erected by his comrades, as a token of respect to one who had served 20 years, and was in the engagements of Alma, Balaclava, Inkermann, and Sebastopol'. As for the old Irish Staff Sergeant-Major Samuel McCarraher, a veteran employed in the Leeds Recruiting District, we can see him rise before our eyes with his soldier's ramrod bearing and his chest clinking with campaign medals, as we read the epitaph composed when he died, at the age of sixty-nine, on 11 August 1867: 'His untiring devotion, probity, and faithfulness, in a military career of nearly fifty-two years, won the respect and admiration of all officers under whom he served, while his social virtues commanded the esteem of all who knew him.'

There is no indication who commissioned the memorial to Private Samuel Cook in 1847, although with a credit of only 18s 11d in the Savings Bank going to his widow Elizabeth, we must assume that it was not she. Since Cook was employed as a servant at the time of his death, it may have been the officer to whom he was batman. Sergeant Horne's gravestone, which proudly describes the peak of his army career ('Served throughout the Crimean War, 1854, 55 and 56') was erected by his family ('He was deeply lamented by his brothers and sisters who places this stone, to his memory, as the last tribute of affection'). James Regan, the second of our sergeants from the 5th Dragoon Guards, received his testimonial from 'the masonic brethren of Lodge 570'. Regan's trade was that of master bootmaker, and when he died his debts exceeded his credits by 12s 10d. He was married but childless, and the last mention of him in the muster rolls conjures up a pathetic vision of his wife Hannah, widowed, alone and penniless after fifteen years of army life far from her own folk: 'A Railway Warrant has been issued (which has not yet been presented for payment),' wrote the paymaster, 'to the wife of the late Sergeant James Regan 5th Dragoon Guards, who enlisted at Dublin on 19 April 1855 and who died at Leeds on 28 January 1870, to enable her to proceed to her home at the first-mentioned place agreeably to Article 51 of the Royal Warrant 1848.'

If his friends did not subscribe to a smart gravestone for him, the departed soldier might at least achieve the solemn splendour of a military funeral, although this could not have been common, since the *Leeds Mercury* of 22 May 1856 thought it worth describing Bernard Brady's.

A MILITARY FUNERAL IN LEEDS.– Yesterday afternoon the interesting spectacle of a soldier's funeral took place in Leeds, when the body of Serjeant Brady, No. 4 Company, Fourth West York Militia, was interred in Burmantofts Cemetery. The funeral cortege started from the Gun Inn,

25. 'From Hand to Mouth – He was one of the Few who would not Beg', by Thomas Faed (1879). The discharged soldier, penniless, was a not uncommon sight.

Barrack-lane, at four o'clock, and consisted of the men of the deceased's company carrying their muskets reversed, the brass and fife bands of the regiment, followed by the hearse, officers, and about one hundred militia-men, who had attended voluntarily. The Dead March in Saul was played by the band alternately with the Sicilian Mariner's Hymn played by the fifes. At the grave the usual ceremony of firing muskets was gone through, after which the military returned to Leeds. In the course of the procession, which went up North-street and down Skinner-lane, many thousands of persons crowded the streets.

Sergeant Brady, who was fifty-two, was buried in a common grave.

The average soldier of the nineteenth century, then, enlisted as a healthy, single, unlettered and unskilled young man. During the course of his poorly paid service he was exposed to unhygienic accommodation, inadequate food, harsh discipline, debauchery and the dangers of battle; eventually he was discharged, probably still unskilled and possibly with little or no financial provision. When he died, he would be lucky to avoid a common grave, or even a pauper burial. The crumbling attestation and discharge papers and the applications for pensions stored at The National Archives tell the stories of some of the soldiers buried at Beckett Street Cemetery, and often these illustrate with particular force or poignancy aspects of life in the Victorian army. We shall now look at some of these army careers.

Not far from the Stoney Rock railings is a low stone inscribed with the name of Nathaniel Wilson, 'late Master Gunner, Royal Artillery', who died in 1870 at the age of eighty-one. There was clearly an administrative muddle here, for the Grave Register carries a different name, crossed out, and a faintly pencilled note, dated 1886 and signed by the Registrar: '26453 is not a grave ... Nathaniel Wilson on stone'. The National Archives has papers for a master gunner of this name and age who may be the same man, although in 1847 he was receiving his pension of 2s 5d a day in Armagh, not in Leeds, and was so sick as to appear unlikely ever to reach the ripe old age of eighty-one. A weaver by trade, brown-haired, blue-eyed and 5 feet 9 inches tall, born at Tynan, Armagh, he enlisted in the Royal Artillery at Armagh in September 1808 when he was eighteen, and served a total of thirty-six years and 214 days, rising slowly through the ranks from Driver to Gunner, from Gunner to Bombardier and Corporal, from Corporal to Sergeant. His service included a spell of nearly ten years abroad, manning the guns under the burning sun of the faraway Cape of Good Hope. Discharged in 1834, three years later he re-enlisted as a master gunner. Lieutenant-General Douglas, in a return to the Master General of the Ordnance in 1824, described the duties Wilson would have performed:

> The general duties of master-gunners are to see that the Ordnance, Carriages, Ammunition, and Stores are preserved in good order and report defects; to keep the batteries clean, to fire salutes where ordered, and hoist the flag; also to render quarterly and annual accounts of the Ordnance and Stores in their charge to the Principal Store-keeper's Office at the Tower. All the master-gunners detailed in this return had served sixteen years or upwards in the Royal Artillery previous to being appointed master-gunner.[119]

When Wilson was finally discharged in 1847 at Chester, he bore the marks of his long years of service. Surgeon Ellson wrote: 'Master Gunner Nathaniel Wilson has suffered from pectoral complaints and chronic rheumatism for the last 4 or 5 years – accompanied latterly with considerable emaciation and general constitutional debility – which render him totally incapable of performing his ordinary duties. I am of opinion that the above disability is the result of his long military services.' A second opinion agreed: 'The Cough, short-breathing, and palpitations of the heart continue; the Rheumatic pains are unabated, and his constitution is greatly impaired ...' His conduct was judged to be exemplary, and his superiors were happy to sign a form stating that his case was not attributable to Neglect, Design, Vice or Intemperance, but nevertheless only a partial pension was awarded, it being the Board's opinion that 'he was able to contribute something towards his livelihood'. Even though the army had admitted ruining the man's health, its attitude remained one of practicality, not philanthropy.

On 14 August 1891 a Crimean veteran, sixty-six years of age, was buried at Beckett Street. Maurice (or Morris) White had enlisted in the 13th Light Dragoons at Cahir in 1844 as a nineteen-year-old labourer; he was discharged from the army in 1872, and as a labourer, old, worn-out and with disease of the heart, he battled on in Leeds through his last sad days. In July 1891 his case was taken up by the *Mercury* in a demand for more generous treatment by the War Office of the survivors of the Crimean War and the Indian Mutiny, of whom there were said to be over thirty in Leeds alone. Although these were 'nearly all old men, weak and ailing', the Secretary for War, just like a government minister of the present day, declared that 'the scheme was impractical, and would cost a million of money'. The *Mercury* said of White on 9 July 1881:

He received the Crimean War medal, with four clasps, for Alma, Balaclava, Inkerman, and Sebastopol; afterwards served two-and-a-half years in Canada, and was discharged in Leeds after 26 years' service, with fifteen-pence a day. With such a record, and six good conduct badges, and the medal for long service, he obtained employment as a labourer, and continued in it until two years ago, when his health failed. With his pension and what he drew from the sick fund of the Discharged Soldiers' Friendly Aid Society, he struggled through 1889 and 1890. The funds of the little association could support him no further, and he had to depend then on his fifteen-pence per day, out of which he paid 4s. 6d. a week for the rent of his house. Sixty-four years of age, with a sick wife, and himself now suffering from heart disease, how can there be any delay here? A year hence, and in all probability he will be in his grave.

He was; and no thanks to HM Government that his memory is still kept green by the name which survives on the guinea grave headstone.

A man who ended his army career with better hopes than White was Frederick Short, who rests under a splendid military memorial carved with a shako and crossed cavalry swords. Sergeant-Major Short of the 4th (Queen's Own) Hussars came of a military family, for his father had survived the heroic Charge, and of his sons one, an eighteen-year-old corporal of the 1st Royal Dragoons, fell in South Africa, while the other served in his father's and grand-father's regiment. When Short enlisted at Canterbury in 1869, aged eighteen, he was employed as a groom, and was just under 5 feet 7 inches in height, with grey eyes and brown hair; thirty-three years later he was discharged at Taunton, aged fifty-one, two inches taller, but rather surprisingly with blue eyes and fair hair! Perhaps his eight years under the glare of the Indian sun had had a bleaching effect. His army record, apart from one early lapse at Christmas 1870, when he spent a week in the cells, was exemplary. Army education did something for Frederick Short. He earned six Good Conduct Badges and the medal for 'Long Service and Good Conduct'; achieved the Certificate of Education, Second Class; passed classes of instruction in fencing (to such effect that he was appointed Sergeant Instructor in Fencing himself), gymnastics and reconnaissance; and completed a successful certificated course at the School of Musketry, Hythe. In 1884 he was transferred to the West Somerset Yeomanry (established in 1794), where he was promoted to Regimental Sergeant-Major ten years later. The Yeomanry regiments were originally raised as volunteer cavalry, often the tenants or employees of the gentry, who officered them and provided them with a horse and uniform; they were not originally required to serve overseas, only to defend their country if called upon, but they did unfortunately find themselves on many occasions coming to the aid of the civil power against their fellow citizens – a delicate task which, as at Peterloo, they sometimes sadly botched. However, their assistance, even if ham-handed, was provided easily and not entirely at government expense, and the Yeomanry continued in existence, stiffened by the experience and dedication of seconded regular NCOs such as RSM Short. In 1903, after nearly thirty-four years' service, Frederick Short finally took his discharge, and his commanding officer wrote on his form, under

26. The memorial to three generations of the Short family. Under the words 'late Sert. Maj. of the 4th. Q.O. Hussars' can be read 'ONE OF THE SIX HUNDRED'.

'Special qualifications for employment in civilian life', the noble recommendation:'Qualified for any position of trust'.

Richard Worger's discharge papers describe his conduct as 'very good', which makes one wonder what sort of behaviour would have earned the description 'very bad'. After twenty years' service he was in possession of only two Good Conduct Badges, and the papers continue, 'His name appears 12 times in the Regimental Defaulters' Book, and he has been four times tried by Court Martial. He has been sixteen times Drunk. He is not in possession of a Certificate of Education.' Worger, born in Devonport, had enlisted in the Royal Artillery at Woolwich in 1848 at the age of fifteen. He was 5 feet 8 inches tall, of sallow complexion, with grey eyes and brown hair, and on both enlistment and discharge the form stated 'Trade None'. His first three years of army service, when he was under age, did not count towards his pension or prospects, but from 1851 his career consisted of a kind of military Snakes and Ladders in which a slow haul up to promotion and a Good Conduct Badge was followed by misconduct and a rapid demotion. Promoted Bombardier in April 1858, he was awaiting trial in the New Year of 1859, and was tried and reduced to Gunner on 15 January. After a year his Good Conduct penny-a-day was restored, but in August 1864, just after re-engaging for a further term of service, he was back in the garrison cells. He was again promoted Bombardier in March 1868 – only to find himself 'awaiting trial' again six months later. Back he went to Gunner, with his Good Conduct pay (which at this stage had reached a munificent 3*d* a day) reduced to 2*d*. Again he struggled up to the rank of Bombardier, but he held it for less than a year before the Christmas spirit (probably literally) overcame him in 1872 and he went AWOL on 27 December, which resulted in another slide down the army snake.

We do not know why Worger was court-martialled four times. Courts martial came in three degrees of severity, the Regimental (convened by the Commanding Officer and consisting of three officers), the District (with seven officers) and the General (with nine officers empowered to pass sentence of death or penal servitude). A Regimental court martial was obligatory for any crime carrying a penalty of more than seven days' imprisonment, but for milder infringements the Commanding Officer could impose lesser penalties, such as fines and confinement to barracks, without the formal apparatus of a court; from 1869 a system of fines for drunkenness was commenced, which had the effect of reducing the number of days spent in confinement for this offence. In an examination of cavalry Regimental court martial records over three years (1865–7),[120] it was established that two-fifths of the 2,541 cases concerned men who had gone absent without leave; desertion was the next most frequent crime, and habitual drunkenness took third place (from 1866 the 'habitual' drunk was one who had offended four times or more). It would seem very likely that drink was Richard Worger's undoing. Of his twenty-one years' service, no less than sixteen had been spent abroad – four at the Cape of Good Hope, one in the Crimea, and nearly twelve in India - and, as Lord Anglesey comments, commanding officers found they had far more cases of drunkenness to try in India than at home because 'the men had nothing to do'. When Worger was buried at Beckett Street Cemetery in 1906, a stone's throw from the grave of the upright Frederick Short, his occupation was given as 'labourer'; for the baptisms of his son and daughter in 1876 he had been described as 'wool scourer', not a particularly lucrative employment. However, he must have kept off the drink and done all right for himself at some periods of his life at least, for he had erected a comparatively expensive memorial to his wife Sarah Ann in 1889. Despite all the punishments and humiliations he endured in the ranks, Worger was undoubtedly one of those who saw his army service as the peak and crown of his life: 'He Served in the Crimea, Sebastopol, and the Indian Muitiny.'

What of the active service on which these men were engaged? From the struggle against Napoleonic France to the 'war to end war' – and, alas, beyond – the records of military conflict dot the memorials at Beckett Street Cemetery.

In 1798 maungey British babies were being hushed with the horrid threat that 'Boney' would get them. Perhaps this was not taken so seriously by little Joseph Pheasey in Wolverhampton, safe in the heart of England; but in February 1815 Napoleon Bonaparte escaped from exile on the island of Elba, landed in France, and, gathering massive support as he went, was soon marching in triumph to confront his hastily mustered enemies over the Belgian border. A dull, wet dawn in June found the British and French armies, who had skirmished the previous day, facing each other across a valley of young wheat near the village of Waterloo. Napoleon was anxious to pound the British into submission before their Prussian allies could join them, and, after his foot-soldiers had been driven back by Wellington's heavy cavalry, he threw his own cavalry against the British infantry on the ridge, hastily formed into their traditional squares, spiky with bayonets. Outside the squares, Pheasey and the other artillerymen loaded, rammed and fired with desperate haste until the last possible moment, when they abandoned their guns and ran to shelter within the squares until each wave of attack had passed and the French horsemen were finally driven back. All day the two armies struggled, until the arrival of the Prussians brought a lifting of morale to the weary British; and at last, late in the afternoon, with the dead and dying sprawled everywhere among the trampled and blood-stained crops, the final heroic effort of the veteran columns of Napoleon's Imperial Guard collapsed. With the gloomy day drawing to a close, the elite of the French army broke on the Allied swords and bayonets, turned and fled. Napoleon's last throw had failed. The carnage had been appalling; of the 72,000 Frenchmen on the field 40,000 were casualties, while the British had lost 15,000 and the Prussians half as many again. 'Napoleon did not manoeuvre at all. He just moved forward in the old style, in columns, and was driven off in the old style,' laconically commented the Iron Duke.

Joseph Pheasey survived to retire from the army which Wellington himself described as 'the scum of the earth', and to settle in Leeds, living to the venerable age of seventy-four. No doubt he recounted over and over to open-mouthed listeners the story of that vivid and bloody day which his headstone recalls proudly for future generations: 'He was Present on the 17th and 18th of June 1815, at the Memorable Battle of Waterloo, in the Royal Artillery.'

Forty years later, in the changing kaleidoscope of power, the French and British were allies when the Russians attempted to interfere in the crumbling empire of Turkey, supporting the Orthodox clergy who, in a quarrel between Christian sects, claimed sole rights of guardianship over the Christian shrines of the Holy Land. When Russia occupied two Turkish provinces, war fever grew in England and France, and the people of the two nations (one concerned with a possible threat to the overland route to the 'Jewel in the Crown', the other looking for revenge for Napoleon's retreat from Moscow) clamoured for the destruction of Sebastopol, the mighty naval base on the Black Sea from which the Russians had destroyed a Turkish flotilla with the loss of 4,000 lives. On 27 March 1854 Britain declared war on Russia,[121] and the business of embarking her ill-prepared and ill-equipped troops began. It was September before the 57,000 Turkish, French and British allies finally landed, unopposed, on Russian soil, to begin the roundabout march on Sebastopol, thirty miles away.

The first hurdle, the crossing of the River Alma against Russian resistance, was successfully accomplished, but no attempt was made to follow up this victory with an immediate attack on Sebastopol, which many thought might have fallen at that time; instead, the armies tethered their horses, put up their tents, lit the fires under their cooking-pots, and prepared for a long siege. Our old friends were there with their regiments: Frederick Short senior of the 4th Light Dragoons, Richard Thompson Chambers of the 11th Hussars, and a whole gaggle from the 13th Light Dragoons – Maurice White, James Malanfy, James Cunningham and William Notley. They were not left in peace for long. On 25 October the Russians made their first attempt at getting rid of the invaders by an attack on the port of Balaclava, the supply base to the rear of the British Army. A gallant charge by the cavalry of the Heavy Brigade checked the assault, but the heroism of this action was soon submerged and all but forgotten in the excitement of the most glorious and foolhardy episode of the entire war.

Neither the French nor the Russians could believe their eyes when they saw 600 smartly uniformed men of the Light Brigade line up in perfect formation, bridles jingling, to trot and then gallop down the North Valley straight towards the death-dealing rage of the Russian guns. The onlookers watched with tears streaming down their faces, and General Bosquet murmured words which would never be forgotten: '*C'est magnifique, mais ce n'est pas la guerre!*'

> Cannon to right of them,
> Cannon to left of them,
> Cannon in front of them
> Volleyed and thundered:
> Stormed at with shot and shell,
> Boldly they rode and well,
> Into the jaws of Death,
> Into the mouth of Hell
> Rode the six hundred,

wrote Tennyson immortally after reading the report in *The Times*. But everybody who watched – and everybody who took part – knew that something was wrong.

> 'Forward the Light Brigade!'
> Was there a man dismayed?
> Not though the soldier knew

Someone had blundered.
Theirs not to make reply,
Theirs not to reason why,
Theirs but to do and die:
Into the valley of Death
Rode the six hundred.

The story of the clashing personalities of Lord Raglan, the Commander-in-Chief, Lord Lucan, commanding the Light Brigade, and the flamboyant Captain Nolan, who carried between them the loosely worded order to 'try to prevent the enemy carrying away the guns', is well known. Lucan saw only the guns at the end of the valley, not those up on the Causeway Heights to the south; Nolan arrogantly refused to enlighten him; and so some 660 men, among them Chambers, Short and Cunningham, were launched on a crazy and hopeless enterprise from which less than one-third returned mounted and unhurt. On 18 November the *Leeds Intelligencer* printed the letter home of an officer who survived the Charge, written from camp on 27 October:

We all knew that the thing was desperate before we started, and it was even worse than we thought ... However there was no hesitation, down our fellows went at the gallop – through a fire in front and on both flanks, which emptied our saddles and knocked over our horses by scores. I do *not* think that *one* man flinched in the whole brigade – though every one allows that so hot a fire was hardly ever seen. We went right on, cut down the gunners at their guns (the Russians worked the guns till we were within ten yards of them) – went on still, broke a line of cavalry in rear of the guns, and drove it back on the third line. But here our bolt was shot: the Russians formed four deep, and our thin and broken ranks, and blown horses, could not attempt to break through them, particularly as the Russian cavalry had got round our flanks, and were prepared to charge our rear (with fresh men). We broke back through them, however, and then had to run the gauntlet, through the cross fire of artillery and Minié rifles back to our own lines, with their cavalry hanging on our flank ...There is no concealing the thing – the light brigade was greatly damaged, and for nothing; for though we killed the gunners and the horses of nine 12-pounders, we could not bring them away.

The *Mercury* of the same date had words of praise for the bravery of the men and the romantic glory of the exploit, but added, with Yorkshire commonsense, 'England deplores the loss of so many of the bravest of her troops, at a time when they can be so ill spared'. The newspaper hailed the battle of Balaclava as a 'brilliant victory', but the advantage was to the Russians, who, despite the heroic conduct of their enemies, had succeeded in cutting the only good road between the British and their base at Balaclava.

After the bloody hand-to-hand struggle on the fog-shrouded heights round the ruined village of Inkerman ten days later, when the Russians were driven back once more into Sebastopol, the British soldiers found themselves facing enemies almost more deadly – the cruel Russian winter and the inefficiency of their own commissariat. A terrible gale ripped tents to rags and sent to the bottom the ships full of supplies in Balaclava harbour; thereafter it rained or snowed constantly, turning the ground into a slough of mud. The men were cold, hungry and miserable on their diet of mouldy biscuit and salt pork; the raw coffee berries issued to them could not be roasted, since the plain had long been stripped of every stick that would serve as fuel. Their clothes had degenerated into filthy rags, and they were lucky men who stumbled across dead Russians whose uniforms and knapsacks could be appropriated. The medical department had collapsed. The harbour was a scene of total chaos, awash with the carcasses of pack animals, stores piled everywhere, spilling and rusting and decaying in the rain; yet even the stores that were there could not be disbursed unless rigid regulations were satisfied. The red tape was mind-boggling.

For the first time in the history of war, the folks at home could follow, with vivid realism and at a lapse of only a few days, the sufferings of the troops. There were war correspondents with the army, their news travelled fast by electric telegraph, and photographers sent back real pictures of the distant scene. *The Times* (which reported the war in such detail that the Tsar is said to have commented, 'We have no need of spies, we have *The Times*') brought the plight of the soldiers to breakfast tables in Britain, and the British public was devastated. The government fell, funds were set up to bring comforts to the troops, Miss Nightingale took out her party of forty nurses, and spring came to the Crimea. In a last bloody attack on the Sebastopol fortifications in September the British were driven back but the French succeeded in carrying the Malakoff, and the Russians, realising that the loss of this dominating position made it impossible to hold the town, quietly evacuated. Peace was not signed till the following year, but to all intents and purposes the Crimean War was over.

Our Crimean heroes went their ways, some of those who had ridden in the Charge becoming members of the Balaclava Commemoration Society and attending the first Reunion on 25 October 1879. The Dubliner James Cunningham served out his twenty-four years, following his time in the Crimea with a three-year spell in Canada, and settled down in Leeds, where he was buried in a common grave at Beckett Street Cemetery on 21 August 1875. Richard Thompson Chambers, a Leeds man, was discharged in 1870 after a stroke, and died on 5 December 1882; the inscription on the plinth of his memorial cross makes no mention of his moment of glory. Frederick Short died in Somerset, but is commemorated on the stone over his upright son's grave: ONE OF THE SIX HUNDRED. William Notley and Richard Worger, too, as we have seen, have left a record for posterity of their struggles and victory.

Transported with the 3rd Battalion of the Royal Artillery from the Crimea to the merciless, maddening heat of India in the hot season, Worger must have sometimes remembered almost with affection the rain, snow and gales of a Russian winter. The spark which sent the Bengal Army and part of India up in flames was the introduction of the new Enfield rifle, loaded through the muzzle with the bullet and a charge of powder which were contained in a heavily greased cartridge; the rumour was soon rife that the grease used was animal fat, either from the cow, which was sacred to Hindus, or from the pig, which was unclean to Moslems. The real cause of conflict was the violent collision of two utterly different cultural systems. British reforms, such as the forbidding of the custom of 'suttee', whereby widows burnt themselves alive on their husbands' funeral pyres, and the expropriation of landowners who could not prove their title, interfered with Indian custom and beliefs. Missionaries were busy with a hard sell of the Christian religion, and, whereas the early settlers had been content to intermarry with the native population, a new race of *memsahibs* to whom Britain was 'home' had now descended, grumbling about the heat, the dirt, the nasty habits of Indians, and the infuriating restrictive practices of servants enmeshed in the caste system.

Insurrection broke out at Meerut, white officers and their families were murdered, and the mob of mutineers marched on Delhi, where they reinstated the aged king and ran amok in the town, massacring Europeans wherever they could be found. At Cawnpore, an important trading-post between Delhi and Benares, the few hundred British held out for two miserable weeks of starvation and bombardment before accepting the bland offer of safe conduct to Allahabad from the Nana Sahib, a prince with a financial grievance against the British. As they started to board the waiting boats at the riverside, the sepoys opened fire on them and virtually all the men were killed, while the women and children, dazed and terrified, were taken back into the town and imprisoned. There, as the British soldiery marched through the gruelling heat to their rescue, the captives were most cruelly murdered and mutilated and the bodies, some still breathing, thrown down a well. No event of the Mutiny had so great an impact on the British as this atrocity, which lost nothing in the telling.

Lucknow was another major focus of rebellion; there 1,700 men and 500 women and children held out for four months in the collection of buildings known as the Residency. Many starved or died of cholera or wounds before the town could be recaptured in March 1858. Meanwhile, the regiments encamped for months on the ridge outside Delhi, impatiently waiting for sufficient reinforcements, were at last able to scale the walls, force the gates, and fight their way hand-to-hand through the streets until by 20 September 1857 the whole city was once more in British hands.

By 1859 the insurgents had been fairly brutally mopped up and the country was quiet again, although it was a long ten years before Richard Worger's artillery battalion finished its tour of duty and returned to Britain; meanwhile, the government had passed from the East India Company to the Crown. The British remained in India for a further ninety years, and now, in an unexpected reversal of history, the rows of back-to-backs around Beckett Street Cemetery are occupied by the great-great-grandchildren of the men and women over whose country those Victorian soldiers fought.

During the whole reign of Queen Victoria there were not more than a few scattered periods of two or three years at a time when the British Army was not fighting somewhere in the world – in China, in New Zealand, in Malaya, in Abyssinia, in Afghanistan. The final major conflict of the century began in 1899 with the Dutch-descended Boers who had the upper hand of British settlers in South Africa. Described as 'the last imperialist war fought by Britain' and disapproved of by many influential people at home, the struggle lasted three years and involved some spectacular and confidence-shaking defeats for the British before ending in victory and the annexation of the two Boer republics. The South African War is noted for the successful use by the Boers of guerrilla tactics, the origination by the British of the concentration camp, the new word 'mafficking', and the rise of Baden-Powell of Boy Scout fame. There were nearly 10,000 dead on both sides, among them young Frederick Francis Short, grandson of the Light Brigade hero, who died at Naauwpoort in the New Year of 1901.

The occasional memorials of the wars of Empire are few compared with those of the cataclysm of 1914, which indelibly marked every cemetery in the land. When the Armistice was signed in the early morning of 11 November 1918, just over half of the men mobilised by all countries had been killed, wounded or taken prisoner; Britain alone had suffered nearly a million dead and over two million wounded. On the fields of France and Flanders and in the other theatres of war in Europe and Africa, a generation of young men had been wiped out. Their remains had been gathered compassionately and respectfully into the great war cemeteries of the Imperial War Graves Commission, the inspiration in 1915 of the energetic and humanitarian Red Cross worker Fabian Ware. An early and controversial decision of the Commission had been the ensuring of equal treatment for all who had made the equal and supreme sacrifice, by the refusal to allow those who could afford it to repatriate the bodies of their relatives; rich and poor were interred in the lands where they had fallen. Many of the grieving families commemorated their dead *in absentia*, on the kerbs or at the foot of family stones; in Beckett Street Cemetery, as everywhere in the country, the bugles call, sad and far away. '2nd Lieut. Edmanson J., 7th KOYLI, killed Ypres 1916 aged 23 … Harry Tuting, who died of wounds received in Gallipoli November 3rd 1915 aged 22 years … Pte. Norman Douglas Fletcher who fell gloriously at Cambrai, Nov. 22 1917, aged 21 years … Albert Edward Jackson, killed in action at Passchendaele Ridge, France, October 9th 1917, aged 26 years … Robert Levitt who died of wounds at Bagdad, July 7th 1917, aged 24 years … Pte. Clifford Morley, 2nd West Yorks. Regt., killed in action July 1st 1916, at the Battle of the Somme, in his 20th year.'

Some were later able to visit the graves of the menfolk they had lost, but that consolation was denied to James and Carrie Reyner, who lie in the shade of a grand horse chestnut tree at the cemetery. Their son had volunteered eagerly for one of Kitchener's 'Pals' and 'Chums' Battalions, so popular in the northern industrial cities, where lads from the same neighbourhood would enlist and serve together.

> Off to the green fields, springy turf and towering trees,
> Into crystal air, under blue skies and zephir breeze.
> Leaving our families, our jobs, our Susies and our 'Sals'
> Jolly fun to be swinging along, marching with the 'Pals'…

wrote 'Leeds Pal' Private Pearson jauntily.[122] The first day of the Battle of
the Somme put an end to the happy dream; among the 60,000 British dead,
wounded or missing was counted every officer but one of the 15th Battalion
West Yorkshire Regiment or 'Leeds Pals', and all but forty-seven of the 800
NCOs and men. The casualty lists in the local newspapers were soon covering a column and a half. Home after home was thrown into mourning, and
the Reyners were among those who received, first the dreaded War Office
telegram, and months later the official letter which ran: 'Sir, It is my painful
duty to inform you that no further news having been received relative to ...
who has been missing since 1.7.1916, the Army Council have been regret-
fully constrained to conclude that he is dead ...' All that was left of their son
was his name, and this they had carved on their own memorial: 'PRIVATE
BURNETT REYNER, "LEEDS PALS", PRESUMED KILLED IN FRANCE, 1ST. JULY
1916, AGED 23.' Private Pearson, saved by two tins of shrapnel-deflecting
bully beef in his knapsack, was one of the very few who came through to
write his verdict on the Great War.

> What had I to show for my four years service – 2 crossed flags
> Three wound scars, one wound stripe, and a craze for fags.
> But what a lifetime had been crammed into those hectic years
> Friendship first, then travel, sand and mud, blood and ghastly fears.

Some survived injury long enough to be shipped back across the Channel
and brought home to die. In Leeds, the East Leeds War Hospital was formed
by the temporary sequestration of some of the Workhouse buildings, and
many a coffin was borne on a gun carriage across the road to the cemetery.
The presence of these war dead is announced by the Cross of Sacrifice,
designed by Sir Reginald Blomfield, which stands guard – here minus its
stolen bronze sword – over all burial-grounds where the Commonwealth
War Graves Commission has been at work. Scattered around the cemetery
are the familiar small, simple slabs of white English stone with the name,
rank and number of the deceased, his regimental badge, and sometimes an
inscription chosen by the family: 'Ever remembered' (Pte. H. Boyce, Royal
Defence Corps, 1918). The memorial design had provoked another hornet's
nest of controversy; to some it was too humble, to others insufficiently religious, and the Commission's intended impression of immaculately ordered
rows like soldiers on parade was often thwarted in the old cemeteries at
home (as at Beckett Street, where there are twenty-eight such stones) by the

necessity of inserting them piecemeal among others, instead of being able to have a special plot. Nevertheless the Commission carried on with its task. 'Not least,' writes Philip Longworth in *The Unending Vigil*,[123] 'it serves as a reminder of more than a million debts which can never be repaid.'

Chapter Eight

Just a Song at Twilight

As a poet he stood unequall'd.

Michael Hall, 1848

The patriotic pride and high-spirited rivalry of provincial cities in the nineteenth century were manifested in a crop of remarkable public buildings across the land; one of the most satisfying of all is the Town Hall at Leeds, a winning design by the young Hull architect Cuthbert Brodrick, opened on 7 September 1858 – amid the usual festive crowds – by the Monarch herself. The wide white flight of steps to the entrance is guarded by four recumbent lions, designed by William Day Keyworth junior, and remarkably like those of Trafalgar Square. The pleasure their commission gave to the Yorkshiremen who were responsible for the building and its trimmings was not merely aesthetic. On the installation of the second set of lions in 1867, Councillor Addyman felt that he and his colleagues were to be congratulated; not only had the noble beasts impressed him with ten times greater force than the Landseer lions guarding Nelson's Column, but 'the latter cost £11,000, while they had four lions in Leeds for £600'. In fact, as the chairman of the meeting pointed out, it was only £550, which was even better value (although it must be admitted that the cut-price stone lions have worn considerably worse than their bronze London cousins).[124]

The primary function of the new Town Hall was, of course, as a setting for the deliberations of the Council, but its main component, the splendidly garish Victoria Hall, quickly developed a most important secondary use as a major concert hall. Despite the shortcomings of the basic education system, there was an extraordinarily wide spectrum of cultural activity available to the Victorians of the provinces. Theatre ranged from serious drama to the crudest of music-hall; music from the classical concert series inspired by Hallé in Manchester to the homely evening of ballad and piano. Talks and lectures, sometimes with lantern-slides, entertained or improved the audience. Books could be borrowed under the new Public Libraries Act (adopted in Leeds in 1868), and the municipal art galleries were busy acquiring masterpieces by Frith or Fildes while *Bubbles* and *Monarch of the Glen* graced parlour wall and biscuit tin. The new art of photography ranged from careful composi- tions by talented amateur members of local photographic societies to the professional production of millions of *cartes de visite* glued into thousands of albums throughout Victoria's reign, and at the end of the century the historic flickering of the first moving film captured moments of a sunny day on Leeds Bridge.

What sort of entertainment was on offer, for instance, in the dull, slushy post-Christmas weeks of January 1868? Advertised in the *Leeds Mercury* of 11 January, after the church and religious meetings, was Dr Spark, Town Hall organist at a salary of £200 a year, who was to perform for an hour on the Grand Organ (the white and gold splendour of which dominates the Victoria Hall) a programme mainly consisting of Mendelssohn's *Lieder ohne Worte*, Book 8, 'for the first time in Leeds'. The following day the Victoria Hall would resound to one of Mr Charles Hallé's Grand Concerts, with a strong operatic flavour: arias from Mozart's *Don Giovanni*, Flotow's *Martha*, Verdi's *La Traviata*, and ballads such as Balfe's 'My love for thee' were inter- spersed with piano solos played by Mr Hallé himself (Beethoven's *Grand Sonata in A flat*, Opus 26, and Schubert's *Valse Caprice in A minor*), while pian- ist Mr Santley, although pipped at the post, still insisted that he was offering Mendelssohn's *Lieder ohne Worte*, Book 8, 'for the first time in Leeds ...' Ten days later, at the same venue, the Leeds Madrigal & Motet Society were to give a Grand Performance of Handel's oratorio *Judas Maccabeus* under the baton of Dr Spark, while those thirsty for immediate cultural gratification could hear, that very night, 350 Juvenile Voices of the Leeds Band of Hope League (accompanied on the Victoria Hall organ by the indefatigable Dr Spark). The Royal Amphitheatre, grandiosely developed from a music hall known as the Royal Casino, was showing what 44,000 people had pro- nounced 'the best panto in or out of London'. *A Apple Pie* had:

The most amazing and superb scenery ever seen.

Transformation Scene a marvel of Beauty and a Joy for ever.

Grand Ballet Scene. Magnificent Palace of Toys. Wonderful!

THE FATHERS' PANTOMIME!

THE MOTHERS' PANTOMIME!

THE CHILDREN'S PANTOMIME!

EVERYBODY'S PANTOMIME!

THE MOST GORGEOUS PANTOMIME IN THE PROVINCES!

Gompertz's Spectroscope was entertaining crowded houses, and Thornton's Varieties offered a premier Baritone and Buffo supported by acrobats, ballet 'etc.' The Princess Concert Hall, obviously appealing to a less well-off patron than the Royal Amphitheatre, drew attention to 'The Greatest Sixpennyworth in the World', with the Alhambra Ballet, a Cavern of Ice with Real Water, and introducing Alexander's Corps de Ballet and Infant Dancers, natives of Leeds, on a scale of splendour; concluded every evening with the Scotch Carnival, the Gathering of the Clans. (Next Monday's special attraction was to be 'the African Blondin'.) Back to earth with a bump, for the advertisements continued: 'DISTRESS IN LEEDS. PROPOSED OPENING OF THE SOUP KITCHEN IN YORK-STREET.'

Although Dr Spark's organ recital and the children's Temperance songs could be heard for as little as 3*d*, the prices of tickets for the Hallé concert ranged from 1*s* to 7*s* 6*d*, and *Judas Maccabeus* required an outlay of at least 6*d*, well beyond the reach of most working men, who might have to support the entire family on a pound a week. There were efforts to bring musical culture within the reach of the lower orders with the work of the Leeds Rational Recreation Society, a development of the mid-Victorian 'people's concerts' movement pioneered in Glasgow and Birmingham. The immediate stimulus was provided by the disgust felt by Town Missionary Samuel Barbour and another minister at the (unspecified) nature of the entertainment provided by the Royal Casino, and with the support of half a hundred eminent citizens the Society was launched in 1852 and went on to sell nearly 90,000 tickets during the next six years of its short existence. Organising concerts which were well within the musical broadstream and largely vocal (therefore less expensive), it aimed to wean the working man from the convivial public house, elevate his musical taste, and stiffen his moral fibre by allowing him to mingle with a better class of person (for it was expected that music-lovers from all grades of society would attend). Many of its officers have already appeared in these pages; John Hope Shaw, for instance, twice served as president. The Leeds Rational Recreation Society, according to its historian, David Russell,[125] was not altogether successful in its aims, since it made more appeal to the artisan class, it being unlikely that the unskilled labourer would have even 3*d* to spare and that, if he did, he would prefer Beethoven in the vast and alien splendour of the Town Hall to beer in the Dog & Gun up the York Road; yet during the 1850s the Society 'helped found a tradition of popular concert life that was to benefit the musical enthusiasts of Leeds at least until the outbreak of the First World War'.

Nobody who has walked along the main path of the Unconsecrated portion of Beckett Street Cemetery can fail to have noticed the unusual name of the infant commemorated on the grey granite obelisk. 'Vieuxtemps Haddock' seems a hard burden for a child to bear, but a little enquiry into the life of his father, whose name is on the east side of the memorial – George Haddock, Professor of Music – reveals why the baby was so christened and provides an astonishing glimpse of the intensity of musical activity in the towns and cities of the North. George's father had come from the North Riding village of Boltby, where he had played the oboe in the little church orchestra, to Killingbeck near Leeds, the birthplace of his son George in 1823; his eldest son Thomas became a talented cellist, and it was not long before his second son was manifesting a great aptitude for the violin, so impressing the local farmers on visits to his Thirsk relatives that one remarked: 'Bless me, little 'un, but it's grand. T' first haaf hour as I have to spare I'll larn to play t'fiddle myself.' In spite of the musical atmosphere which the family breathed - hearing Paganini play at the Music Hall in Albion Street on his visit to Leeds in 1832, being involved in the first performances in Yorkshire of Beethoven quartets, keeping in communication with Mendelssohn's German publishers, who had instructions to send them everything of his as soon as it appeared - it was decided that George should make a career, not of music, but of law. However, the strongboxes, deeds and sealing-wax of Mr Samuel Hick's offices in Briggate received little attention from the young clerk, who smuggled in his violin to practise, and it was not long before he abandoned the post.

During his long life George Haddock's influence on the performance and teaching of music in the North was remarkable. He was able to persuade the great Belgian violinist Henri Vieuxtemps (after whom that child was named) to take him as a pupil and to teach him the secret of his method of bowing, which training he in turn imparted to the 4,000 pupils (among them Delius) who passed through his own hands. For twenty years he played with the Hallé Orchestra and for twenty-five with the Liverpool Philharmonic; engaged at Bradford for two years, he organised the great first performance there of Mendelssohn's *Elijah*, at which the Mayor was so impressed by the overflowing crowds wishing to attend that Bradford subsequently acquired a Concert Hall; he was leader of the Leeds Choral Society and the West Riding Choral Union; other towns such as Dewsbury, Halifax and Harrogate benefited from musical events inspired by him; he knew the great performers, conductors and composers of his time – Vieuxtemps and Joachim, Hallé, Sullivan, Spohr and Sterndale Bennett. His teaching activities (he was still nominal Principal of the Leeds College of Music, his family foundation, when he died, and he was the author of *A Complete Practical Violin School*) continued throughout his busy life. He also possessed a magnificent collection of instruments, including the 'Emperor' Stradivarius of 1715. At his death in 1907 his family received a message of sympathy from Queen Alexandra, and every Leeds paper carried an obituary. His son Edgar looked back in 1916 on his father's lifetime as a golden age - despite brushes with some local performers whose attitude was more practical than professional, like the violinist who arrived late for a performance of Haydn's *Creation*; refused admittance by the janitor on Mr Haddock's orders, the musician urged, 'They have not got much past t' "Chaos" yet, and every one knows that's nowt. Only let me in, and as I am a very fast player I'll overtake them all, long before they get to t' "Marvellous Work".' (He was kept out.)

Edgar Haddock was convinced of his native city's high standing in the musical world of the nineteenth century. 'There is full evidence to prove that the town of Leeds was considered to be a centre of such sufficient importance as to receive recognition, on at least one occasion of their artistic journeyings, from most of the specially great stars who flashed periodically across the musical firmament.'[126] From this slightly qualified remark, it can be inferred that Leeds did not attract quite such attention from the great as did London, Paris, Berlin or Milan, but it is also very evident that the industrial cities of the North were no cultural deserts, and that a ready and enthusiastic welcome awaited the visiting celebrity.

There were doubtless many, many lesser luminaries who delighted the inhabitants of Victorian Leeds (or otherwise, to judge by the joke reprinted by the *Mercury* from *Punch* in 1868: 'WITHOUT AND WITHIN. He grinds his organ in the street. I grind my teeth in the house'). Although he was only buried in a common grave, the newspapers announced the death in June

1849 of Thomas Leadbeater, 'a celebrated blind violin player', while in 1856 there was an inquest on the body of Edward McCabe, a travelling musician aged fifty-six, 'who picked up a living by playing from pothouse to pothouse upon the Irish bagpipes'. There is music in the cemetery, too, and very much in accordance with English taste; little Emma Bowes, whose memorial probably dates from 1860, has the notation and words of 'O rest in the Lord' from *Elijah*, and in 1856 Joshua Cawthra's musical friends subscribed to a stone with Handel's 'I know that my Redeemer liveth' finely carved on a slate tablet. The *Leeds Intelligencer* described the funeral of Mr Cawthra, for many years the first tenor of the Parish Church choir.

> The remains ... were interred in the consecrated portion of Burmantofts Cemetery, on Sunday afternoon, in the presence of upwards of 2000 persons. The Parish Church choir, and the vocalists of the borough generally, were present, and sang the anthem, 'I heard a voice from Heaven saying', and Luther's hymn, 'Great God what do I see and hear.' Previous to the funeral cortege leaving Mr. Cawthra's house, in Somers-street, the choristers sang a funeral piece in the street.

Music was not always welcome everywhere; in 1887 the Burial Grounds Committee had to deal with a complaint from Mr George Jesson about the high-handedness of Mr Sheard, Superintendent of the cemetery, who had stopped a brass band at an interment. Mr Jesson was soon seen off, since the Superintendent 'had acted in accordance with the provision of the Act of Parliament relating to the Ground'.[127] Apparently it was all right to sing, but not to play the trombone.

A Beckett Street Cemetery musician wreathed in mystery is David Ripley, alias 'Hamilton Winter'. Traced in successive censuses as a nineteen-year-old labourer in a felting mill, living at 21 Calls with his shoemaker father John and stepmother Maria (1851), and as the head of a family, a cordwainer by trade and aged twenty-nine, at Railway Street (1861), then described in the Burial Register as a 'currier of leather' (1879), he seems ordinary enough; yet he comes complete with family legend of noble descent, tradition of first stage appearance at the Argyle Theatre, Birkenhead (now demolished) as a singer of 'Scotch ballads', and gold cross passed down to descendants and inscribed: 'PRESENTED TO MR. HAMILTON WINTER BY A FEW FRIENDS AT THE BRICKLAYERS ARMS YORK ROAD LEEDS 10TH JULY 1868.' A photograph captioned 'Hamilton Winter', showing him

27. 'Hamilton Winter', alias shoemaker David Ripley (1831–79), in theatrical costume and wearing the cross presented by friends at the Bricklayers' Arms.

in Highland garb, with the cross pinned to his lapel and a dangerous-look-
ing claymore (also still in the possession of the family) in his hand, pads out
the image, as do a few of those scraps of information which are the tantalus
and relish of the family historian (he wore a velvet smoking-cap and always
travelled first class); but without the meagre family memories there would
be no hint that David Ripley was anything other than the simple shoemaker the records reveal.

Painting and drawing, like music, could be carried on at any level from
the domestic pastime to the full-time profession. In 1857 a great art exhibition had been mounted in Manchester, and eleven years later Leeds
followed suit. There was no art gallery, and the pictures were hung, with
careful attention to natural lighting, in the large wards – as yet empty of
patients – of Mr Gilbert Scott's noble new Infirmary. After the excitement
of the grand opening on 19 May 1868 by the Prince of Wales, visitors could
admire works by Raphael, Tintoretto and Caracci; linger before fleshy
Rubens; enjoy Reynolds' *Strawberry Girl* and (of course) several paintings
by Landseer; feel themselves transported as if by magic carpet to the mystic
East in the 'Indian Court'; or marvel at the incalculable value of the collection of exhibits shown in the Museum of Art – Celtic, Roman, Greek
and Egyptian antiquities, Wedgwood, Burmantofts faience. There was a
gallery of 'Yorkshire Worthies', which quirkily included, among the dry
divines and the scions of local armigerous houses, the portrait of the well-
known Yorkshire racehorse 'Flying Childers'. The *Mercury* was unable to let
the day pass without a side-swipe at Manchester, the Leeds exhibits being
judged 'equal, if not in extent, at all events in excellence, to those shown in
Manchester in 1857'.[128] However, Manchester, Liverpool and Birmingham
all had proper municipal galleries before the inspired and single-minded
Colonel Harding (also donor to the city of Lady Butler's dramatic view of
the cavalry charge, *Scotland for Ever!*) got the Leeds City Art Gallery opened
in 1888. Art was perhaps not of such significance to Leeds as music; the 1868
Exhibition apparently did not succeed in making a profit, and the organis-
ers of the course of lectures proposed to accompany it seem to have found
it difficult to attract sufficient subscribers at a guinea each.

Two of the gravestones at Beckett Street Cemetery commemorate artists.
John Bracewell's 1874 entry in the Burial Register describes his occupation simply as 'painter', but from the delicately carved palette, brushes and
mahlstick we can assume he painted pictures rather than window-frames.
Joseph Fountain, who died in 1887, also has a palette and brushes (now

flaking sadly), 'erected by his Friends', commemorating his work in one field of artistic production which does seem to have been fully appreciated – that of the theatre poster.

The earliest playbills consisted of fairly densely packed print, the title of the play and the names of the actors standing out in lettering of graduated sizes. The inclusion of a woodcut scene, which by the nature of the process was somewhat crudely done, more readily attracted the attention of passers-by; and the next major development was the expensive but extremely attractive method of chrome lithography. In this the design was drawn with a greasy crayon on a flat slab of porous limestone, the stone was dampened and ink was rolled on to it. As the wet sections repelled the ink while the greasy parts attracted it, paper could then be laid over it and the picture printed in a press, but each different colour area had to be drawn separately and the inking and printing procedure repeated. Posters produced in this way were works of art, a world away from the dry text of the playbill. In 1887 the *Yorkshire Post* carried an obituary on Joseph Fountain, from which it seems that he came somewhere in between the woodcut and the chromolithograph.

Mr. Fountain may be considered the actual pioneer of the new extensive industry of designing and printing of theatrical 'posters'. Before he set to work the only mural decorations giving the public an idea of the scenes from popular plays were the small, coarse, and common, woodcuts, illustrating scenes from Sweeney Todd, Maria Martin, and other popular horrors, which even until lately were to be seen occasionally on the hoardings of the theatres in the mining and manufacturing districts. When, however, many years ago Mr. John Coleman was about to produce some piece at the Leeds Theatre Royal in Hunslet Lane, Mr. Fountain suggested to him that the public would be attracted by actual pictures of scenes from the play on the walls of the town, and the idea proved such a success that it was rapidly developed, and much artistic work from Mr. Fountain's pencil followed in the days before the present elaborate and costly chrome-lithographs were seen upon our hoardings.

Isaac Fountain, Joseph's father, was a tailor, originating from Wisbech in Cambridgeshire. His children were all born in Leeds; in the 1851 census his sons Joseph and Isaac, twenty-three and nineteen, are described as 'engravers' and Edward as a 'lithographic printer' – an interesting and inexplicable change of direction from the father's trade. For many years

Fountain's ran a successful business in Leeds, but at the end of his life Joseph seems to have suffered financial, physical and possibly also mental deterioration, and his affairs got into such a state that he had to be rescued by a benefit performance at the Grand Theatre (consisting of the triple bill *The Colour Sergeant*, *Clerical Error* and *Chatterton*, produced and acted in by the theatre's lessee Wilson Barrett). The artists gladly gave their services and the audience its money, for genial Joe, president of the Albion Club, was a popular man, intimate with and respected by the most prominent members of the theatrical profession, and, as the *Yorkshire Post* continued warmly, 'his large knowledge of the world, his artistic ability, and his unfailing fund of good humour endeared him to an unusually large circle of personal friends'.

The production of theatre posters by chromolithography from the mid-1860s came too late for one of Beckett Street Cemetery's actors, John Langford Pritchard, who died in 1850 at the age of fifty-two. 'Alonso, MR. PRITCHARD' features in very small print on an 1835 playbill for the Theatre Royal, Covent Garden, well below the thick black capitals of the title 'PIZARRO!' Pritchard, the son of a naval captain, was born at sea, and inevitably entered the service as a midshipman, but amateur dramatics soon lured him away to join a company of professional actors. He toured widely, and was particularly successful both professionally and socially in Edinburgh, where he was a founder member of the Edinburgh Shakespeare Society. He is described on his gravestone as 'for many years a principal dramatic performer at the Theatres Royal Covent Garden, Dublin and Edinburgh', and in his final years he retired to the North to become lessee of the York Theatrical Circuit, a grouping of local theatres comprising York, Leeds and Hull (in the orchestra of which circuit the ubiquitous George Haddock later played his violin). The *Dictionary of National Biography* seems to damn the poor actor-manager with faint praise: 'He was a sound, careful and judicious actor, but only just reached the second rank.'

Some never made it at all. Does one scent a whiff of the classic Victorian paterfamilias about the case of young William Ruddock, who committed suicide at his father's home in 1868 by taking laudanum? 'For some weeks past the deceased had drunk heavily, and had frequently remarked that he wished he was dead,' ran the *Mercury*'s account of the inquest. 'He had kept the company of theatricals, and had expressed a strong desire to become an actor.' William, aged twenty-two, was the son of William Petty Ruddock, a respected Leeds surgeon, and it seems hardly likely that his parents would have embraced with any notable enthusiasm the idea of a stage career for their son, especially as he was already embarked on his medical studies. William junior was 'in the habit of drinking laudanum as a stimulant', and knew what to expect from it; on the eve of his death he went the round of the local public-houses, came home, and topped up the alcohol with the deadly drug. Next morning he was found expiring on the hearthrug in the sitting room. Was he really desperate to go on the stage, taking his life as a last dramatic gesture in protest against the straitjacket of a profession for which he had no affinity, or was he just a weak-willed young man brought up in some luxury, who did not really know what he did want, except that it wasn't what he had got? We shall never know.

Equal obscurity might easily have shrouded Michael Hall, whose 1848 headstone grandiosely claims unparallelled literary and domestic virtues. 'As a Poet he stood unequall'd ... As a Husband, a Father and a Friend he was esteemed by all who knew him. The star of genius now has Death o'ercast, No more he'll send the merry laugh along; He's gain'd his home of everlasting rest And sings aloud, prepare to follow on.' The verse may be forgiven as the product of a lesser hand, but the name itself arouses no echoes in the memory. The *Dictionary of National Biography* knew him not, nor did the obituary columns of the local newspapers. A lucky contact with his descendants brought his work, his life and even his portrait to light. Here was a man who, like John Langford Pritchard, made his living by entertaining, yet who differed from that better-known and rather serious-sounding worthy in every way. Michael Hall could do anything – sing, dance, play, write, act, compose – and his versatility seems to relate more to the tradition of the amateur home entertainment, and to the later immensely popular music hall, than to the professional boards which Pritchard trod. His work gained him a livelihood, but it did not make him rich; after his death his friends organised a Memorial Benefit Night at the Palace Inn, East Street, in aid of his widow and children.

Miles Naylor, a Leeds basket-maker, gave the address, summarising the facts of Hall's early life and creating a vivid picture of a kind, clever, witty and honest man. Hall had been born in London in 1807 and at an early age had gone to sea for four years, after which he had decided to take to the stage, establishing himself in a six-year engagement at the Marylebone Theatre as 'a comedian of the first order'. He devised and acted in sketches, composed and sang songs, wrote and delivered recitations. His first literary production, according to Naylor, was 'a sort of allusion to his own stature, in the Song of the Devil and little Mike'. The mood of his compositions[129] varied from the satirical humour of 'The Song of my kind Relations' (inspired by the refusal of a request for a trifling loan), through the elegiac grandeur of such recitations as 'Mighty Frost', to the pathos of 'Granny Gray', in which a poor old woman, sick, sad and starving, creeps out from her 'time-shattered dwelling' on the seashore to seek help from her neighbours.

> Their hearts were as hard as the stones where she knelt.
> No succour they gave her, nor pity they felt.
> Tho' weary and dying, they turned her away,
> And spurned for a witch, was poor granny Gray.

> Now death thou art welcome, poor Granny did cry
> While tears of old age trickled forth from each eye
> Her clothes that were torn, in the bleak winds did play
> While homeward despairing, crept poor granny Gray.

> She entered her hovel heart-broken and weak
> Where food, and for shelter, in vain did she seek.
> Then fell to the earth, with her limbs cold as clay
> When death's heavy hand relieved poor granny Gray.

The tears froze to icicles on her cheeks, the snow drifted over her, and Michael Hall drew his moral:

> And when the cold winter again doth appear
> All you in your mansions with glorious cheer
> Then know – while you sport with the giddy and gay
> There's thousands as wretched as poor granny Gray.

The language is simple yet dramatic, with its repetition of the key themes of cold, cruelty and hunger mirrored in the images of stones, clay and icicles, and even a hint of the rigours of the New Poor Law in the reference to death 'relieving' the old woman; meanwhile, the beat of the metre leads us relentlessly on towards her end. Although recitation itself has become alien to us as an art form, and modern taste scoffs at Victorian sentiment, we can appreciate that, performed by a man of talent and personality, this must have been an effective and moving piece.

28. A versatile entertainer: Michael Hall (1807–49).

Michael Hall was also master of the comic, as can been seen from his surviving sketches. In *Catching a Gorilla* the underpaid and much put-upon servant John, whom we first meet making up medicines for his master, Dr Calomel, gets his revenge for being exploited and called an 'infernal monkey'. A satisfied customer, one of the few Calomel has not poisoned, sends him a newspaper containing an advertisement by the Royal Zoological Society of Humbugshire offering 1,000 guineas for a gorilla, and the Doctor, who has already obtained several stuffed animals for his own museum, becomes wildly excited as he works out how he can get hold of a gorilla and the reward. John disguises himself as a sailor and spins a yarn about how he has wounded and captured a gorilla which he mistook for a hostile native. An offer of one hundred pounds from the almost hysterical Calomel is raised to three, and John goes off with the first instalment in his hands, promising to deliver the gorilla at four bells. Sooner than expected a large box arrives, which the Doctor cautiously opens. Out springs a creature which belabours him, jumps on his back, runs round the room smashing windows and bottles and creating mayhem, till at last Calomel is supine on the floor and the animal, chattering at him from the chair on which it is perched, pulls off a mask and reveals itself to be – John. His employer is suitably chastised for his foolishness and greed, and, having been given back his money, promises a reformed attitude towards his servant in future. This sparkling little sketch is interspersed with comic songs ('I own I was a prince of ninnies Counting upon a thousand guineas ... I'll stay at home And ne'er will roam In search of the gorilla') and is full of dreadful Victorian puns ('Is that draught ready for Mrs. Wheezer?' 'Ye-e-s, Sir.' 'That's right. I'll take a draft on the bank from her.') There is plenty of knockabout fun, and at the end, again, the author points a moral as he makes Dr Calomel say: 'Damn the gorilla! When a man follows an honest profession for the good of his fellow-man he has no business to be following monkeys!'

In his Benefit Night speech Miles Naylor drew attention to the skills of his friend's children, for entertainment was a family business; the violin playing of his son Michael and the dancing of his son Edward offered further confirmation that evening of the ability of the father who had taught them. Naylor continued: 'Where's the man that could spend an evening with him and listen to his Duetts with Miss Hall, his Irish Sketch and Comic songs, and not be carried with an impetuous stream of fun and wit till he forgot the cares of the World and gave himself up to laughter

29. Nineteenth-century fireworks: 'Geoffrey, Percy and Jessie witnessing the pyrotechnic display', from a story in *The Leisure Hour* (1859).

and amusement?' Clearly good company and a man of ability and charm, Michael Hall comes alive again for us as a versatile entertainer typical of the early Victorian age.

   The strangest skills lie buried at Beckett Street Cemetery; most are never guessed at, some glow weirdly and without explanation through the pages of the newspapers or the Burial Registers. Thomas Irvine and his son Edward, of Byron Street, were firework makers. Simple fireworks had been known in the East since very early times, and pyrotechnic displays had grown popular in Europe from the seventeenth century as a dramatic means of brightening up national celebrations, or, later, as an added attraction to places of entertainment such as Vauxhall and Ranelagh Gardens in London. Fireworks consist of a paper container charged with a mixture of which at least one ingredient contains a readily liberated supply of oxygen for burning; for a long time saltpetre (potassium nitrate) was used for this purpose, but the resulting colour, a 'greenish' or 'reddish' flame, was not sufficiently spectacular. Early in the nineteenth century potassium chlorate was discovered to be a more effective substitute, and further improvements in the brilliance of the colours came with the introduction of magnesium (about 1865) and aluminium (1894) – too late for the Irvines, for Edward, aged nineteen, died a week before his father, who was buried on 5 November 1863. Is it possible that the date is merely an unkind coincidence? Yet if there was an explosion in a cellar in Byron Street it passed unnoticed by the Leeds newspapers. All we are offered is a tantalising announcement in the Deaths column of the *Intelligencer*, which goes to show how little we really know of the entertainers who sleep at Beckett Street:

On the 1st. inst., aged 50, MR. THOMAS IRVINE, fire-works manufacturer, known as MONS. DAVALLE, tight-rope dancer.

Chapter Nine

Gone to the Bad

Resolv'd in Folly's path to go,
Led captive by my stubborn will ...

William Henry Townsley, 1851

'It is not infrequently the lot of pious parents to have family trials of no common order,' sorrowfully observed the Revd Henry Marles, biographer of Jabez Tunnicliff, in 1865. His words would have been equally applicable to Christopher Dove, respected merchant, philanthropist and patron of the Leeds Town Mission, on whose house the blackest of horrors had fallen nine years before.

Christopher and Mary Dove were natives of Darlington, County Durham, where most of their children were born – Mary, Elizabeth, Christopher (in 1820), Sarah (in 1823) and their second son William about 1828. The last child, Jane, was born in 1833 in Leeds, where her father and uncle had set up in partnership in a leather business. Mr Dove soon gained a prominent position in the town and among his co-religionists. His commercial activities were extremely successful, enabling him to live in comfort in Park Square, in the best area of town, and to give financial help to his children, each of whom received, during his lifetime or under his will, at least £1,000. His sound and sensible investments involved property, life policies and shares in the Leeds Banking Company, the New Gas Company and the Leeds and York Fire Insurance Office. He was a pillar of the Wesleyan comunity, acting as a trustee for the new Oxford Place Chapel, and he was also interested in politics, although his ambition of a place on the Town Council was not realised. His elder daughters all married satisfactorily, two of them wedding Wesleyan ministers; Sarah's husband was the Revd John Sloggett Jenkins, a teacher at the Methodist school of Woodhouse Grove. But there were, nevertheless, dark clouds and deep sorrows in the lives of Christopher and Mary Dove, brought upon them by their two boys.

Christopher junior was a saint. A kind, cheerful and generous lad, who regularly received money from his parents to distribute as alms, he was orderly and industrious, loved learning, and devoted a great deal of time to his God. In a memoir of his life a little story is told of his missionary activity towards his brother, then a mere child:

> Christopher's heart now yearned with pity over his brother William, who still remained in distress of soul, shut up in unbelief; and while the company were taking tea, he had him, unperceived by any, into another room, and there prayed with him, and for him, till his timid and wounded spirit was enabled to repose a believing trust in Him of whom it is said, 'A bruised reed shall he not break, and smoking flax shall he not quench, till he send forth judgment unto victory.' When William found that his load of guilt was gone, and that his soul was strangely filled with peace and joy, Christopher was in raptures; and, running to his mother, exclaimed, 'O mother, all your children are converted to God!'[130]

Sadly, as Christopher was preparing to enter the family business, the first signs of tuberculosis began to show themselves. After an illness which he bore prayerfully and uncomplainingly, he died on 6 February 1836 in the sixteenth year of his age, and was the first person to be interred in the burial-ground at Oxford Place. Exactly twenty years later at York Castle his brother William, convicted of murder, was dangling at the end of a rope.

William's conversion had not lasted long, and his perplexed parents, whose faith in the Lord must have been bitterly tested by being left with William in place of Christopher, tried one means after another to get him to settle down and make something of his life. A succession of schools and colleges showed him to be an unpredictable, unpleasant dunce; his father abandoned any hope of training him up to the leather business, and in desperation apprenticed him to a farmer. William showed no more aptitude for this work than he had for his books, and emigrated to America, but after two years he was home again, and there seemed no other possibility but to establish him on a farm of his own and hope for a miracle. Perhaps marriage would stabilise his character? In 1851 he met a young lady of the same age and of respectable family from Plymouth, Harriet Jenkins, who was staying with friends at Apperley Bridge. Harriet's father was connected with the leather trade, and her brother, who was later to marry William's sister, regarded the alliance with the Doves as an honour. So in 1852 William and Harriet were married, and returned to Bramham, outside Leeds, to live on the young man's farm. It was not a successful union. Despite moments of kindness and playfulness, William's behaviour was often brutal and violent, and he drank, while Harriet nagged. They were so unhappy that Mrs Jenkins came up from Plymouth to try to arrange a separation, but unfortunately for her daughter, she was talked out of it. William went from bad to worse; in August 1854 he was actually taken into custody for threatening his father and attempting self-destruction, and soon afterwards he took up with Henry Harrison, a sinister character known as 'the Leeds Wizard'. On Christmas Eve old Mr Dove died, in deep trouble of spirit over his wayward child; his bequest to William was tied up in a way that struck contemporaries as peculiar, since the money was put in trust for his maintenance and support, the income to be payable to his wife or other persons 'thereby to secure as far as possible his personal enjoyment thereof and prevent the same from becoming the property of any alienee'. With an assured income, the young couple gave up the attempt at farming and moved into the city, to a house in Cardigan Place.

Early in 1856 William Dove was showing an obsessive interest in the Staffordshire poisoner William Palmer, whose recent trial and conviction had been headline news. In February he went to Mr Morley's surgery in Park Square to buy ten grains of strychnine to kill the cats which frequented his yard. A grey and white cat died on 15 February, and Dove went back for five more grains. Harriet Dove fell ill, with strange 'twitches' and convulsions which came and went painfully for a week. Mr Morley, a premier Leeds surgeon who had been treating her since December for slight disorders of the stomach and nervous system, was puzzled by these new and violent symptoms, and prescribed dark, bitter anti-spasmodic medicines. On Saturday 1 March Mrs Dove was well enough to take a mutton chop for tea. At about twenty to eight in the evening, in the presence of Jane Witham, a neighbour, and Mary Wood, an old servant of the Dove family, William Dove gave his wife a dose of medicine, carefully washing out the glass afterwards. 'Oh dear, it is very disagreeable and very hot,' complained Harriet, asking Mrs Whitham for a peppermint lozenge to take the taste away. Half an hour later the poor woman was in agony, her back arched, her eyes protruding, and dreadful moans issuing from between her clenched teeth. William, who smelt of porter, went for medical aid, but by the time Mr Morley reached his patient all was over: Harriet Dove was dead. She was buried on 5 March, not at Oxford Place with other members of the Dove family, but in an unmarked grave at Beckett Street Cemetery; in a possibly deliberate attempt at obfuscation to confound sensation-seekers, Burial and Grave Registers do not correspond, and there is now no means of telling where she lies.

The inquest opened at Fleischmann's Hotel, Leeds, on 7 March, with the finger of suspicion laid heavily on William Dove. Although the Coroner, Mr Blackburn, was at pains to point out that an inquest was merely an inquiry to establish the cause of death, there was at that time an obligation on the Coroner's jury to name any person found guilty of causing that death, and on the Coroner to commit such person for trial. The atmosphere was, therefore, electric. Mrs Whitham, Mrs Wood and Mrs Fisher (the mother of the Doves' servant-girl, who had been helping out while her daughter was poorly at home) all testified with only minor inconsistencies to the attacks that Mrs Dove had suffered during her last week, to the food and medicines which she had ingested, and to the fact that her husband kept poison for cats in the razor-case in his bedroom. Mr Morley and Mr Nunneley described Mrs Dove's condition and detailed the findings of their post-mortem examination; their evidence was so lucid and competent that it earned praise from the national press, and when doubt was cast on the accuracy of chemical analysis to prove the presence of strychnine they proceeded to a further series of experiments in which, with the contents of poor Harriet's stomach, they poisoned two mice, two rabbits and a guinea-pig. Both Mr Morley's pupil, John Elletson, and the surgery boy, James Peacock, recalled conversations Dove had had with them about the poison used by Palmer and the possibility of concealing the use of strychnine. Henry Harrison caused a furore with his account of Dove's asking him, on the Thursday after Harriet's death, whether a grain and a half of strychnine could be detected. 'I said, "Why, have you given your wife some?" He said, "No, but I may have spilt some."' (Sensation.) Dove was reported by Mr Morley and by another pupil to have insisted that his wife had forbidden a post-mortem in the event of her death (a claim directly contradicted by the servant-girl), and this, coupled with his later anxiety to discover from the doctors whether any poison had been found, was most damaging. There was not much Mr Barret, defending, could do for his client other than to try to shake the medical evidence and suggest heart disease or tetanus as the cause of death, but this line was firmly rebutted.

On 17 March the Coroner summed up. If the evidence before the jury satisfied them that Harriet Dove had died of poison, they must decide whether she had taken her own life, or whether the poison had been administered accidentally, or whether it had been given deliberately. Expressing his opinion that there was no reason at all to suppose the case was one of suicide, and drawing attention to the claim that the strychnine had been kept safely in the razor-case, he felt that the jury must turn their attention to the third possibility. Carefully, point by point, he went once more through the evidence which had been laid before them.

> If you are satisfied that strychnia was the cause of death, it will be your duty to say that it was designedly administered to her by some one; and considering the fact of the prisoner being in possession of the poison and the further fact, that he must have been present when the poison was given, you will have to determine whether, under all the circumstances of the case, you can have any reasonable doubt that he administered it to his wife on the night of her death. If he did not administer it, can any other person be suggested? If not, if all the world be excluded except the prisoner, you must find a verdict of wilful murder against him.

The jury retired at ten past one, and it took them only half an hour to reach a conclusion. 'We find that HARRIET DOVE HAS DIED FROM THE EFFECTS OF STRYCHNIA, WILFULLY ADMINISTERED BY HER HUSBAND, WILLIAM DOVE.' (Sensation.)

As the Coroner had explained, the inquest was not a trial, and that ordeal had still to be undergone. William Dove was tried for his life at York in July,[131] and witness after witness came forward to state that the prisoner was not of sound mind. Here is Richard Hiley, who taught the eleven-year-old for a year at his school in Leeds: 'I had reason to suspect that he was not "altogether there". He was not generally teachable. His conduct was generally very bad, and he was fond of mischief for its own sake,' and, significantly, 'He was regardless of the consequences of his own acts – in fact he appeared to be deprived of reason.' William was expelled for purchasing a pistol with the declared intention of shooting his father and Mr Hiley. His next school, again for only a year, was the Wesley College in Sheffield, and the former Principal, Revd John Manners, came to York to testify. 'He put on a sort of vacant stare, and it appeared as though it was of very little consequence whether he was chastised or not. I believe his parents were requested to remove him. I can't recollect why.' Revd William Lord, of Woodhouse Grove School, had attempted to give him religious instruction.

> He listened quietly, but I could get no rational answer. His father consulted me as to how he should deal with him in his will. The prisoner was not at that time in a state to deal rationally with any amount of property. He could not be introduced into company without great mortification to the family, on account of the state of his mind ... He was irrational, he could not follow up an action to its result.

Mr Lord had attempted to intervene with Miss Jenkins' brother in order to prevent her becoming Mrs William Dove.

Vicious, crazy and sometimes drunken freaks were described by his acquaintances and colleagues. Farmer Aaron Frankish, to whom he had been apprenticed, spoke of kittens blinded by vitriol, fences burnt down, cows strung up with ropes by their hind legs to beams, cats painted with phosphorus to make them glow. James Shann, who had also tried to teach William farming, testified to his obsessive fear of burglars and his dangerous ways with loaded guns. Housemaid Emma Spence's life had been threatened, and she had seen Harriet flee next door while William put a pistol into his mouth and then fired it out of the window to deter the non-existent but ever-expected intruders. Mary Peck, the housekeeper, had had her cap set on fire – on her head. His words were as irrational as his actions; the Normanton schoolmaster and brewer Joseph Abbott told the court, 'He once told me a rambling story about some black potatoes; but the story was so monstrous that I could not believe it.'

Mr Bliss, his defending counsel, pleaded: 'It is more just and merciful to take care of him, than to put an irresponsible agent like an insane man to death.' William Dove could, under the Criminal Lunatics Act of 1800, have been acquitted on grounds of insanity and detained in a suitable place, but the York jury, though recommending him to mercy on the grounds of defective intellect, found him guilty of wilful murder, and appeals to the

Home Secretary failed to save him from the gallows. In the condemned cell he was visited for the last time by his family, and in traditional style the *Leeds Mercury* offered its public the aged mother's convulsive sobbing, the clerical brother-in-law's fervent prayers, the prisoner on his knees for forgiveness. The newspaper printed, too, William's 'FULL CONFESSION',[132] in which he admitted the crime, but laid a good deal of the blame on Henry Harrison for casting his horoscope and promising him, if he got rid of his first wife, a second who would have auburn hair, a light complexion and a good fortune. The execution, which to modern eyes seems most unjustified, took place at noon on Saturday 9 August 1856.

It was not long before the Leeds Wizard got his comeuppance. In October[133] he was prosecuted on three charges, namely: obtaining 6d by fortune-telling, obtaining 5s by undertaking to restore a girl's sweetheart to her, and committing a rape upon her person. A rather foolish twenty-year-old, Eliza Croft, in service at the New Cross public house in Meadow Lane, had gone to Harrison's house at South Market to ask him to put a spell on her young man, John Stephenson, whose attentions had decreased in fervour. In the eerie room, with its mysterious egg-shaped pieces of glass, astrological cards and books on fortune-telling, the wizard propositioned her; the spell for which she had paid could not work unless she bestowed her favours on him. Eliza refused, Stephenson remained neglectful, and the silly girl persisted in going to Harrison to ask for help until she was assaulted, after which the story spread like wildfire and she lost her place. A private prosecution was then instigated, paid for by public subscription, for until 1879 the office of Director of Public Prosecutions did not exist; an aggrieved person had to bear the cost, inconvenience and lost time of bringing his own prosecution (which might well fail over some technicality) or lick his wounds in silence. Harrison attempted to besmirch Eliza's reputation by falsely claiming that she had come to consult him over 'a loathsome disease', and more fairly defended himself by producing the well-attested alibi of a pub-crawl to Colton and back. Everything hinged on the timing, and Eliza's evidence was shaky, for she claimed at first that the rape had taken place at seven in the evening, with candles burning, and then changed her story to midday; but her uncertainty did not help Harrison. Mr Lupton, the examining magistrate, speaking of her 'great want of comprehension, and an almost entire absence of the knowledge of time', simply attributed the discrepancy to the lack of education among the poorer classes of Leeds, and sentenced Harrison to nine months' hard labour for deception and rape.

The salacious details of the trial aroused great interest, although the *Mercury* declined to print them all, and the females in the gallery over the Bench at the Courthouse were sent out during certain exchanges. 'As soon as this part of the evidence was closed, the doors were thrown open, and they again rushed in with an eagerness, which drew down upon them the unmistakeable disapprobation of the great body of the men in the gallery, who hissed them loudly.' Feelings ran strongly against Harrison; one of the subscribers to the prosecution fund was the wife of a police constable who was supposed to be his friend. The verdict was greeted with tremendous enthusiasm. Better-educated citizens disapproved strongly of Henry Harrison, whilst the credulous mob attributed to him evil beyond his actual powers, and his part in Harriet Dove's death was not forgotten. The *Schadenfreude* rose to a peak when, the following month, the Leeds Wizard was convicted of bigamy.[134] Jane Harrison, *née* Brayshaw, a 'meanly-attired, middle-aged woman' came to testify that she had married him at the Parish Church in 1833; he had acquired a second Mrs Harrison at Rothwell in 1846 and a third at Wakefield four years later. Penal servitude for four years was his punishment, and this unsavoury person fades from our pages.

An important role in the downfall of the Leeds Wizard in 1856 was played by the police. Law and order had once been maintained by parish constables – unpaid, annually elected citizens, sometimes less than eager to serve. Large towns later paid a 'Watch' to guard the streets, especially at night; these men, known familiarly as 'Charleys', were not always noted for their youth and vigour. The tremendous increase in urban population from the early 1800s demanded a more professional force, and London established the model in 1829 under the Metropolitan Police Act. In 1835 the Municipal Corporations Act, which in Leeds replaced the previous undemocratic merchant oligarchy with an elected Council, made it obligatory for all incorporated boroughs to establish police forces under a Watch Committee, and the County and Borough Police Act of 1856 compelled the setting up of such forces throughout the country. The men recruited in Leeds under the 1835 Act, earning 18*s* a week, were expected to be literate, even-tempered, honest, sober, active and intelligent, and at least 5 feet 7 inches tall; even more difficult, they were required to deposit £3 in case they succumbed to a sudden temptation to run off with the uniform of top hat, white duck trousers and military-style blue coat provided.[135] Like so many nineteenth-century institutions, what was intended as an improvement aroused alarm over the burden on the rates and the possible infringement of personal liberties; when the newspapers had occasion to praise the conduct and usefulness of the early force, they often did so in terms of faint surprise.

In 1843 Leeds and Hunslet were organised into three divisions. 'A' Division, with headquarters first at the Town Hall and later at Millgarth Street (where the charming Victorian building was destroyed in the 1980s and today's monolithic West Yorkshire HQ looms up over the rubble), covered areas to the west of Briggate (the main north–south street); 'B' Division took in some eastern areas (including Burmantofts) and extended south of the Aire; 'C', with its main station at Sheepscar, filled in the segment between these two, while 'D', added in 1869, covered Wortley in the southwest. The number of men employed, including headquarters staff, was 279 in 1869, which was reckoned at one policeman to 787 inhabitants. The loyalty of the officers was not only to the force in general, but also to their own division, proudly indicated on gravestones at Beckett Street Cemetery, like that of William Thackrah in 1900: 'Late Inspector, Leeds City Police A Division. Joined the Force 1857, Retired 1894. BELOVED IN LIFE, IN DEATH NOT FORGOTTEN.'

The task of the Leeds police was made easier in 1868 by a marvellous new development: the stations were linked by telegraph. Readers of the *Mercury* learnt of this apropos of the drowning in June of a young cartman, Thomas Horner. That evening a reporter called at the Town Hall to enquire whether the body had been recovered, and the somewhat perfunctory regret in his account is overwhelmed by the novelty of the occasion. Every word of the pedestrian communication is excitedly retailed:

In reply to the query the officer on duty stated that he did not know, but courteously said that he would inquire immediately. He then signalled the Hunslet police station, and the response 'All right' speedily came. 'Has the body been found?' asked the officer. 'Yes' was the reply without hesitation, 'and removed to his parents' home in Snowdrop-walk, Bank.' Supplementing the six o'clock telegram, the operator at Hunslet added, 'He was drowned whilst bathing.' 'What is his age?' again asked the officer at the central station. 'Twenty-two', was the answer from Hunslet, and the communication was then closed. The operation – which did not occupy more than five minutes – was a striking indication of the immense benefit these police telegraph wires will be in the event of any sudden and serious disaster, such as a fire, requiring speedy additional assistance, occurring in any of the suburbs, and the step that has been taken by the Corporation in having them fixed is one that must be viewed with great satisfaction.

Another police duty in the nineteenth century was fire-fighting. The horse-drawn engines were stationed at various points, including the Town Hall, and there was some friction between the police and the private brigades maintained by the various insurance companies, particularly when there was a question of a £10 gratuity being awarded to the first brigade to reach the fire! Early manual pumps required thirty-four men to work them, but the Corporation's first 'steamer', purchased in 1876, was a great improvement, delivering 150 gallons a minute to the height of the Town Hall clock; 1910 saw the first motor engine, and by 1922 all the horses had gone.[136] The men were regarded as policemen rather than firemen, as can be seen from the following obituary of 1868:

SUDDEN DEATH OF A LEEDS POLICE INSPECTOR. – Mr. Frankland, who was well known in connection with the fire brigade of the Leeds Corporation, died very suddenly yesterday at his own residence. He had been a member of the police force for the long period of 27 years, and for the last 10 years had filled the post of sub-inspector.

George Frankland, aged fifty-four, who had joined only a few years after the Leeds force had been set up, is entered in the Burial Register as 'police inspector'. It was not until 1948 that the Fire Brigade became a separate institution.

Traffic control was another police function, with a policeman stationed at the south end of Briggate as early as 1878 to help pedestrians through the heavy cross-traffic. Ewart Clay, in *The Leeds Police 1836–1974*, gives the figures for 1911 of people killed by vehicles in central Leeds: ten killed by motor and four by horse-drawn vehicles, four by tramcars, totalling eighteen. In 1928 the first automatic traffic lights in Britain were installed at the junction of Park Row and Bond Street.

The first port of call for the arrested drunk or vagrant, or the malefactor apprehended *in flagrante delicto*, was the police lock-up, originally at the Court House. From 1858 it was in the new Town Hall, and it was here that little John William Lanigan died, because even in a police cell a Victorian child was a private and not a public responsibility. His mother was taken into custody in Meadow Lane one Saturday night in 1866 after falling down with him, so helplessly drunk that two policemen had to 'paddle' her to the Town Hall, while the seven-week-old baby was carried by a passer-by. At the lock-up the child was given into the care of another prisoner, but cried so much (no doubt from hunger and discomfort) that he was given back to his mother. Five hours later she was thought to have sobered up enough to give her name and address and was removed to the office for that purpose, where it was discovered that John William was dead, accidentally suffocated, as Mr Price the surgeon discovered, by his snoring, reeking, intoxicated parent.

The prisoner who had a case to answer would appear before the magistrates at the Quarter Sessions, or, for a more serious offence, before a judge and jury at the Assizes. If found guilty of one of the capital offences, by mid-century reduced from a large number of crimes to the four of murder, treason, piracy and arson in the royal dockyards, he would be hanged (but not, after 1868, in public); if convicted of something lesser, he might be sent to gaol or fined. The reluctance of the colonies to continue to accept endless drafts of British convicts led to a reduction from 1841 in the number of criminals sentenced to be transported, and the substitution of sentences of penal servitude; transportation was finally abandoned in 1867. Meanwhile, the government convict prison at Pentonville had been built in 1842 to the new single-cell design, and during the decade some fifty local prisons were constructed or remodelled along similar lines. One of these was the Leeds Borough Gaol, which, although intended to serve its own locality and financed out of the borough rate, rented some of its cells to central government before the nationalisation of the entire prison system in 1877.[137] White's 1853 Directory reports on this new institution, completed six years previously at a cost of £40,000:

> This extensive prison is pleasantly situated near Armley, on the south side of the picturesque valley of the Aire, more than a mile W. of the town. It is of massive masonry, and its numerous cells and wards are constructed according to the most improved system of prison discipline. It has a noble castellated appearance when viewed at a distance, and is second to none of its class in the kingdom.

Mayhall[138] adds that there are about 334 separate cells, in which the prisoners follow the occupations to which they have been accustomed, or, if without a trade, pick oakum or make matting to defray the cost of the ratepayers' hospitality. Today the fierce, squat Norman castle still dominates its surroundings but, despite extensions, it is now one of the most overcrowded prisons in Britain, and its 1,000 inmates doubtless find it neither pleasant nor picturesque.

In the early years of the gaol's existence, prisoners who died before completing their sentence were sometimes buried at Beckett Street Cemetery. The first of these, as will be seen from Appendix D, Part 3, was in every way typical of the inmates of the prison in the middle years of the century. Jesse Goodrich, aged twenty-four and single, was an almost illiterate labourer who received a seven-year sentence at the Central Criminal Court on 3 January 1848 for larceny (his third conviction). He was sent to Leeds Borough Gaol in July, but he never completed his sentence, for he died, and was buried on 7 May 1849. Larceny was one of the commonest of Victorian crimes, when offences against property were not viewed with the unhappy resignation which they seem to command today; David Philips, in a study in *Crime and Authority in Victorian England* of committals for trial in the Black Country between 1835 and 1860, finds that 78.9 per cent were for this offence.[139] Those who did not die were released to offend again – or perhaps not; a *Mercury* journalist covered the visit to the prison of the Bishop of Ripon in April 1855,[140] and was much struck by the tears which coursed down the cheeks of many male and female inmates during the episcopal address. 'We cannot but feel convinced that the system of prison discipline which can produce such results as were apparent in the whole conduct and demeanour of the prisoners on this occasion, must of necessity exercise a most salutory influence on the after lives of a large number of those who are subjected to it.'

There must be many buried at Beckett Street Cemetery who have taken unknown criminal histories to the merciful silence of the grave. Those which come to light here are, of course, only those which are connected with death, and our city study must, in this respect, give a distorted picture. The newspapers are full of shoplifting, cruelty to horses, arson, bigamy, pocket-picking, vitriol-throwing and even violent assaults by mushroom gatherers, but we must restrict ourselves to murder, homicide (such as we have seen in the 'Irish Row'), suicide and one or two rarer crimes.

Inquests on suicides were often reported in the newspapers of the day. Suicide was a crime, and therefore doubly newsworthy; if the perpetrator survived his attempt, he could be tried for it. Of eighty-one inquests held before the Leeds Borough Coroner and reported in the *Mercury* between 1866 and 1868 whose subjects lie in the cemetery, nine brought in a verdict of *felo de se*. The reasons for the crime generally fall into simple categories:

30. Leeds Borough Gaol at Armley, as it appeared in the late 1840s.

delusions, business worries, health problems and drink or drugs. Joseph Haigh, a well-known and respected chemist and druggist of fifty-two whose place of business was in Briggate, believed himself to be in pecuniary difficulties, and no amount of reasoning by his family and friends could dissuade him, so one Sunday morning, on his usual visit to his shop to open the letters delivered that day, he swallowed a large dose of prussic acid. Mr Nunneley, who was passing, was too late to save him. The solicitor who was asked by the Coroner to examine Mr Haigh's books reported sadly that 'there was nothing in the state of his accounts to warrant the delusion with which the deceased had been haunted'. John Priestley, a former miner who was thirty-eight years of age and partially paralysed, eked out a living by supplying mill-hands with coffee from a stall on a piece of vacant land near his house; one day he was told the land was required for development, and was ordered to move. He fastened a rope to a projecting stair-end in his cellar, and hanged himself. Poor Matthew Atkin, aged fifty-nine, suffered from failing eyesight, fatal to his trade of tailoring, and in his depression went down to the cellar and cut his throat. John Cooke, an alcoholic weaver, hanged himself from his own loom with a hank of worsted thread while in a fit of delirium tremens; he left a wife and six children, presumably to the workhouse. An engine driver in the service of the Midland Railway Company, Samuel Birchall, who was addicted to opium and gambling, succeeded in doing away with himself despite the attentions of Mr Ruddock and his colleague Mr Woodhead with emetics ('when these remedies were being persisted in, the deceased swore energetically at Mr. Woodhead, and endeavoured to strike him') and the stomach-pump.

Haigh, Atkin, Cooke and Birchall are all buried in the Consecrated portion of the cemetery. *Things you ought to know, clearly explained*, a most helpful Victorian vademecum,[141] elucidates the situation after the passage of the Interments (*Felo de Se*) Act of 1882:

> Suicide 'while of unsound mind' is not a disqualification for Christian burial, which can only be refused to those suicides who are presumed to have been of sound mind when the act was committed. Formerly, when a verdict of 'felo-de-se' was recorded, the suicide was buried at cross roads, or in some lone place indicative of degradation; but that course is no longer legal, and the burial ground, even though consecrated, must receive the body if required to do so.

In 1849 Elizabeth Goy, a twenty-four-year-old prostitute who had left a husband in Hull to cohabit with a fish hawker and fiddler named Brown, was found by the latter, on his return after an eighteen-hour absence, violently ill in bed. After half an hour she admitted that she had taken poison; she continued to get worse, and died the same day. At the inquest,

> it was stated by a female who lives next door, that she had accompanied the deceased on the Wednesday to the shop of a druggist at the end of Cornhill, where she purchased and took home a pennyworth of arsenic, which she said she wanted for the purpose of killing black beetles, which swarmed in the house. This person did not leave her till ten o'clock at night, when she appeared to be in her usual health, and in excellent spirits. Nothing transpired during the day to excite the least suspicion either of insanity on the part of the deceased, or the intention of destroying herself. The jury under the

circumstance felt themselves justified in returning a verdict of 'Felo-de-se'. The remains of the deceased were interred in the Burmantofts Cemetery, between eleven and twelve o'clock on the night of Thursday, without the observance of any religious ceremony.

Although she was accepted into the Consecrated portion, Elizabeth Goy clearly did *not* receive a Christian burial; she was shovelled into the ground under cover of darkness, with no words of hope or consolation to mark her passing.

Since the end of Victoria's reign, the suicide rates have shown no dramatic change; the Mortality Statistics of the Office of Population Censuses & Surveys (Serial Tables 1841–1980) inform us that an annual average of 101 people per million took their lives in the years 1901–5, while in 1977 the figure stood at 80 per million. The stresses and strains which drive people over the verge today are an unwelcome link with our Victorian past.[142]

The epidemic of 'child abuse' in this century, too, has its counterpart in our vignettes from the past. An unsavoury couple called Motterham deserted their five children in 1864; first the husband disappeared, then the wife decamped with another man, leaving 'an infant at the breast' on a neighbour's doorstep. Henry Motterham was found and brought to book four years later on a charge of neglecting his family, but in the meantime his children, abandoned without any means of subsistence, had ended up variously in the workhouse and at the cemetery. He was sentenced to three months in prison.[143]

The child carried by Hannah Collins, an Irish beggarwoman, when she was intercepted at the top of Briggate by a bunch of excited women on a spring day in 1856, must have been a sorry sight. Four-year-old Patrick was only thirty inches long, a dribbling cretin with thrush and scaldhead, his teeth rotting in his swollen gums, his right wrist dislocated, and his small body apparently legless. The mother and her three children were sitting on a step in Green Dragon Yard, two of the little ones crying with hunger, when Fanny Ellis, wife of an upholsterer living in the Yard, gave her some bread and butter and asked where the child's legs were. Elizabeth Dykes, her outspoken neighbour, wife of a coachman, said the little boy should be taken to a doctor, and then, looking closer, exclaimed: 'Dear me, what have you the child's legs tied up in that way for?' Underneath the ragged wrappings the emaciated limbs were drawn up to the chest and fastened with tape across the knees and under the arms, and there were marks like pinpricks in the flesh. Mrs Dykes snatched Patrick from his mother and handed him to Mary Longbottom, the daughter of the Green Dragon's landlord, who took off the tape and tried to straighten the legs, but the child cried and resisted, drawing them back up to his body. With Mrs Collins screaming abuse, the women searched her and found a large pin, which she claimed she used for pinning her shawl. By this time Mr Gawthorne, a Town Missionary, had joined them, and they got the attention of a policeman who marched the Irishwoman off to the Court House on a charge of gross cruelty, while Mary Longbottom carried the miserable bundle to the Workhouse, where it was examined by Mr W.S. Taylor. Weak and ill, his mouth full of sores, little Patrick gradually sank; five days later he died, and joined the quota of Workhouse corpses in common grave 5607. Meanwhile Hannah had been sent to prison for three months and her husband, an out-of-work farm labourer – 'who, there is reason to believe, has been living on the fruits of his wife's mendicancy, and the torture of his child', was rather unrealistically ordered to pay 5s a week towards the cost of keeping his children in the Workhouse.

The inquest, in the boardroom of the Workhouse, was attended by a Catholic priest on behalf of the Collins family, and opened, under the chilly gaze of the portraits of past Guardians, with evidence in their support. Mary M'Laughlin said Hannah had only gone out begging for the past few months, while her husband had been poorly. Hannah was a good, kind and attentive mother, and Mary had never seen her tie the boy up; he lay naturally with his legs upon his chest. 'I was very much surprised to hear that she had been charged with behaving ill to the child, for I took her to be a very affectionate mother that did all she could for the child.' Elizabeth Kershaw, too, had never seen the legs bandaged, and testified that there was always a bit of linen laid between legs and chest to prevent chafing.

> The child appeared quite destitute of intellect. It was always remarkably clean. She appeared to treat the child with kindness. Whenever she put the knees down a little the child always cried, and drew them back again ... I often felt surprised at its living so long, and once said so, when she said, 'The great God who gave it would take it in his own good time.'

The object of the inquest, as stated by Mr Blackburn, the Coroner, was to establish the extent of the cruelty practised on the child, by whom it had been inflicted, and whether or not it amounted to a criminal act which would render the perpetrator liable to a charge of manslaughter. Mr Taylor, the Workhouse surgeon, was prepared to stake his reputation on the cause of death. He had examined Patrick when he was brought to the Workhouse, and had found the head and mouth in a shocking state and the boy suffering from mesenteric disease. 'On the left leg there were a great many marks, produced by a pin or sharp pointed instrument. These marks were so many that the leg looked like a pincushion. The places had bled. The legs were up, and the arms crooked. Upon straightening the legs and arms the child began to whine – it had not strength to cry.' He was strongly of the opinion – despite John Collins' evidence that the child kept his arms close to his side, driving them against his ribs when in convulsions, and roaring when they were prised away – that the arms, as well as the legs, had been strapped up. The cramping of the lungs and heart would account for all the other conditions, including the lack of speech. On the final day of the hearing the big guns were brought in, in the shape of Mr Samuel Smith, Senior Surgeon at the Infirmary and a gentleman of considerable prestige, who agreed with everything Mr Taylor had said except for the most important part of his evidence. As far as Mr Smith was concerned, the child was born an idiot and his malformations were largely due to rickets; an opinion to which Mr Taylor had gracefully to yield. The Coroner felt that it would be a waste of time to continue with the case (although, surprisingly, the matter of the pinpricks was not pursued, Mr Blackburn commenting that it was 'very suspicious, but that was all'). It was always possible that she had been putting on a cunning act, but there was plenty of evidence to show that Hannah Collins had been a loving mother to Patrick and none that she had deliberately crippled and pricked him to aid her in her cadging; in view of the difference of opinion in the medical profession, it would be going too far to deprive her of her liberty on a charge of causing his death. The jury returned a verdict of 'Died from natural causes', and the sobbing mother was taken back to prison to complete her original sentence.

Young, defenceless children suffered at the hands of mercenary or sadistic employers, none more so than the climbing-boys; it took thirty years for Lord Shaftesbury's campaign against the use of child chimney-sweeps to achieve its objectives. The Act of Parliament of 1840 was a dead letter, as was that of 1864, since most people fancied that the sweeping-machines would drop more soot than the boys did, or objected to having to have their chimneys widened to take the machinery. A master-sweep from Nottingham gave evidence to the Children's Employment Commission in 1863. 'I have myself lost a great amount of custom which I should otherwise have ... I have been sent away even from magistrates' houses, and in some cases even by ladies who have professed to pity the boys, for refusing to use them ... I did for a time try to bring up one of my own children to it, but my wife and I felt that we could not stand it any longer, and that we would sooner go to the workhouse than suffer what we did from it.' He continued by describing the methods used to toughen the boys' skin.

> This is done by rubbing it, chiefly on the elbows and knees, with the strongest brine, as that got from a pork-shop, close by a hot fire. You must stand over them with a cane, or coax them by promise of a halfpenny, etc. if they will stand a few more rubs. At first they will come back from their work with their arms and knees streaming with blood, and the knees looking as if the caps had been pulled off. Then they must be rubbed with brine again, and perhaps go off at once to another chimney.[144]

The children often slept, black and verminous as they were, under their soot sacks, and in addition to the deformities produced by the climbing and the tortures of the brine, they were subject to tuberculosis and to a particularly unpleasant form of cancer.

In 1851, twelve years before the Nottingham sweep's testimony, twelve-year-old George Wilson had died in the flue, one foot square, of a brick-kiln in Hunslet, his cap tumbled off his head and his mouth stuffed with soot. It was the tenth chimney he had swept that day; the sweep who accompanied him, Christopher Sheerin, had not brought a machine with him. The Coroner's jury returned an open verdict of 'Found suffocated', but the employer, Benjamin Gozard of York Street, was summoned before magistrates at the Court House two weeks later under the 1840 Act, which laid down fines for persons allowing or compelling youths under twenty-one to sweep chimneys. Seven charges, relating to seven of the chimneys, had been laid. The two magistrates could not agree as to whether Gozard knew Sheerin had no machine with him, and the master-sweep was acquitted; five of the charges against Sheerin were withdrawn, and he was fined £20 on the other two; Taylor, the foreman at the brickworks, who had allowed George to go up the flues, was fined £5.[145] It was to be a generation longer before the death of another boy in identical circumstances near Cambridge proved to be the catalyst which brought about the 1875 Act of Parliament, providing for the annual licensing of sweeps and the end of what has been called 'the long agony of the climbing boys'.

The Motterham children and George Wilson, if not Patrick Collins, were victims of the selfishness and greed of the grown-ups around them; Laura Eliza Thurkill paid the penalty of her own folly in submitting herself to a Victorian abortionist in order to get rid of an unwanted child. This sleazy case illustrates how dispassionately conviction or acquittal could hang on the exact interpretation of the law. Miss Thurkill, a 'professional singer' from Hull, aged twenty-one, was living with a commission agent named Bigger in Fenton Street, and passing herself off as his wife; they had one child. One December evening in 1868 she left the house, telling him that she was going to the baths; it was nearly midnight when she returned in a cab, so ill that she had to be helped to bed. The next day a surgeon, Mr Hayward, was called in, who was so perturbed at what he found that he summoned the magistrates' clerk to her bedside to take her deposition. The sordid story which emerged concerned the payment of £5 to a cleaning-woman, Mrs Jackson, for the name and address of midwife Sarah Barrett (alias 'Mrs Varley') and a further payment to Barrett for an abortion, procured with instruments. This was a felony, punishable by penal servitude for life; but meanwhile Laura Thurkill, who had been improving, suffered a relapse, and crying hysterically 'Don't let me die, Mr Hayward!' she expired, thereby altering the charge to one of murder. Sarah Barrett was brought up at the Spring Assizes before Mr Justice Cleasby on 29 March 1869,[146] where evidence was produced that a woman and a little girl had directed a person of the deceased's description to Barrett's house in Wellington Lane, and that the cabbie Charles Scott had later picked her up, very ill, from nearby, and taken her back to Fenton Street. It was also stated that Miss Thurkill had, on her deathbed (albeit hesitantly, and not until the midwife took her bonnet off), identified Sarah Barrett as the abortionist. Mrs Barrett strenuously denied ever having met the deceased before being taken to the death-chamber, and Mrs Jackson, the cleaner who was supposed to have supplied the introduction, piously declared that she herself had a large family and had advised her employer not to contemplate such a wicked act. However, it was not on the strength of these denials that the midwife (who, it transpired, had narrowly escaped conviction on a similar charge before) was acquitted, but on a technicality: Laura Thurkill's deposition was not admissible, because it was taken in support of the charge of procuring an abortion, which was not the charge (murder) now being pursued. Nor, for the same reason, could her evidence be used in the form of a 'dying declaration'; in any case it did not qualify as such, since she had frequently asked the surgeon if she would live, and therefore could not have been 'under the solemn feeling that the hand of death was upon her'! Mrs Barrett, or Mrs Varley, walked free from the court, to pursue her unsavoury and sometimes lethal calling.

There is no credit, either, in the behaviour of the adults who wrapped a tiny body in a towel and hid it in the toolshed at the back of the North Lodge at Beckett Street Cemetery one wet, wild night in April 1865, while the Registrar, Jabez Tunnicliff, lay feeble and senile within the house.[147] William Henry, Jabez' son, a commission agent aged twenty-seven, married with a son of six and a daughter four years old, had been carrying on the clerical side of his father's work during his last illness – and carrying on with the servant, Selina Hollings, at the same time. Selina's father was a widower who worked as warehouseman in a flax mill and whose house was kept by a very elderly widowed sister. Perhaps it was the lack of a mother's guiding care which allowed Selina to stray into the primrose paths of dalliance with her employer's son, with the inevitable consequences. One evening she went to the house of Mrs Waite, Jabez' married daughter, to work a sewing machine, and when that lady noticed that she did not appear quite herself, she confessed that she was in the family way by Mrs Waite's brother. Mrs Waite appears not to have been unduly surprised or upset, and, having ascertained that Selina needed no help, soon retired to bed, leaving the girl in the kitchen. At 2 a.m. she woke for some reason and went downstairs again. 'It is over,' said Selina baldly. 'Where's the child?' 'It is here' (pointing to the top of the set-pot or copper near the fire). There, on a towel, lay the cold little body of a dead child. 'No further conversation passed between us,' reported Mrs Waite later, 'and I went up to bed again.'

No house in Victorian Yorkshire was properly equipped without its set-pot. This was a square construction of brick in the kitchen, scullery or cellar, containing a firegrate below with a door for access, and a large round iron pot built in above it, in which water was heated for the weekly wash (and Christmas puddings were boiled in December). A circular wooden lid covered the hole in the flagstone topping the pot, and a flue conducted the smoke outside the house. On 12 April, while the rain poured down outside from a leaden sky, the tiny corpse lay hidden in the set-pot in a corner of Mrs Waite's dark kitchen. At nine in the morning young Tunnicliff came, and urgent words passed between him and his sister. 'You know all about it?' 'Yes, Willie, I do.' 'For God's sake don't say anything; if this gets to father's ears, it will kill him.' 'No, Willie, if no one else betrays you, I won't.' The day wore on, wet and stormy. Meanwhile William Henry had gone to the cemetery to help poor forgetful Jabez with the registers and certificates for the day's work. Nervously chewing on the end of his pen, he awaited the opportunity to speak to Joy, the gravedigger. Would Joy agree secretly to bury the evidence of sin? No, he would not, it was more than his job was worth to disobey the law and to cheat the Town Council of its shilling. At last Joy was persuaded, but he was not happy.

It was not thought fit for Selina to be out in such vile weather, and Mrs Waite accompanied her brother that night with the sad bundle. 'I believe it is customary to take stillborn children to the Cemetery by night,' she claimed afterwards. 'I took this because I did not wish my father to know anything about it. I did not take it with the intention of hiding the birth from any person but my father; but I took the body to the Cemetery at night because I did not want any person to see me. I believe there were graves open in the Cemetery at the time I took the body, and that my brother might have interred it that night.'

The baby was left in the toolhouse while Jabez' erring children went into the Lodge to see their father, and later it was gone. That, however, was not the last William Henry Tunnicliff was to hear of his child, for the gravedigger was not at ease. The little box was disinterred and taken to the police, and information was laid against Tunnicliff and Selina which resulted in their appearance that August at the Assizes in Leeds, on a charge of concealment of birth.

The first charge brought against Selina Hollings was one of wilful murder, but the sifting-out system of the time, in which a Bill of Indictment, based on the prosecution's evidence alone, had first to be laid before a Grand Jury to see whether a proper case had been made, threw this one out. The only charge which might stick was that of concealment of birth, for the male prisoner had applied to the gravedigger to bury the body and had not, as was his duty, either entered the interment in what was called the rough notice book, or charged the usual fee of 1s. Mrs Waite was the principal witness, and the *Mercury* reported her account of the conversations quoted above; the prisoners were undefended by counsel. In summing up, the judge had to point out that the charge was not well-founded. After all, Selina had openly admitted to Mrs Waite that she was pregnant; the child had been left in the toolhouse and the gravedigger had been asked to bury it, when the prisoners might have slipped it into a grave already dug. The jury must also have felt that the prosecution was skating on thin ice, for they soon returned a verdict of not guilty, but the judge had sharp words for foolish Tunnicliff:

> You have been guilty of a very gross irregularity. Your duty was to do things properly and in order, and enter in the book provided the interment of any still-born child. Though I am happy to believe that your sister and probably Joy, the gravedigger, had no improper motive, at the same time you have given rise, by your irregular conduct, to the most painful suspicions affecting your sister as well as yourself.

William Henry attempted to speak. 'No, I will not allow you to say a word,' snapped his Lordship, acquitting the couple.

Many of the evils of the Victorian city sprang from a background of poverty, ignorance and habitual crime – influences which can explain, if they cannot exonerate, the heavy case-load at Assizes and Quarter Sessions; but the case of William Henry Tunnicliff, like that of William Dove, shows a weak young man from the most moral of backgrounds 'going to the bad', a disappointment and a shame to his family. We can only be thankful that neither upright father lived to hear his name disgraced in murky gossip on every street corner in Leeds.

Chapter Ten

In Loving Memory

Death is swallowed up in Victory.

Fanny Chappell, 1863

The Hirsts, who went to the cemetery on that day in 1845 when it first opened, would be hard put to recognise it now, with its smoke-blackened walls and ancient, leaning trees, both chapels razed and their sites lying empty, thousands more gravestones packed within the area than they could ever have imagined, and yet thousands more toppled by age, vandals or improving authorities. Outside, whole terraces of small brick houses have sprung up, sheltered the lives of five or six generations within their walls, and crumbled without trace before the demolition men; avenues of trees, like those which once fronted the Workhouse, have grown to maturity and decayed, or fallen victim to road-widening. The city has engulfed Beckett Street with bricks and mortar, steel and concrete, and exploded on, out to Roundhay and Seacroft, leaving the cemetery in the inner city, with inner-city problems. From the Moral and Industrial Training School opposite, once housing and educating 500 pauper children, has grown the largest teaching hospital in Europe. Milthorp & Hodgson's yard has long gone; the police station on the corner of Stanley Road is now the 'Dock Green' pub, and drinkers have replaced the policemen to whom young Cissie Temple used to wave from the landing window. In Stanley Road itself the former Tram Depot has become Council-owned worksheds, and beyond is a large

municipal refuse disposal site. The beck has disappeared from Stoney Rock
Lane, till recently lined with industries – a prominent cleaners and dyers
(giving rise to the old chestnut that in Stoney Rock Lane you stood between
the dying and the dead ...) and the headquarters of a well-known producer
of ready-made clothing, sole legacy of the huge cloth industry which gave
employment to so many of those now at rest in the cemetery. On the fourth
side, Glebe Street has been renamed Shakespeare Street, and over it loom
the fortified concrete tower blocks, on their sterile green lawns, which have
replaced the brick back-to-back homes of a whole community. Coming
back to Beckett Street, the visitor sees the 'Florence Nightingale' pub, once
the Cemetery Tavern, sadly overtaken by today's determination to ignore
realities and sweep death under the carpet.

The tending of the family grave was formerly a duty, and on Sundays
children would accompany parents to the cemetery to clip, weed and tidy
up. Since the last war this custom has fallen into disuse. The fact that most
people die at one remove from their relatives, in hospital, and that 67 per cent
of bodies are not buried but cremated, often with the ashes subsequently
scattered, makes it harder to assimilate death and to find any meaning in the
concept of the 'last resting-place'. In the classic pattern of migration, local
residents have moved out and on to the suburbs, and the incomers who
have taken their place have no connection with the old burial-ground and,
indeed, often worship other gods in other tongues. Income from Victorian
cemeteries has shrunk to nothing; there is no more space to sell, and the
commitments of previous generations (£10 paid over to the Corporation
at the beginning of the twentieth century for 'planting in perpetuity' was
expected to ensure the tending of the grave till the Last Trump!) are seen as
impossibilities and are no longer honoured. Iron dowels rust, stones crack,
cement crumbles away. Mindless louts enjoy the evening sport of smashing
a cross, heaving the slab off a chest tomb, or spraying on gibberish with
brightly coloured aerosol paint. In a desperate effort to balance the books,
the cemetery authorities cut maintenance to a minimum, removing the
resident staff in favour of a team of gardeners who will work, in rotation, in
every cemetery in the city – but will spend least time on the old and infrequently used such as Beckett Street. Vandalism becomes worse; glue-sniffers
move in; people complain that it is no longer safe to go there. The Council
looks for a solution, and decides on clearance.

In January 1984 a small paragraph in a local advertising paper[148] informed
readers that the Municipal Services Committee had agreed on 'improve-

31. Richard and Pauline Freeman, of the Friends of Beckett Street Cemetery, in quiet reflection in 1989.

ments' to Beckett Street Cemetery. Over the following eighteen months the group which was to be named 'Friends of Beckett Street Cemetery' struggled to persuade Leeds City Council to abandon these proposals, which would have involved removing most of the memorials, flattening and turfing the site so as to facilitate mowing, and putting in a few shrubs and benches. In other parts of the country, Victorian cemeteries were being recognised as part of our local history and often, too, as important urban wildlife sites. With the help of petitions, deputations, innumerable letters and all kinds of publicity, and with the backing of local councillors and MPs and of several local and national organisations, the fight was at last won. On 25 March 1985 the proposed 'improvements' were withdrawn, and a public meeting, called by Leeds City Council in June, packed a local school hall and triumphantly demonstrated that the citizens of Leeds wanted Beckett Street Cemetery, its memorials and its wildlife, kept for their enjoyment and for their children's.

By the end of Victoria's reign Beckett Street Cemetery had received three-quarters of its eventual 180,000 burials, and the character it bears today was already stamped out. An early municipal burial-ground in a grimy northern industrial city, it offers in its physical presence the opportunity to scrutinise the conditions, tastes and attitudes of an age gone by, and to compare them with those which dictate the appearance of the Corporation cemeteries and crematoria of today.

The attraction of the Victorian cemetery springs largely from two opposing tendencies: the framework of homogeneity and the pull of individualism. The impossibility of conveying heavy materials over inadequate roads had left the churchyards of the eighteenth century dependent on local stone for memorials – slate in Devon, granite in Scotland, limestone in Derbyshire. Despite the development of rail transport and the improvements in road-making, it remained cheaper and easier to use the stone produced by the many local quarries, so that the vast majority of the memorials at Beckett Street are of Yorkshire sandstone. Although the surrounding fields were subsequently covered in the dark red brick typical of Leeds, the cemetery itself, within its walls of sooty stone eight feet high, is an entity on which the eye rests gently and with pleasure. The stone 'looks right'. It is local, and it echoes the vernacular building traditions of the West Riding. It has been there a long time, and is consequently lichened, weathered and mellowed. The settling effect is enhanced by the masses of memorials on the guinea graves, made, as we have seen, largely from stone quarried in the Bradford area, and uniform in style.

Within the homogeneity, however, are outbursts of individuality which enliven and fascinate. Apart from some minor regulations such as that of 1852 requiring that 'the most prominent part of the Bases and backs of the stones form a straight line with each other', there seems to have been little curb placed on the imagination of the commemorator – other, of course, than the depth of his or her pocket. There was no restriction on height, material, style or inscription, or even on the siting of the memorial to face east or west. Plenty of grey or pink granite was brought down from Peterhead and Aberdeen and polished to a shiny glow for monuments such as the 1868 pillar to the successful brickmaking family of Boyle, or the slabs marking the twin vaults of the Butlers, well-off painters and decorators (1879). Iron railings – rather few of these – stake out a last terrestrial claim for the residents of the tomb, and guard their privacy; lead letters glint dully forth from their weathering background. Slate, that eminently carvable stone available from Wales or Westmorland, makes a rare appearance in the memorial to Sarah Baines, where the calligraphy demonstrates both the skill of the mason and the excellence of the material; the documentation in the possession of descendants makes it clear that, although Sarah was buried in 1855, the headstone was not commissioned until 1882. The twentieth century saw the mass importation of alien marbles from Italy, and the strange wartime expedient of black 'grancotta', based on fireclay.

From the sea of headstones bursts a riot of crosses, obelisks, broken columns, box tombs, coped stones, pillars bearing angels, crocketed spires and draped urns; even the lowlier stones are carved with clasped hands, bunches of flowers, doves, crowns, lambs and cherubs. It is uncertain how far the choice of such designs was influenced by any particular attitude of mind on the part of the commemorator. Although there was a well-established traditional meaning to many of the architectural and artistic forms (the obelisk standing for eternity, the broken column and the sickle with flowers for life cut short, the inverted torch for life extinguished, the willow for mourning, the hourglass for time passing, the crown for glory, and so on), it was perfectly possible just to choose a pleasant design from the mason's book of patterns, or to ask for one like Mrs Greenwood put up last year for her Joe. Certain styles may be associated with religious affinities; the draped urn, for instance, was widely used in the Georgian churchyard as a plain decorative motif free from any taint of Popery. The common theme of the 'Rock of Ages', the woman with flowing hair and loose garments spreadeagled on a pile of rocks and clutching the base of a crucifix, is derived from the hymn written in 1775 by the Calvinist clergyman Toplady ('Nothing in my hand I bring, Simply to thy cross I cling') and might likewise be said to indicate Low Church tendencies and the abandonment of the baggage of ritual. Conversely, the reinforcement of ritualistic tendencies with the development of the Oxford Movement, the secession to Rome of noted churchmen such as Newman, the establishment in England of a Roman Catholic hierarchy, and the medievalist trend in painting and architecture, might be expected to encourage in those of a 'High' persuasion the choice of a Gothic-styled memorial. Designs of High and Low Church types can, however, be found on both Anglican and Nonconformist sides of the cemetery.

Even within the compass of a headstone of 'normal' size, room could be found for the unusual and even the slightly manic. John Thorp, who died in 1872, is commemorated by an excellent carving of a perky-looking terrier, complete with name disc. These dogs (the name derives from the Latin *terra*, earth) were skilled at rooting into burrows and tunnels after their quarry, and were popular with mill workers and miners on account of their ability to deal with the rats which infested such people's workplaces; the Yorkshire breed was first shown in Leeds in 1861. Whether John Thorp was a breeder of these dogs, or was merely particularly fond of the household pet, we do not know.

A grimmer emblem is the fireman's helmet of James Potter Schofield, killed in 1892 while trying to extinguish the fire raging at the Leeds Joint Station. The sinister brick caverns under the station, known as the Dark Arches, were used at that time as storage by various undertakings, including soap manufacturers Joseph Watson & Sons ('Soapy Joe' to Leeds people). In the early morning of 13 January a fire started in Watson's depot, which contained 1,600 tons of highly inflammable resin, oil and tallow. The men of the London, Liverpool & Globe Company's brigade, among them the brothers Jim and Bill Schofield, both bricklayers, were the first to race their team of sweating horses to the scene, but the conflagration was already beyond control. Jim took the hose from his brother; a minute or two later the platform gave way beneath him, and he plunged among the falling earth and masonry into the pit beneath, where, dazed by the dense smoke, he missed an opening which would have led to freedom, and, crawling into a blind arch, expired. Twenty-four hours later the flames had been mastered, but the debris was still smouldering; an enormous amount of damage had been done, with the eighty-five-foot span of the railway bridge over the canal in twisted ruins, tracks and girders bent and broken, rolling stock reduced to blackened skeletons. On 17 January the remains of Schofield, his charred helmet resting on his coffin, were borne to the grave, and the *Mercury* reported:

> The tragic circumstances of his death, the powerful struggle the poor fellow must have made for his life, together with the recollection of the cruel fate that but for a wrong turning he might have escaped after all, have been common subjects for talk during the last few days, and it was only to be expected that the last rites would be witnessed by a large gathering of sympathisers. But few could have been prepared for the vast tokens of interest shown.

Thousands of people lined the route to see the solemn bands leading the procession of dignitaries in forty-two mourning coaches and of fire-engines from all over Yorkshire, and at the graveside the chorus of the Grand Theatre intoned a lugubrious hymn. Later, Schofield's brothers and sisters were to have his helmet carved, in poignant commemoration, on a costly memorial.

A familiar sight a hundred years ago on the rivers and canals of Yorkshire was the stubby, square-rigged little cargo-boat known as a 'Humber Keel', and two small carvings of these vessels grace headstones at the cemetery – although, given the originals' usual dimensions of a mast almost as high as the length (fifty-five feet) of the hull, a certain amount of artistic licence has been necessary to accommodate the boat within the short triangular or rounded upper segment of the stone. The capacity of the keels was between 110 and 130 tons, and they were crewed by the skipper and a mate, some-times helped by the skipper's wife, who made a home out of the thirty square feet of the after cabin. By mid-century most skippers owned their own boats; where they did not, it was the owner's duty to maintain the vessel and the skipper's to negotiate the cargo and pay the mate, one third of the profits going to the owner. Christopher Burn, master of the *Henrietta*, was only twenty-one when he was drowned in the Ouse off Goole in 1849, and it was a month before his body was recovered and brought back to Leeds for burial. The keel could be a tricky boat to handle. When the *Edward & William*, owned by the timber merchant William Snowden and captained by his son, capsized with its load of wood at Whitton Sands in the Humber in 1885, the *Yorkshire Post* reported the loss of the vessel with all on board except for the mate, who had managed to swim ashore, but the next day there was an even more dramatic tale to tell. Mrs Snowden had not been drowned, but had been trapped in the inverted cabin for seventeen hours, the water up to her neck and three little children clinging about her, her hands raw and bloody from beating on the wooden planks, her voice hoarse with shouting for help. Mercifully Mr Barley, the master of the Whitton lightship, convinced that there was life on the stricken vessel, had persuaded the steam tug *Hecla* to investigate, and the crew had been able with painful care to cut an opening through the former bottom and haul the frozen and exhausted woman out, with her one surviving child; during the dreadful vigil life had ebbed from Elizabeth, aged four, and from baby Edward, and they had slipped quietly away. A stained copy survives of a ballad hawked in the streets to raise money for the devastated family:

The Keel to Leeds returning from Grimsby we are told,
In charge of Captain Snowden a sailor young & bold.
And in the vessel down below his sleeping children lay,
And two with him to sleep in death upon the coming day.

32. Christopher Burn's headstone: the *Henrietta*, 1849.

Soon comes the shock, the keel overturned the husband's spirits fled,
His gallant heart's ceased beating he is numbered with the dead,
The mother clutched her little ones that slept so peacefully,
And tried, so hard to save them but alas twas not to be ...

The water rose about her and higher still it came
Their little arms are round her neck as she calls each one by name,
But when the water sunk again she knew one spirit fled,
And called her little Lizzies name but ah! the child was dead.

At last they hear her knocking and willing hands contrive
To save the mother and the only one she's left alive,
What tongue can tell her feelings or who shall know her grief,
Pray God in all his mercy send her stricken heart relief.

The *Edward & William* and the *Henrietta* now bob for ever, towing their little coggy boats behind, on the stylised stone waves at Beckett Street.

Thomas, eldest son of Leeds labourer Joseph Kidney, flirted with various trades – ironfounder (1851), bricklayer (1871), publican (1881) – before deciding that his true vocation lay in the manufacture and erection of lightning conductors. At first he combined this with duty behind the bar at the Black Swan, but by 1897 he was advertising in local directories from 87 Benson Street as 'lightning conductor and maker, fixed in superior style'. Five of his infants had been buried in common graves, but when his wife Sarah died in 1895 he was able to afford to erect to her memory the most brilliantly individual of the monuments at the cemetery, which was also a highly appropriate tribute to life and industry in the great Victorian cities, for the Kidney gravestone was in the form of a miniature mill-chimney. Thomas joined Sarah below it in 1914, but the business continued to prosper; his son, winner of several gold and silver medals for chimney felling, was proud to describe it to the *Yorkshire Evening News* in 1926 as 'the oldest firm of steeplejacks in Yorkshire',[149] and his great-grandson Tommy made news at the age of five when he was taken up the 120-foot-high steeple of a Scarborough church and stood for half an hour on an eighteen-inch plank, watching the men at work ('I don't like school,' the lad is reported to have said, 'I'd rather be up a steeple').[150] Alas, a family quarrel put paid to Tommy's dreams, and while Thomas Kidney Steeplejacks was sold to strangers, he drove a van until he was called up, dying at twenty-three of disease

33. The unusual memorial to the Kidney family, Leeds steeplejacks from 1854 to 1927 (since stolen from the cemetery; present whereabouts unknown)

contracted on the retreat from Dunkirk. The handsome and unique memorial, too, is no longer with us, having been stolen from the cemetery in the early years of the twenty-first century. As a result of anonymous information received (sadly, too late), its progress was followed from one 'antiques fair' to another; it was last heard of in the hands of a 'dodgy antiques dealer' in Huddersfield, who denied all knowledge of it to the police. Now, robbed of its context and its message from the past, it is probably a quaint little garden ornament for a grave-robber.

The inscriptions placed upon nineteenth-century gravestones offer both contact and contrast with those of our own age. Hackneyed and commonplace as many of them may be, they provided the mourner with an opportunity to make a public statement of affection for the departed, or to laud his character or achievements. A testimony in stone to the agonies of the departed or the grief of the survivor could well have a cathartic effect after sudden loss or long-drawn-out suffering, and the frequent visits to the grave which would follow the death would bring consolation with the repeated reminder that ''tis better to be yonder than here'.

The masses might labour in darkness, but every literate Victorian was familiar with the Bible, which offered a range of suitable epitaphs. For young Emma Sunderland in 1871 there was 2 Kings, Chapter 4, Verse 26: 'Is it well with the child? And she answered, It is well.' Robert Stephenson drowned in the Leamonroyd Lock, Methley, in 1881, and his grave is graced by the beautiful and well-chosen words from Isaiah, Chapter 43, Verse 2: 'When thou passest through the waters, I will be with thee.' Isaiah was also chosen for Adolphe Zelter, Professor of Languages, of whom we know no more than that he died in the Workhouse, aged 40, in 1868. Chapter 51, Verse 14, gives us, rather uncomplementarily to Zelter's adopted city, 'The captive exile hasteneth that he may be loosed and that he should not die in the pit.'

Religious phrases such as 'A sinner saved by grace' surfaced readily, and there is a hymn-like lilt to many of the verses ('Happy voyager, thou are landed Safe on Canaan's peaceful shore ...'); indeed, the consolations of religion were likely to be needed in the frequent bereavements which afflicted the Victorian family. The empty cradle was a grim reality, but its former occupant was idealised as a heavenly being or, very commonly, as a flower. In 1854 two-year-old Hannah Westerman's parents chose 'All knew who gazed on thy sweet face It was an angel's dwelling-place', while Squire Newton, aged five months, was remembered in 1859 by the lines:

> This lovely bud, so young and fair,
> Our hope and joy and pride,
> Was snatched away from our embrace
> To dwell at Jesu's side.

The first line of this verse was extremely popular, and can be found, like other much-loved lines and couplets, in different combinations throughout the cemetery. Lulled by this comforting, sentimental view, we are startled by the dour morality of Mr and Mrs Manks, who lost their four-year-old John James in 1860:

> While my hopes, my desires and my pleasures were free,
> I died in my childhood, yet weep not for me;
> Reserve for thyself all thy sighs and thy tears:
> He who dies in his youth cannot sin in his years.

Parallel with the theme of safety in a better life runs an unstated threat. 'Be ye also ready,' warned William Beasley simply in 1851, while Henry Thompson, despite living to the age of sixty-five, is commemorated with

> Death little warning to me gave,
> And quickly called me to my grave,
> Make haste to Christ make no delay,
> For no-one knows their dying day.

In 1875, the year Thompson was buried, the single greatest cause of death in Leeds was bronchitis, a killer which in its chronic form found most of its targets among the elderly (427 men and women over the age of sixty succumbed); but in the same year many people disappeared much more suddenly from the Leeds scene – fifty-three people died of peritonitis, 145 suffered apoplexy, 142 fell victim to accident and injury, and there were even fourteen adult victims of smallpox.[151] The people who chose such epitaphs had uppermost in their minds the abruptness of their loss, just as others felt, predominantly, a sense of release:

> Afflictions sore long time I bore,
> Physicians were in vain,

But death gave ease when God did please,
And freed me from my pain.

The medieval Church's desire to remind man of his mortality, and consequently urge him to a better way of life, was illustrated by wall-paintings of the Danse Macabre, or by tombs on which stately bishops lay sculpted above their own skeletal, worm-writhed effigies. The verbal admonition which echoed this visual motif, the theme '*Sum quod eris*', survives, interestingly, in the Victorian cemetery.

Oft have I stood, as you stand now,
To view the grave as you view mine,
Think reader, you must lay as low
As I, and others stand and look at thine.

This verse was chosen as late as 1893 for Mary Schofield, aged fifty-two, and there are other examples; yet the single pictorial survival of the ancient theme is the tiny skull carved on the headstone of schoolmaster John Wood (1860).

With the emphasis on bodily decay and on the heavenly mansions goes a desire to affirm one's earthly standing. 'Of Leeds', 'of this town', 'of this city', proclaim countless gravestones; even 'of No. 15, Elmwood Street' (Elizabeth Harrison, 1855). One's loyalties, if one had moved, might lie elsewhere; old Mrs Cowlishaw, buried in 1880, was 'late of Crich, Derbyshire'. Occupations were another confirmation of one's standing in society. With 'wine and spirit merchant', 'music publisher', 'assistant surveyor', 'tailor and outfitter', one slotted neatly into some kind of niche. These were facts (though the chimney-sweep of the Burial Register, like William Butterfield in 1858, could be transmogrified on stone into a 'soot merchant'); less quantifiable were the virtues, although the Georgian habit of decorating the church wall with laudatory screeds had become comparatively watered-down by the age of the municipal cemetery. 'She was a sincere Christian, a truly affectionate wife, and an exemplary mother,' summed up Charlotte Moore's widower succinctly in 1863.

The nineteenth-century burial-ground testifies to the physical mobility of the nation in the days of Empire. In 1878 Alfred Roberts, as the family stone informs us, died 'at Madras, India, of sunstroke, aged 27 years'. George Waterworth, aged twenty-one, was 'accidentally drowned whilst crossing a river in South Africa' in 1861. Henry Gilbert Jackson was Resident Medical

Officer of the Collingwood Lunatic Asylum, Melbourne, Australia, and was buried at the Borooudora Cemetery in 1869. John William Wadsworth died at Bahia, Brazil, in 1870, in his thirty-first year, but two years earlier on in his travels, his little daughter Margaret Emma had been buried in Melbourne. His widow returned home to bury a second young child in Leeds in 1871.

One of the favourite destinations of the young Englishman starting a new life abroad was the United States.[152] In 1851 emigration thither reached a peak of 267,000 persons out of a total of 336,000, far exceeding the 43,000 who went to Canada or the 21,000 bound for Australia and New Zealand. Ten years later emigration, following cycles of economic depression and upturn as it did, was at a low point, but still 50,000 people – the equivalent of the population of a fair-sized town – made their way to America in 1861. Among the emigrants of mid-century who found not gold but death at the end of the trail was a young Leeds cloth-dresser, son of the aged labourer who in June 1865 met with a fatal accident on the Great Northern Railway, at Birkenshaw. Old John Groundwell had toiled all his life, working on the land, carrying hods of bricks, unloading ballast – any job requiring physical strength and a tough constitution. One act of folly cost him his life, for when the ganger warned that the train on which the men were working was about to move forward, John, instead of standing in a safe position with the others, attempted to sit on the edge of the truck, and when the train stopped he was jerked out and the wheels ran over his arm. Amputation followed at the Infirmary, but he sank rapidly, probably as a result of septicaemia. It was the last sad chapter of a life which had seen several tragedies. John and Elizabeth Groundwell had reared a large family in nearby Gildersome before moving to Leeds, where, in September 1849, John lost his wife, his young son-in-law and his daughter, all within the space of two weeks, perhaps from cholera. The 1851 census shows John, a widower, living in Grey Street with his four cloth-dresser sons aged between twenty-six and fifteen, his two daughters, of whom the elder was employed as a flax-spinner, and his little orphaned granddaughter Alice. Ten years later the household had contracted to four; John, the youngest son, had become one of the emigration statistics, and was never to see Leeds again. The Groundwell headstone commemorates the three 1849 deaths and the decease of John's father, and continues: 'ALSO JOHN GROUNDWELL ... WHO DIED WHEN A PRISONER OF WAR AT ANDERSONVILLE GEORGIA UNITED STATES, AMERICA OCTOBER 12TH 1864 AGED 28 YEARS.'

On 12 April 1861 the guns had opened fire at Fort Sumter in South Carolina, in the cause of keeping America united. The economic, political and cultural differences between North and South had focused on the issue of slavery, which was the mainstay of the economic system by which the South produced its cotton and other crops, but which the North was determined to abolish. A cruel civil war raged for five years, in which young John Groundwell from Leeds gave up his life.

The name of Andersonville,[153] once a remote little hamlet of thirty inhabitants, still provokes bitterness and controversy in the USA. In the first years of the war there had been a system for exchanging prisoners, but by 1864 this had broken down, and huge numbers had to be accommodated in prison camps on both sides. At Andersonville, Union soldiers were herded in ever-larger crowds behind the seventeen-foot-high palisade of pine trunks, punctuated by watchtowers, which enclosed an area originally almost exactly the size of Beckett Street Cemetery and designed to hold 10,000 men. Water was obtained from a sluggish and contaminated branch of the ironically named Sweetwater Creek; the prisoners sheltered in wretched 'shebangs' constructed out of blankets or clothing strung on whatever branches or sticks they could find, and existed on a diet which often consisted of nothing but corn meal, with the indigestible cobs mashed into it. The swampy area designated for latrines filled up rapidly with filth which could not be flushed away, so that the smell from the camp wafted two miles over the countryside. The collapsing Confederate economy was unable to supply its own army with adequate food and medicines, let alone the 32,000 unwanted prisoners who were corralled in Andersonville at its nadir in August 1864. In the hot, damp Georgian summer, infections, malnutrition and untreated wounds killed a hundred men a day; altogether 13,000 of the 52,000 who passed through its gates were buried in the mass trenches of the camp cemetery. When Atlanta, Georgia's capital, fell to the Union forces, many of the prisoners were sent to camps further away, and by October only 5,000 remained, mostly too ill to travel. It was then that John Groundwell died, too soon to be helped by the resumed exchange of prisoners in March 1865, or the capitulation of the South at Appomattox on 9 April, or the hanging of the camp's Swiss-born commandant in November. We shall probably never know why he came to be fighting under the Union banner instead of dressing cloth at home in Leeds. His name is not in the records at the Andersonville National Historic Site, and we must assume that he is one of the 400 prisoners who rest there under chunky white marble tablets engraved simply 'UNKNOWN U.S. SOLDIER'.

To Leeds came German merchants like Edward Sigismund Lehmann, born in Strelitz, Mecklenburg, and working as a wool broker with a firm in Moorgate, London; on a business trip to the North he died, aged forty, and is commemorated with a headstone raised by Edward Stavenhagen – perhaps the senior partner. Travelling in the opposite direction from the empire-builders arrived, perhaps as servant to some retired India merchant, a young man who was to die in the Infirmary in 1865 at the age of nineteen, far indeed from the land of his birth: 'Deenoo, a Hindoo'. There came, too, men whose crafts were specialities of their native lands, such as Giuseppe Galli, silversmith, and others of his family who were jewellers or toy-merchants. Many were following the finger of God, like the charismatic Welsh preacher Henry Edmund Phillips, incumbent of Christ Church. 'Heb saeth, heb fraw, heb ofn,' lyricises the memorial erected by the latter's personal friends in 1859: 'Without arrow, without fright, without fear, without worry and without pain, singing in front of the throne of the pure glory of the Lamb, in the midst of myriads and myriads, loving all without ebbing, the anthem is love, and love to continue.'

It is sometimes claimed that the art of the Victorian cemetery is a crude and debased anticlimax to the history of memorialisation. At Beckett Street Cemetery there is, undeniably, repetitious material, unsuccessful sculpture (like the two reclining children, Annie and George Pearson Turner, of 1860, where the younger child resembles nothing so much as the Pig Baby from *Alice in Wonderland*), and atrocious verse such as George Russell's 1887

We miss thee when the morning dawns,
We miss thee when the night returns.
We miss thee here, we miss thee there,
Father, we miss thee everywhere.

This was an age of sentimental effusion, and at the same time an age of mass production. Yet, despite the occasional failure with an over-ambitious design, or lapse in spelling or punctuation (like Worger's 'muitiny' and John Henry Gallagher's 'ti's better'), the standards of the stonemasons remained high, and in the choice of styles and the variety of epitaphs thousands of lost voices still have their say. The modern mason, by contrast, however skilled he may be, suffers under severe restrictions from cemetery and church authorities as to material, form and inscription, and it must be admitted that he is not helped by customers who ask for soppy carvings and for verses like 'Silent thought, Tears unseen, Were your absence but a dream'. The giving of interesting factual information, other than name and dates, has been thoroughly out of fashion since the Great War; in any case, the present predominance of cremation has inevitably led to the full-size headstone's becoming an endangered species. The historian of our own times will find very little joy in his 'gatherings from graveyards' as he wanders among uniform Loving Memories of strictly limited size and style created from alien, glossy stone, or crawls on hands and knees down the paths of the crematorium grounds, inspecting the small plastic commemorative plaques which line the kerbs.

Let us be thankful for the survival of at least some of the cemeteries established and patronised by our Victorian ancestors, and for the way in which, in the midst of death, they resurrect for us the nineteenth-century urban scene and the people who made the cities we inhabit today. Here are rich and poor, young and old, wise and foolish, people we should have loved to know and others we should have loathed: the whole diversity and fascination of a century and a half of humanity, gone but not forgotten. Burial-grounds like Beckett Street Cemetery are places for considering and remembering, for resting and reviving, places for the living as well as for the dead.

'Pause! Reflect! Pass on!'

Notes

1 Minutes of the Burial Grounds Committee (hereafter BGC), 19 January 1848.
2 R. Baker, *On the State and Condition of the Town of Leeds in the West Riding of the County of York*, Leeds, 1842, pp. 21-2.
3 BGC 19 January 1848.
4 James Stevens Curl, *A Celebration of Death*, London, 1984, p. 295.
5 BGC 9, 23 February, 25, 26 March 1844.
6 BGC 5, 27 January, 6 May 1844.
7 BGC 5, 10 June 1844.
8 BGC 21 April 1859.
9 Report to the Burial Grounds Committee by their Sub-Committee, appointed on the 30th December, 1881.
10 BGC: General Report, Leeds Burial Ground (Consecrated Portion), Burmantofts, 1885.
11 BGC 29 November 1844.
12 Mayhall, *Annals of Yorkshire*, Leeds, 1878, 25 April 1842.
13 Reply of the Burial Grounds Committee of the Leeds Town Council to the Charges made by the Vicar of Leeds in his Reply to the Memorialists, Leeds, 1847.
14 BGC 11 February, 7 March 1851; Mayhall, *Annals*, 1 March 1851.
15 BGC 11 July, 15 September 1851.
16 BGC Visiting Sub-Committee 2 December 1881; BGC 27 January 1882.
17 BGC Visiting Sub-Committee 1 April 1884.
18 BGC 12 September 1878.
19 BGC 30 June, 31 July 1879.
20 BGC 11 September 1879, BGC Visiting Sub-Committee 15 September 1879.
21 BGC 4 June 1869.

22 BGC 15, 16 July 1881.

23 BGC 18 February, 29 April, 5 May, 18 June 1880.

24 Sylvia M. Barnard, interview with Mr Stanley Temple, July 1986.

25 M.W. Beresford, 'The back-to-back house in Leeds, 1787-1937', *Time and Place*, London, 1984, p. 367.

26 *Ibid.*, p. 370.

27 Baker, *Town of Leeds*, p. 11.

28 *Leeds Mercury* and *Leeds Intelligencer*, 25 August 1865.

29 *Leeds Mercury*, 16 April 1866.

30 Dr John Simon, *City of London Medical Reports*, 'Special Report on Intramural Interments', 1852 (quoted in E. Royston Pike, *Human Documents of the Victorian Golden Age*, London, 1967).

31 E. Chadwick, *Report on the Sanitary Condition of the Labouring Population of Great Britain*, 1842, p. 159.

32 *Leeds Mercury*, 23 June 1849.

33 *Leeds Intelligencer*, 11 August 1849.

34 *Leeds Mercury*, 11 August 1849.

35 BGC 16 November 1849.

36 *Leeds Mercury*, 5 January 1860.

37 R.V. Taylor, *Supplement to the Biographia Leodiensis*, London, 1867, pp. 679 and 697.

38 F. Burgess, *English Churchyard Memorials*, London, 1963; Great North of Scotland Granite Co. Ltd., price list, 1911.

39 BGC 26 August 1881.

40 A.T. Wilson and H. Levy, *Burial Reform and Funeral Costs*, Oxford, 1938, pp. 28-9.

41 *Ibid.*, p. 26.

42 Mrs M. Pember Reeves, *Round about a Pound a Week*, London, 1913.

43 *Yorkshire Evening Post*, 21 September 1984.

44 BGC 30 June 1882.

45 *Leeds Mercury*, 10 August 1865: 'The alleged concealment of birth at Leeds'.

46 W.N. Yates, *The Oxford Movement and Parish Life: St Saviour's, Leeds, 1839-1929*, York, 1975.

47 *Leeds Mercury*, 19 March 1868.

48 N. Yates, 'Religious Life in Victorian Leeds', ed. D. Fraser, *A History of Modern Leeds*, Manchester, 1980, p. 250.

49 *Ibid.*, pp. 260-1.

50 *Leeds Mercury*, 4, 13 December 1856.

51 BGC 11 April 1877.

52 BGC 31 July 1879.

53 BGC 1 October 1883.

54 BGC 25 January 1884.

55 *Leeds City Mission Annual Reports* 1839-1955.

56 Dr A.M. Mitchell, MD, 'Plural births in connection with idiocy', *Medical Times & Gazette*, 1862, II, 646.

57   *Medical Reports of the Privy Council,* No. 6, 1863, Appendix 14 (quoted in Pike, *Victorian Golden Age*).

58   H. Fletcher, *A Life on the Humber,* London, 1975, p. 46.

59   Dr F.T. Roberts, MD, BSc, MRCS, *The Theory and Practice of Medicine,* London, 1873, pp. 921-2.

60   *Leeds Mercury,* 25 November 1856.

61   *Minority Report of the Royal Commission on the Poor Laws and Relief of Distress,* 1909 (quoted in E. Royston Pike, *Human Documents of the Lloyd George Era,* London, 1972, p. 94).

62   James Greenwood, 'A night in the Workhouse', 1866 (reprinted in P. Keating, ed., *Into Unknown England: Selections from the Social Explorers,* Glasgow, 1976).

63   Pike, *Lloyd George Era,* p. 96.

64   D. Fraser, 'Poor Law politics in Leeds 1833-55', Thoresby Society, XV, Leeds, 1971.

65   Pike, *Lloyd George Era,* p. 85.

66   Samuel Smiles, *Self-Help,* with a centenary introduction by Professor Asa Briggs, London, 1958.

67   J.F.C. Harrison, *Social Reform in Victorian Leeds: the work of James Hole,* Thoresby Society, Leeds, 1954.

68   *Leeds Guardian Society Annual Reports* 1822-1908.

69   Mayhall, *Annals,* 16 October 1848.

70   P.M. Pennock, 'The evolution of St James's 1848-94', Thoresby Society, LIX, Leeds, 1986.

71   *Leeds Mercury,* 27 December 1856.

72   Mayhall, *Annals,* 15 July 1857.

73   S.T. Anning, *The Leeds School of Medicine 1831–1981,* Leeds, 1982, p. 19.

74   See R. Richardson, *Death, Dissection and the Destitute,* London, 1987.

75   S.T. Anning, 'Leeds House of Recovery', *Medical History,* XIII, 3 July 1969, p. 230.

76   Mayhall, *Annals,* 20 August 1864.

77   See G. Best, *Mid-Victorian Britain,* London, 1971.

78   Report of the Royal Sanitary Commission, 1871 (quoted in Best, *Mid-Victorian Britain,* p. 59).

79   B.J. Barber, 'Aspects of municipal government 1835-1914', ed. Fraser, *History of Modern Leeds,* p. 301.

80   *Leeds Intelligencer,* 16 August 1851.

81   A. Mattison, *Tom Maguire: a Remembrance,* Manchester, 1895.

82   This account of Jabez Tunnicliff is taken from Revd H. Marles, *Life and Labours of the Rev. Jabez Tunnicliff,* London, 1865.

83   *Leeds Mercury,* 9 July 1874.

84   R. Freeman, Survey of memorials of Beckett Street Cemetery (manuscript).

85   A.L. Bowley, *Wages in the U.K. in the Nineteenth Century,* Cambridge, 1900.

86   J. Dodgson, *An Historical and Descriptive Guide to the Borough of Leeds,* Leeds, 1879, p. 32.

87 W. Hamish Fraser, *The Coming of the Mass Market*, London, 1981, p. 34.
88 *Ibid.*, p. 38.
89 J. Burnett, *Plenty and Want: a Social History of Diet in England from 1815*, London, 1979, p. 70.
90 *Leeds Mercury* 28, 31 July; 17 August; 1, 20, 25, 27 September 1866.
91 C. Lackey, *Quality Pays: the Story of Joshua Tetley & Son*, Ascot, 1985, p. 135.
92 *Leeds Mercury*, 12 September 1866.
93 *Yorkshire Evening Post*, 27 September 1917.
94 W.G. Rimmer, 'Occupations in Leeds 1841-1951', Thoresby Society, L, Leeds, 1967.
95 E. Baines, 'Account of the woollen manufacture of England', *Yorkshire Past and Present*, London, 1870.
96 A. Ure, *A Dictionary of Arts, Manufactures & Mines*, London, 1878.
97 *Leeds Mercury*, 10 November 1866.
98 E.M. Sigsworth, 'Leeds and its industrial growth: the development of dyeing', *Leeds Journal*, I, 26, Leeds, 1955.
99 W.G. Rimmer, 'The Leeds leather industry in the nineteenth century', Thoresby Society, XLVI, Leeds, 1960.
100 Reports of HM Inspector of Mines for the Yorks. & Lincs. District (No. 5) for the years 1877; 1878; 1880; 1881; 1883; 1885; 1886; 1888 to 1892.
101 A. Lockwood, 'Leeds Gas Light Company', Thoresby Society, Miscellany XVII, Leeds, 1980.
102 Fraser, ed., *History of Modern Leeds*, p. 319.
103 *The Unfortunate Genius, by a Factory Girl*, London, 1853.
104 J. Soper, *Leeds Transport*, Wetherby, 1985.
105 B.S. Puckle, *Funeral Customs: their Origin and Development*, London, 1926, p. 125.
106 A.R. Skelley, *The Victorian Army at Home*, London, 1977, p. 246. Much of the following is based on this full and fascinating study of army life.
107 *Hard-up Husband: James Turner's Diary*, Halifax, 1881/2.
108 F. Richards, *Old-Soldier Sahib*, London, 1965, p. 19.
109 R. Edmondson, *Is a Soldier's Life Worth Living?* (quoted in Skelley, *Victorian Army*, p. 249).
110 Skelley, *Victorian Army*, p. 184.
111 Report of the Army Sanitary Commission (1857-8) (quoted in Skelley, *Victorian Army*, p. 30).
112 Skelley, *Victorian Army*, p. 22.
113 The Marquess of Anglesey, *A History of the British Cavalry*, I, London, 1973, p. 125.
114 *Ibid.*, p. 131.
115 Skelley, *Victorian Army*, p. 130.
116 *Ibid.*, p. 89.
117 1871 Census RG 10/4558, ff. 93-104.
118 The National Archives WO 12/340, 341.

119 Col. K.W. Maurice-Jones, *The History of Coast Artillery in the British Army*, London, 1959, pp. 137-8.

120 Anglesey, *British Cavalry*, II, p. 285.

121 For useful accounts of the Crimean War and Indian Mutiny, see C. Hibbert, *The Destruction of Lord Raglan*, London, 1961, and *The Great Mutiny*, London, 1987.

122 *Summoned by Duty*, manuscript verse autobiography by A.V. Pearson.

123 P. Longworth, *The Unending Vigil: A History of the Commonwealth War Graves Commission*, London, 1985, p. 254.

124 *Leeds Mercury*, 8 June 1867.

125 D. Russell, 'The Leeds Rational Recreation Society', Thoresby Society, LVI, Leeds, 1981.

126 *Yorkshire Weekly Post*, 16 September 1916.

127 BGC 25 November 1887.

128 *Leeds Mercury*, 20 May 1868.

129 Manuscripts in the possession of the family.

130 P. M'Owan, *Memoir of Christopher Dove junior, of Leeds*, Leeds, 1837, p. 68.

131 *Leeds Mercury*, 19 July 1856.

132 *Leeds Mercury*, 12 August 1856.

133 *Leeds Mercury*, 25, 28 October, 1 November 1856.

134 *Leeds Mercury*, 8, 11 November 1856.

135 E.W. Clay, ed., *The Leeds Police 1836–1974*, Leeds, 1974.

136 Leeds City Council Fire Brigade Committee, *The City of Leeds Fire Brigade: its Development and History*, Leeds, 1952.

137 S. McConville, *A History of English Prison Administration*, London, 1981, I, p. 215.

138 Mayhall, *Annals*, 29 July 1847.

139 D. Philips, *Crime and Authority in Victorian England*, London, 1977, p. 142.

140 *Leeds Mercury*, 7 April 1855.

141 *Things You Ought to Know, Clearly Explained*, by One Who Knows, London (undated), p. 264.

142 See O. Anderson, *Suicide in Victorian and Edwardian England*, Oxford, 1987.

143 *Leeds Mercury*, 15 July 1868.

144 Children's Employment Commission, First Report, 1863 (quoted in Pike, *Victorian Golden Age*, pp. 140-1).

145 *Leeds Mercury*, 5 July 1851.

146 *Leeds Mercury*, 26, 30 March 1869.

147 *Leeds Intelligencer, Leeds Mercury*, 10 August 1865.

148 *Leeds Skyrack Express*, 27 January 1984.

149 *Yorkshire Evening News*, 14 January 1924.

150 *Yorkshire Evening News*, 16 February 1924.

151 Robinson and Goldie, *Sanitary Condition of Leeds*, Reports 1866-77.

152 G.M. Young, W.D. Hancock, eds., *English Historical Documents* XII (1) 1833-1874, London, 1956, p. 204.

153 *Blue & Gray Magazine*, III, 3, Columbus, Ohio, 1986.

Death Notices, Obituaries and Inquest Reports

from the *Leeds Mercury*, *Leeds Intelligencer* (later *Yorkshire Post*) and *Yorkshire Evening Post*

ATKIN	Matthew	LM	7 February 1868	204
BARRAN	John	LM	4 May 1905	111–12
BEDFORD	Matthew	LM	20 September 1856	39
BIRCHALL	Samuel	LM	6 June 1866	204
BREARY	George	LM	30 September 1849	45
BREASLEY	Benjamin	LI	10 February 1855	88–9
BROUGHTON	George	LM	12 June 1856	143
BROWN	George Henry	LI	19 March 1864	93
BROWN	Susannah	LI	25 Aug, 1 Sept 1849	45–7
BURNS	John	LM	28 Aug, 23 Dec 1856	91
CAWTHRA	Joshua	LI	8 January 1856	180
COLEMAN	William Henry	LM	2 February 1856	84
COLLINS	Patrick	LM	12, 22, 24 April 1856	205–7
COOKE	John	LM	6 March 1866	204
CORDINGLEY	John	LM	5, 7 June 1856	85
CRAVEN	Ellen	LM	11, 18 August 1849	42–3
CRYER	Samuel	LM	2 October 1856	84
DEWSE	Jemima	LM	14 January 1867	99
DOVE	Harriet	LM	8, 11, 13, 18 Mar 1856	193–6
DUCKWORTH	Mary Jane	LM	23 September 1856	87
DUNNING	John	YP	15 July 1873	94
FAWCETT	Elizabeth	LM	23, 25 May 1866	134
FOLEY	Bridget	LM	26, 28 May 1868	155

FOUNTAIN	Joseph	YP	12 October 1887	182–4
FRANKLAND	George	LM	23 May 1868	200
GARRICK	Joseph	LM	28 December 1850	87–8
GOY	Elizabeth	LM	23 June 1849	204–5
GRAYSHON	Hannah	LM	28 July 1849	42
GROUNDWELL	John	LM	29 June 1865	226–7
HADDOCK	George	YEP	12 September 1907	178–9
		LM	13 September 1907	
		YP	13 September 1907	
HAIGH	Joseph	LM	3 June 1868	203
HICK	George	LM	14 May 1866	148
HORNER	Thomas	LM	22 June 1868	199
HULME	Charles Denton	LM	26 July 1856	89–90
IRVINE	Thomas	LI	7 November 1863	189–90
JACKSON	Thomas	LM	20 November 1856	39
JENKINS	John	LM	11, 15 July 1865	93
JONES	Joseph	LM	16 September 1865	91
KEELEY	William	LM	8 December 1849	93
KEIGHLEY	Joseph	LI	28 July 1849	139
KELLY	William	LM	4 September 1856	84
KIRK	Mary	LM	9 March 1865	84
LANIGAN	John William	LM	1 May 1866	200–1
MAGUIRE	Tom	LM	9, 11 March 1895	113–5
MAY	Sam	LM	29 March 1856	83
McCARTHY	John	LM	16 June 1849	42
MENZIE	John	LM	16 October 1856	92
METCALFE	Thomas	LI	23 September 1848	105
MITCHELL	John	LM	8 September 1868	91
M'LARIN	Hugh	LM	22 May 1856	133
MOSLEY	Thomas	LM	14 December 1871	112–3
MOUNSEY	James	LM	25 September 1856	91
MURPHY	Michael	LM	16 September 1865	86–7
NEWBOUND	Walter	YP	1 November 1897	
		YEP	1 November 1897	86–7
NOLAN	Margaret	LM	14 June 1856	84
PEARSON	Samuel	LM	29,30 Mar, 5 Apr 1866	142–3
PHEENEY	Sarah	LI	3 February 1855	83
PRIESTLEY	John	LM	16 June 1868	203–4
RIDER	John	LI	27 January 1855	88
RITCHIE	Sarah	LM	21 June 1856	92–3
ROPER	John	LM	26 January 1869	93–4
ROWELL	Frederick	LI	14 October 1865	62
RUDDOCK	William	LM	2, 4 April 1868	184–5
SCATCHARD	Jane Ann	LM	10 August 1866	130

SCHOFIELD	James Potter	LM	13, 14, 15 Jan 1892	218
SHEPHERD	Dorothy	LM	25 August 1849	44
SMITH	James	LM	2 October 1856	142
SMITH	Mark	LM	4 August 1849	42
SNOWDEN	Edward	YP	14, 15 May 1885	219–21
STAMPER	George	LM	22 December 1849	83
STRACHAN	John	LM	30 Mar, 3 Apr 1911	131–2
THURKILL	Laura Eliza	LM	23, 28, 29, 30 December 1868, 5 January 1869	209–10
UNKNOWN	man	LM	16 September 1856	85
WAINWRIGHT	Joseph	LM	1 July 1865	141
WHITE	Joseph	LM	5, 7 June 1856	85
WHITLING	John	LM	12 July 1856	87
WHITWAM	Henry Pearson	LM	20 September 1879	87
WILKINSON	Benjamin	LM	29 March 1866	143
WILSON	George	LM	21, 28 June 1851	208–9

Appendix A

Mid-century burial law and the development of municipal cemeteries in England and Wales

Private and local Acts of Parliament
The earliest nineteenth-century cemeteries were commercial undertakings; from 1825 several joint-stock cemetery companies were constituted under individual Acts of Parliament. In the 1840s, however, a handful of Town Councils obtained Acts enabling them to use money from the rates for the provision of burial facilities.

Cemeteries Clauses Act, 1847
In a climate of opinion still favourable to the commercial cemetery, this Act provided guidelines for the establishment and running of such cemeteries.

Burial Act, 1852
This Act provided for the setting up of Burial Boards in parishes within the metropolis; these Boards were empowered to spend money from the Poor Rate to establish public cemeteries.

Burial Act, 1853
The provisions of the previous Act were extended to parishes outside the metropolis, and full burial grounds could be ordered to close.

Burial Act, 1854
Town Councils were enabled to form Burial Boards, using the borough rate, to establish cemeteries deemed to be for the parishes within the borough.

The following table lists the first municipal cemeteries in a number of towns, cities and London boroughs. While not comprehensive, it demonstrates clearly the urgent need for new burial-grounds in the expanding urban areas, and the consequent dramatic response to the enactment of the legislation of the 1850s.

Town	Current name of cemetery	Date	Approx present acreage	Approx no. of burials
Leeds	Beckett Street	1845	16	180,000
Leeds	Hunslet	1845	10	72,400
Southampton	Old	1846	26	116,700
Coventry	London Road	1848	43	180,000
Leicester	Welford Road	1849	28	213,100
Islington	Islington	1854	77	NK
Lambeth	Lambeth	1854	42	NK
Middlesbrough	Old Linthorpe	1854	8	11,000
Newport, Gwent	St Woolos	1854	80	210,600
Poole	Poole	1854	18	25,100
Portsmouth	Eastney	1854	17	55,500
St Pancras	St Pancras	1854	123	385,400
Westminster	Hanwell	1854	24	100,400
Huddersfield	Edgerton	1855	27	80,800
Ipswich	Old	1855	70	NK
Kensington	Kensington	1855	18	77,900
Preston	Old	1855	80	141,000
Putney	Lower Common	1855	3	7,500
Bolton	Tonge	1856	39	114,800
Camberwell	Old	1856	40	282,500
City of London	City of London	1856	200	483,400
Doncaster	Old	1856	10	55,800
Hillingdon	H'don & Uxbridge	1856	20	36,000
Liverpool	Toxteth Park	1856	55	191,000
Norwich	City	1856	85	NK
Swansea	Danygraig	1856	20	62,500
Blackburn	Whalley New Rd	1857	34	200,000
Brighton	Borough	1857	20	NK
Gloucester	Old	1857	32	75,300
Oldham	Greenacres	1857	36	103,500
West Ham	West Ham	1857	20	278,400
Deptford	Brockley	1858	15	89,600
Lewisham	Ladywell	1858	20	131,100
Peterborough	Broadway	1858	6	25,700

Tottenham	Tottenham	1858	50	123,100
West Bromwich	Heath Lane	1858	28	73,800
Cardiff	Cathays	1859	112	118,200
Sheffield	Attercliffe	1859	4	14,300
Battersea	Battersea	1860	14	33,200
Bradford	Scholemoor	1860	60	106,800
Stoke-on-Trent	Hanley	1860	25	93,000
Croydon	Queen's Rd	1861	22	78,300
Ealing	South Ealing	1861	25	24,600
Halifax	Stoney Royd	1861	23	43,000
Birmingham	Witton	1863	103	448,700
Fulham	Palace Rd	1865	13	98,200
Exeter	Higher	1866	32	69,100
Manchester	Philips Park	1867	46	97,200
Twickenham	Twickenham	1867	21	33,500
Rotherham	Wath-upon-Dearne	1868	14	10,300
Hammersmith	Margravine Rd	1869	17	83,300
Hounslow	Hounslow	1869	8	14,200
Bristol	Greenbank	1871	35	96,300
Blackpool	Layton	1873	18	49,900
Hull	Hedon Rd	1875	4	86,700
Nottingham	Basford	1875	6	34,500
Hampstead	Hampstead	1876	35	64,100
Wandsworth	Wandsworth	1878	34	95,800
Oxford	Headington	1880	6	4,900
Swindon	Radnor Street	1881	8	33,000
Putney	Putney Vale	1891	42	96,000

Source: information supplied by officers of local authorities.

Note: The establishment of a new cemetery usually took two or three years, and this should be borne in mind when correlating the above list with the legislation of the 1850s. In the case of some towns and cities the existence of adequate and suitable private or ecclesiastical provision may have delayed the foundation of a municipal cemetery (even, as with York's Fulford Cemetery of 1915, until the next century). Cemeteries created by parish Burial Boards will now usually be found to be run by the local authority of the area (e.g. Greenbank, Bristol, opened in 1871 and transferred to Bristol Corporation in 1885).

Appendix B

The Cost of Death

Table B.1: Charges for burial at Beckett Street Cemetery
(12*d* = 1*s*, or 5p in decimal money; 20*s* = £1.)

	1857	1881	1915	1921
Land for private grave	£2–3	£1–3	£1–3	£2–5
Interment in private grave	15*s*	8*s*–£1	9*s*–£1 5*s*	£1 5*s*–£2
Stillborn interment in private grave	2*s* 6*d*–5*s*	2*s* 6*d*–10*s*	4*s*–12*s* 6*d*	£1 5*s*
Guinea grave (incl. stone and 36 letters)				
for person 7 and over	–	£1 1*s*	£1 2*s*	£2
for person under 7	–	£1 1*s*	11*s*	£1
Interment in public grave, according to situation and depth	7*s*–14*s*	7*s*–14*s*	7*s*–14*s*	£1 (under 7:10*s*)
Stillborn interment in public grave	not given	not given	not given	6*s*
Interment in 'lock-up' grave according to situation of grave and age of person	3*s* 6*d*–5*s*	3*s* 6*d*–5*s*	4*s*–6*s*	–
Stillborn interment in 'lock-up' grave	1*s*–5*s*	1*s*	2*s* 6*d*	–
Right to erect headstone or monument	5*s*	£1 1*s*	12*s* 6*d*– £1 1*s*	7% on cost

Sources: BGC 5 March 1857; Report to the Burial Grounds Committee 1881; printed table of fees 1915; Leeds, Hunslet and Holbeck Cemeteries, Rules and Regulations, 1921.

Note: There were three categories of 'public graves'. Prices for 1915 list 'graves over which a Gravestone is to be erected' (the guinea graves), 'graves to be filled up after each interment' and 'graves not to be filled up after each interment'. The second category is self-explanatory; prices were charged according to the depth of the interment and, consequently, the amount of work involved. The third category seems to correspond to what is known in the registers as 'lock-up' graves, which were considerably cheaper, with charges for persons over seven years old, persons under seven years old, and stillborn babies. It appears that these graves were only filled to a level which covered the current interment and was appropriate to receive the next. A wooden 'door' was then locked in place on to a framework around the grave, and when the grave was full, the superfluous contraptions were removed so that it appeared like any other. The last mention of 'lock-up' graves in the minutes kept at the Civic Hall (which extend to 1905) is in 1891. At some point thereafter the wooden framework was superseded by a concrete slab, known as a 'coffin cover', as used today over interments in common graves. The 1921 price list refers only to 'common graves', but uses the same tripartite age divisions as the 1915 'lock-up' graves. Mr Stanley Temple, who was born and brought up in Beckett Street Cemetery, has no recollection of the name or practice of the 'lock-up' graves.

Table B:2: Proportional interments for sample years, showing the reflection of the growing prosperity of Britain in the increasing use of graves either private or at least provided with a memorial.

Year	Total burials		Common graves No. (%)	Guinea graves No. (%)	Private graves No. (%)	Total % private and/or with memorial
1851	1,680	Con.	1,091 (89)	–	137 (11)	
		Uncon.	346 (77)	–	106 (23)	
		Whole	1,437 (85)	–	243 (15)	15
1871	2,540	Con.	1,302 (80)	–	329 (20)	
		Uncon.	690 (76)	–	219 (24)	
		Whole	1,992 (78)	–	548 (22)	22
1891	3,323	Con.	1,029 (58)	435 (24)	323 (18)	
		Uncon.	940 (61)	355 (23)	241 (16)	
		Whole	1,969 (59)	790 (24)	564 (17)	41
1911 [a]	1,787	Con.	650 (75)	–	222 (25)	
		Uncon.	318 (35)	386 (42)	211 (23)	
		Whole	968 (54)	386 (22)	433 (24)	46
1931 [b]	594	Con.	–	–	95 (100)	
		Uncon.	131 (26)	202 (41)	166 (33)	
		Whole	131 (22)	202 (34)	261 (44)	78

Source: Burial and Grave Registers

Notes:
[a] The last guinea grave in the Consecrated portion is dated March 1908.
[b] The last common grave in the Consecrated portion is dated May 1913.
The discontinuance of these categories was the result of the filling up of the
Consecrated portion, which by the end of 1907 had received 90,444 bodies as
against 57,555 buried in the Unconsecrated portion, where the same number of
graves was available. An Anglican wishing to inter in a guinea grave after 1908, or in
a common grave after 1913, was obliged to use the Unconsecrated portion (many
did), or to choose another cemetery.

During the years when nearly half the burials were in private or guinea graves,
however, approximately one person in every five interred was the object of
disbursements by the Board of Guardians. Lists survive of payments by the Guardians
between 1907 and 1917 for the burials of paupers who died in the Workhouse
Infirmary or at home on out-relief. No list relating to the Workhouse itself has been
found, but by adding the total number of entries in the Burial Registers during these
years where the address is given as 'Workhouse' we can arrive at a possible figure for
pauper burials. (The true figure will probably be lower, since in some cases bodies
were claimed by relatives and buried at their expense.)

Table B.3: Burial costs and Poor Relief

Burials at Beckett Street Cemetery 1908–16	No.	%
Total burials	15,074	100.0
Burials from Leeds Union Infirmary	1,359	9.0
Burials on Out-relief	544	3.6
Burials from Leeds Union Workhouse	1,309	8.7
Estimated total burials paid for by Guardians	3,212	21.3

Source: Burial Registers; Account Book for interments paid by Board of Guardians
1907–1917.

The cost to the Guardians of the burial of a pauper was a far cry from the bill for
the funeral of an even moderately well-off citizen. On Wednesday 27 November
1889, the body of John Robinson, aged seventy, a maltster from the firm of William
Naylor & Co. of Railway Street, Leeds, was removed from his red-brick terraced
house in the suburb of Potternewton, and taken in a hearse followed by four
mourning coaches and a carriage containing the clergyman to private grave 22467
in the Unconsecrated portion of Beckett Street Cemetery. The bill of undertakers
John Wales Smith & Sons, which included items such as the customary gift of black
gloves to friends and relatives, the hire of frock-coats and gloves for the six bearers
and six drivers, and the personal attendance of Mr Smith with his assistant, is given in
full below. One week later, on Wednesday 4 December, the body of Charles Flesher,

aged sixty, a former mason, was trundled across the cobbles of Beckett Street on the Workhouse bier to the 'open' (lock-up) grave 10529 in the Consecrated portion of the cemetery. The irreducible minimum costs of the 'coffin and dues' which had to be provided by the Guardians are also set out below, assuming Mr Flesher to have been a man of average height. (Mr Henry Wright of Prussia Street was contracted, according to a minute of the Guardians' meeting on 25 September 1889, to supply coffins to the Workhouse at prices graded from 2s for a coffin 2 feet or less in length to 7s 6d for one 6 feet long or more.) Relieving Officers were able to authorise a hearse and bearers for 5s, but this would not have been necessary for a funeral which had only to cross the road.

Table B.4: Paying for the funeral

Funeral of John Robinson Esqre. from 6 Reginald Terrace to Burmantofts Cemetery

	£	s	d
Polished Pitch Pine Coffin Lined with Flannel and Ruching with rich Ormolu Furniture	8	8	0
Flannel mattress and pillow		15	0
Fine Flannel Robe trimmed with Satin	1	1	0
Attendance to put on do.		5	0
Ormolu Breast Plate with inscription		15	0
Conveyance of Coffin with Bearers &c.		18	6
2 pairs 2 B[utton] Best Kid Gloves		11	0
1 pair Servant's 4B 2nd do.		3	6
4 pairs Men's Calf Gloves		13	0
3 Elastic Cloth Hatbands		3	9
19 Burial Services		6	4
Funeral Car and pair Horses	1	11	6
4 Landaus (shutters up) and pairs	5	0	0
Brougham for clergyman		15	0
State Cloth, Violet Trestle Cloth and Trestles		10	6
Horsesheets, Wands, Girths &c.		8	6
12 pairs Blk Berlin Gloves for men		12	0
Loan of 12 Coats		18	0
6 Bearers and 6 Drivers	2	14	0
Attendance	1	11	6
Funeral [cemetery] dues	1	0	6
Rev. F.C. Kilner	1	1	0
Wreath		14	6
Mr Blenkin, Beckett Street, for lettering of Tombstone &c., 5 doz. gilt letters at 2s 3d		11	3
	31	8	4

Funeral of Charles Flesher from Workhouse to Burmantofts Cemetery

	£	s	d
Coffin		7	0
Cemetery dues		5	0

Sources: Leeds City Archives, Account Books of John Wales Smith, Undertakers; Board of Guardians Minute Books, PL/1/1.

Appendix C

Morbidity and Mortality

Table C.1: Ages at death of persons buried at Beckett Street Cemetery in sample census years.

Year	Total buried	Under 1 year	1–4	5–14	15–29	30–49	50–69	Over 70
1851	1,678	482	400	122	175	204	195	100
(%)	(100)	(28.7)	(23.8)	(7.3)	(10.4)	(12.2)	(11.6)	(6.0)
1871	2,528	799	439	138	224	365	375	188
(%)	(100)	(31.6)	(17.4)	(5.5)	(8.9)	(14.4)	(14.8)	(7.4)
1891	3,317	892	599	135	231	458	685	317
(%)	(100)	(26.9)	(18.1)	(4.1)	(7.0)	(13.9)	(20.7)	(9.6)
1911	1,787	483	236	60	74	243	421	270
(%)	(100)	(27.0)	(13.2)	(3.4)	(4.1)	(13.6)	(23.6)	(15.1)
1931	595	71	27	9	25	58	194	211
(%)	(100)	(12.0)	(4.5)	(1.6)	(4.2)	(9.7)	(32.6)	(35.5)

Source: Burial Registers.

Note: In view of the decline from the early years of this century in the death rate of infants under one year, the figure for 1911 is exceptionally high. This is undoubtedly attributable to diarrhoea, a major killer of babies, which was usually at its worst in the late summer, and resulted from a combination of warm weather and poor food hygiene. Figures fluctuated widely from year to year with climatic conditions; in the very hot weather of 1911 482 Leeds infants died of diarrhoea, but only ninety-one succumbed in the cold, wet summer of 1912. The problem was national – Mrs Pember Reeves, writing in London, refers to 'the deadly month of August 1911'. At Beckett Street Cemetery that year, burials of children under one averaged 28.5 per month from January to July, and 28 per month from October to December. In August there were 111, in September 64. See F.B. Smith, *The People's Health 1830–1910*, London, 1979, and Leeds MOH Reports, 1911–16.

The first Medical Officer of Health appointed in Leeds began his reports in 1867, in which year the total number of deaths in the borough was 6,261.

Table C.2: Deaths from some major diseases in different age-groups, 1867

Disease	Under 1 year	1–4	5–14	15–29	30–49	50–69	Over 70	Total all ages
Smallpox	17	13	5	6	5	0	0	46
Measles	1	26	1	0	0	0	0	28
Scarlatina	4	50	15	1	0	1	0	71
Diptheria	4	10	11	1	2	0	0	28
Whooping Cough	82	75	11	0	0	0	0	168
Typhus	7	41	44	62	60	29	12	255
Diarrhoea	295	81	7	7	4	7	6	407
Phthisis*	18	24	55	299	212	52	6	666
Convulsions	416	95	7	2	0	0	0	520
Bronchitis	197	140	12	18	92	226	130	815
Pneumonia	72	79	6	19	40	28	5	249

* Pulmonary tuberculosis ('consumption')

Source: Robinson and Goldie, *Sanitary Condition of Leeds*, Reports 1867–77

Appendix D

Victorian Institutions

1: *Leeds Union Workhouse*

The 1871 Census shows 576 inmates (313 males, 263 females). In addition there were sixteen male vagrants in the Casual Ward that night; 276 children aged from three to eighteen (175 boys, 101 girls) were housed in the Moral & Industrial Training Schools for Pauper Children next door.

Table D.1: Ages of inmates

Under 20	20–39	40–59	Over 60
57 (9.9%)	128 (22.2%)	139 (24.2%)	252 (43.7%)

Table D.2: Birthplaces

Leeds	Elsewhere in Yorkshire	Ireland	Other/Not known
203 (35.2%)	161 (28%)	112 (19.4%)	100 (17.4%)

Table D.3: Marital status

Unmarried	Married	Widowed
247 (42.9%)	102 (17.7%) (includes 7 couples)	227 (39.4%)

Note: The 576 occupants of the Workhouse were there because of mental or physical infirmity, or because they were unable to make a living in the world outside. In 1871 they included eighty-four people described as 'imbecile', 'imbecile from birth', 'idiot' or 'lunatic', and four who were blind or deaf (eighty-eight handicapped inmates, or 15.3% of the total). The 252 elderly residents included seventeen who were also 'imbeciles', possibly suffering from dementia. There were, too, twenty-five young mothers (9 married, 15 unmarried, 1 widow) with thirty-two dependent children between them; these fifty-seven people formed 9.9% of the total.

Source: 1871 Census RG 10/4558, ff. 104–117.

2: *Leeds Cavalry Barracks*

266 unmarried privates of the 5th Dragoon Guards occupying the Barracks on 2 April 1871 have also been identified in the muster for that date.

Table D.4: Ages of soldiers

Under 20	20–29	30–39	Over 40
59 (22%)	160 (60%)	44 (17%)	3 (1%)

Table D.5: Birthplaces

Ireland	Yorkshire	London	Other
54 (20.3%)	51 (19.2%)	27 (10.1%)	134 (50.4%)

Table D.6: In receipt of Good Conduct Pay for all or part of period

Yes	No
76 (28%)	190 (72%)

Note on discipline during the 91 days of the muster:
Fifty-three men (20% of total) had pay mulcted (average 3.3 days' pay lost per man). Twenty-two men (8% of total) spent time in cells; of these six were also confined in civil or military prisons or prison hospital (624 days' imprisonment, or an average of 28.4 days per imprisoned man).
One man was discharged as a Bad Character, one committed suicide and one was reclaimed by the 33rd Regiment as a deserter.

Source: 1871 Census RG 10/4558, ff. 93–104; Pay Lists WO 12/341.

3: *Leeds Borough Gaol*

The cost of establishing the gaol at Armley fell on the Leeds Borough rates, as did the running costs until nationalisation in 1877. It also received criminals at government expense from their places of conviction at sessions and assizes all over Britain. The Home Office register of these convicts runs initially from 1848 to 1855, and contains 497 male names. These men had committed crimes serious enough to warrant sentences of four to ten years, or life.

Table D.7: Ages of prisoners

Under 20	20–29	30–39	Over 40
92 (18%)	278 (56%)	89 (18%)	38 (8%)

Table D.8: Degree of instruction

Neither read nor write	Read only	Read/write imperfectly	Read/write well
110 (22%)	109 (22%)	245 (50%)	33 (6%)

Table D.9: Occupation

Labourer	Other manual	Skilled	Professional
197 (40%)	124 (25%)	166 (33%)	10 (2%)

Table D.10: Previous convictions

None	Tried and acquitted	Previously convicted	Previously transported
93 (19%)	48 (10%)	336 (67%)	20 (4%)

Table D.11: Crimes for which sentenced

Crime	No. sentenced
Larceny	278 (56%)
Offences against property, committed with violence (robbery, housebreaking)	122 (25%)
Receiving stolen goods	8 (2%)
Fraud, forgery, currency offences	21 (4%)
Offences against the person	36 (7%)
Riot and public order offences	3 (1%)
Malicious damage or injury	12 (2%)
Other	17 (3%)

Source: Register of Leeds Prison, HO 23/3
Note: Sixty-one of the convicts registered in HO 23/3 are also listed in the 1851 Census (HO 107/2314, ff. 562–70) under 'Leeds Borough Gaol and House of Correction'. A total of 299 prisoners were in the gaol on that occasion, 252 of them male and 47 female. 50 per cent were Yorkshire men and women and 15 per cent were of Irish birth, although, interestingly, Irishwomen formed 34 per cent of the female prisoners. Almost half were in their twenties, but there was a greater number of teenagers than in HO 23/3 and even two children aged nine and ten, presumably reflecting their conviction by lesser courts for less serious crimes. More than a quarter of the men were described as 'labourer'.

Further Reading

Anderson, O. *Suicide in Victorian and Edwardian England*. Oxford, 1987.

Briggs, A. *Victorian Cities*. London, 1963.

Brooks, C. *Mortal Remains: The History and Present State of the Victorian and Edwardian Cemetery*. Exeter, 1989.

Burnett, J. *Plenty and Want: A Social History of Diet in England from 1815*. London, 1979.

Crowther, M.A. *The Workhouse System 1834–1929: The History of an English Social Institution*. London, 1981.

Curl, J.S. *A Celebration of Death*. London. 1980.

Curl, J.S. *The Victorian Celebration of Death*, Newton Abbot, 1972.

Finnegan, F. *Poverty and Prostitution: A study of Victorian Prostitution in York*. Cambridge, 1979.

Fraser, D. (ed.) *A History of Modern Leeds*. Manchester, 1980.

Gilbert, A.D. *Religion and Society in Industrial England: Church, Chapel and Social Change*. London, 1976.

Harrison, B. *Drink and the Victorians: The Temperance Question in England, 1815–1872*. London, 1971.

Litten, J.W.S. *The English Way of Death: the Common Funeral since 1450*. London, 1991.

Morley, J. *Death, Heaven and the Victorians*. London, 1971.

Philips, D. *Crime and Authority in Victorian England: the Black Country, 1835–60*. London, 1977.

Pike, E.R. *Human Documents of the Victorian Golden Age (1850–1875)*. London, 1967.

Skelley, A. R. *The Victorian Army at Home: The Recruitment, Terms and Conditions of the British Regular, 1859–1899*. London, 1977.

Smith, F.B. *The People's Health 1830–1910*. London, 1979.

Waller, P.J. *Town, City and Nation: England 1850–1914*. Oxford, 1983.

Index

NB. Death notices, obituaries and inquest reports from the local press are separately listed in alphabetical order on pages 236–238